THE
AMERICAN
UNITY PLAN

BOLD AMERICAN SOLUTIONS FOR
A DIVIDED COUNTRY

ALAN NAGER

Design and distribution by Bublish
Published by American Unity Publications

ISBN: 978-1-647047-06-1 (eBook)
ISBN: 978-1-647047-07-8 (paperback)
ISBN: 978-1-647047-08-5 (hardcover)

CONTENTS

PART III
THE UNIFIERS

INTRODUCTION
THE NEED FOR UNITY

A merica is more divided now than ever in our lifetimes. Republican versus Democrat, red state versus blue state, rural versus urban—it is clear people are increasingly retreating into competing camps and geographies. Initiated by the pandemic, people are "voting with their feet," making red states redder and blue states bluer by fleeing to their respective corners of the country. The increasing number of Congressional votes along strict party affiliation is growing proof of a disturbing trend. In addition, the electorate is increasingly voting for Congressional positions and the presidency along strict party lines. Some believe we are heading for a second civil war, where the winner dictates the terms of living in America.

Yet the majority of Americans still look for real solutions that are bold and based on American principles. Uniquely American solutions that appeal to conservatives, progressives, libertarians, moderates, independents, and classical liberals are still possible. The criterion for good governance is when a cross section of the ideological spectrum votes for a policy solution, even if for different reasons.

If a solution gains popular support, the most ideological, incumbent politicians will vote accordingly, and meaningful change will occur.

Change is more than a political slogan, and something does need to change. Change itself can be a unifying force in America if most Americans agree on the policy solution—not our form of a representative republic, which has stood the test of time, but policies within our republic that divide us. We require change without losing our freedoms enshrined in our Constitution, which are under attack from both sides of the political aisle.

This book is about uniting Americans from across the political spectrum to solve major problems facing us that our politicians are ignoring or cannot muster the political will to resolve. However, this is a book on policy, not politics. I am not a politician, journalist, talk-show host, or pundit. Nor am I a lawyer, and I will never run for office. My wife and I have four great adult children who vote along the entire political spectrum or maybe not at all. I read a lot about philosophy, history, finance, and politics when I can stand it. We sent our kids to both public and private schools, even when we could not really afford it, to give them educational opportunities. We give to charities more than most and less than we should because we worry about the future and taking care of four living generations. In short, I believe I am one of the tens of millions of normal, hard-working, get-up-every-day, and do-what-you-are-supposed-to-do Americans who care about the future of our country.

I am an engineer by training. Engineers are problem solvers. We define problems, research, analyze data, and develop solutions. I was born and raised in New York City and educated and live in the South. I have worked in various businesses solving problems in supply chain and manufacturing, design and construction, and commercial real estate. I am an entrepreneur, having built a consulting business to service my clients around whatever skill sets I have that they are willing to pay for, and I know what it means to make payroll, be in debt, and pay taxes. I am not rich but did better than my parents and well enough to retire at age sixty.

This book will propose bold, modern, American solutions for problems plaguing this country, whether they are currently politically viable or not. It will propose solutions that require compromise at a scale not seen in America in generations. It will not use cliches or modern cultural terms or name-drop politicians. It is not about bringing Democrats over to the Republican side or vice versa. It uses references and quotes from all perspectives, from progressive to conservative. It will be direct and honest, with no political agenda other than to create a more united country.

Many people who vote for one party or the other do so out of their own sense of compassion rather than ideology, power, or control. They want change that will benefit society. As such, this book has two simple goals:

1. Present bold solutions using fundamental American principles to solve real-world problems that pose some of the greatest economic, national security, and social risks to America.

2. Unite people around these solutions to drive popular legislation and fix systemic problems.

Some of the ideas presented here are new; others are great ideas from the past that have never been implemented. I have integrated both old and new ideas into one proposal called the American Unity Plan. This plan is in alignment with the American principles we seem to share, and its messaging as a platform to voters is devised deliberately to gather support across political lines.

As we have seen in recent years, change via executive order is populist and short-term expedient. Unless they are enacted with long-term perspective through legislation, popular ideas that win elections are transient if the next election is lost to the opposing party. The bolder the solution enacted by Congress, however, the more difficult it is to change if the next election is lost. For example, the Affordable Care Act (ACA) is far-reaching, passed through Congress, withstood legal changes, and has benefited millions.

Whether you agree with ACA as good legislation is not the point. It became law due to the legislative process, with fierce deliberation. On the other hand, tax-rate cuts or increases, without changing the structure of the underlying tax code, are transient and discussed every time we change presidents or Congressional control. The same can be said for changes to military spending, social benefits, immigration, and many other generational issues that are debated annually without a long-term strategy. Once a bold solution becomes accepted as beneficial to society at large, it is difficult to change course.

It is not enough to rally around the next great politician who can bring short-term votes and make expedient changes. The goal is to legislate, regardless of the party in charge, through both policy and communication, by working together. Solutions sell, and solutions founded in core American principles (which will be discussed in the next chapter) work. We need both leadership and policy working hand in hand with an articulated and resonating message. Good solutions become permanent through consistent and systematic change toward a clear vision or goal and when rooted in foundational principles, whether scientific, economic, or social.

We need bold solutions that are supported across the political landscape. We require unity from traditional liberals who believe in free speech and the Bill of Rights, conservatives and libertarians who believe in limited government, progressives who want a robust social safety net and opportunities for many Americans currently left behind, and independents and moderates who want practical balance and honesty.

Americans these days only seem to unite when there is a tragedy or a war, and this expedient unity is temporary, as everything becomes politicized over time. The beginning of any policy solution must be grounded in something else. Policy must be based on American principles that unite us, whether we recognize these principles or not. Can American principles such as fairness, equality under the law, and reasonable accommodation be applied to solutions that address many of America's greatest needs?

There have been many books defining our country's impending doom. Some of the disasters that may happen within our lifetimes are not hard to identify. Many are talked about endlessly, with little to no progress on the horizon. You've likely been hearing a lot about some or all of the following pressing national issues:

- Government and private debt levels are increasing, which leads to inflation, recession, and eventually stagflation.

- The Social Security and Medicare systems are going bankrupt within ten to fifteen years, which will lead to higher taxes or reduced benefits for tens of millions of seniors who have already paid into the current system.

- The tax burden is affecting the middle class more than ever, while the social safety net is evaporating for the poorest Americans.

- Immigration is draining local resources across the country and leading to social unrest.

- After decades of reform, there are still almost thirty million people without healthcare insurance, and costs continue to rise while services diminish, especially with an aging population.

- Our public education system was broken before the pandemic and now many students have lost years of learning and assimilation into society due to the prolonged lockdown.

- Many believe we are headed for environmental disaster, yet we must rely on fossil fuels for the foreseeable future to ensure we maintain and grow our economy while fighting inflation.

- In all areas of life, our constitutional freedoms are being eroded due to government overreach.

We know the problems, but where are the solutions? More specifically, where are the big ideas? We must face the fact that incrementalism will not work. We know that attempts to solve one problem cause unintended consequences elsewhere. Environmental issues cannot be resolved without addressing inflation. Inflation cannot be tackled without addressing governmental expenditures. The social safety net cannot be maintained without addressing immigration and taxation.

Unfortunately, most proposals are presented along ideological lines. These ideas may have unity within a party, but they do not have support across the aisle. These proposals give half the country something to vote for and the other half something to vote against. They do nothing except promote reelection for failed politicians.

Rather than an incremental approach, the American Unity Plan is a fully integrated, bold solution to tackle some of America's most pressing long-term problems. It provides something for *all* Americans to vote for. There will be parts that individual citizens will like and dislike. Rather than breaking it apart, it must be viewed holistically. The American Unity Plan will resonate with most Americans from across the political landscape who want to achieve real, lasting, positive change to solve problems that seem insurmountable and divide us a nation. It is a uniquely American road map for long-term success.

PART I
THE PRINCIPLES

1

★ ★ ★

AMERICAN PRINCIPLES – UNITER OR DIVIDER?

We hold these truths to be self-evident, that all men are created equal, that they are endowed by their Creator with certain unalienable Rights, that among these are Life, Liberty and the pursuit of Happiness.

— US Declaration of Independence, July 4, 1776

What are American principles, and are they still applicable today or are they a relic of the past? Do American principles cross the political spectrum? Without getting into specific issues and policies or having a legal and historical discussion of the Constitution, we first need to start by defining unifying American principles. Principles serve as the foundation for behavior and reasoning. We are attracted to policies and solutions aligned with what we believe.

The preamble to the Declaration of Independence provides the basis for establishing American principles. It establishes equality of rights of those governed ("the People"), but those rights come from nature, not government, and therefore can never be taken away. The Constitution forms the basis of establishing the framework for government and lists specific rights, including freedom of speech and the press, the right to assemble peaceably, and the right to petition the government.

Rights are different than principles and values. Rights are protected by our federal laws and cannot be infringed by either the federal government or the states, but they can be regulated, within reason, at both the federal and state level. For example, the Second Amendment provides the right to bear arms, but we regulate that right at the federal level and in various states through background checks, minimum age requirements, licensing mandates, and more. Rights are portable from state to state, whereas laws and regulations can be changed through our federal and state governments.

Progressives will argue the Constitution is a living document, and our principles should reflect the times, whereas conservatives will argue the Constitution is as written, timeless, and can only be changed by the Constitutional Amendment process. Regardless of your point of view, the average voter is not a legal scholar. When proposed solutions emanate from our politicians, our default position is not to debate the legality or the intent of the Founding Fathers, but to align with our personal beliefs. Unfortunately, many default to "What's in it for me?" (or WIIFM) when deciding issues because the solutions presented by politicians are often ideological and not in the context of principles.

Laws and regulations based on strict ideology or legacy party platforms, instead of principles, cause division. On the other hand, I believe there is a core set of principles that build unity and cut across political ideology. Our politicians rarely articulate principles that align with Americans across the political spectrum. Without principles, people act (vote) to their own benefit. People evaluate policy solutions based on principles. It is common to hear the term "I agree with that in principle." Principles may not always be articulated or aligned to legal rights, but they "feel right" based on our own life experiences and how we want to treat others and be treated.

Here are what I believe are foundational American principles, not from a legal or constitutional basis but from a life perspective.

- <u>Protection of human rights</u>. The federal government is limited in its scope by the US Constitution, and the primary responsibility of the government is to ensure liberty and freedom. This freedom provides unlimited opportunity without any guarantee, and success is defined only by the individual. It is our responsibility to chase our dreams. We do not want the government dictating the direction of our life or defining our pursuit of happiness. However, with freedom and opportunity comes personal responsibility for our actions.

- <u>Equal opportunity and protection under the law</u>. The federal government must be neutral in treating citizens. We want a "level playing field" to compete for the opportunities America offers. People must also be held accountable under the rule of law, applied equally to all without exception.

- <u>Fair and reasonable accommodation to both the majority and the minority</u>. The government should take no position on the morality of how one chooses to live and should protect the individual's right to be treated fairly and equally under the law while giving no advantage to any group or person over another. Providing benefits to some must not incur "negative rights" on another.

Although similar, these principles are different than American values or traits, such as a sense of American pride, innovation, charity, dedication, hard work, self-reliance, competition, respect, assimilation, acceptance of others, and much more. These principles are also a subset of the legal rights guaranteed to us by the Constitution, although without our constitutional protections these principles would not have evolved. These principles are based on America's collective sense of right and wrong. These principles are how we think about solutions to everyday problems. In a sense, they are our combined American morality.

Most Americans will argue with specific wording, and the subject of principles could be broadened to fill an entire book on its own. That is not the point. In general, it would be hard for most Americans to argue with the basic sentiment unless one wants to benefit specifically from a policy (WIIFM) and is not concerned about the harm inflicted on others. Some do not believe in equal protection and opportunity under the law but rather outcome, which is unfair and incurs negative rights and therefore makes it difficult to build unity.

To be clear, this is not to say all Americans believe the law *is* applied equally, but the fundamental, unifying American principle that we strive for is equality of opportunity and treatment. We accommodate the disadvantaged, but American principles unite us when we do so without harming others. America and American citizens give proportionately more to charities than other nations because we do so out of the need to help, not due to mandate or confiscation of wealth by the government. When dealing with public policy, many times we move away from individual accommodation toward a one-size-fits-all approach, which harms many in the process of targeted assistance to some.

We tolerate solutions that affect us more than others, so long as they are deemed fair. For example, we expect those with more financial resources to pay more in taxes than those without the means. However, the manner of taxation is where we disagree, especially if some people are perceived to pay disproportionately than others who receive more benefits, incur unnecessary costs just to pay taxes, or believe the government is intruding into their lives.

Whatever solution or policy is proposed, it should be viewed in the context of American principles. Is this fair and reasonable in accommodation to both the majority and the minority so our rights are protected? Does it provide for equal opportunity and protection under the law? Does the benefit to one incur negative rights on someone else? To provide unity around policy and solutions, we must ensure the debate remains focused on principles. It is acceptable to debate different solutions that are all based on common principles. We become divided as a country when any proposal violates American principles because it is viewed as favoring one side or the other politically, mostly to buy favor or win elections.

From this point forward, we will review past policies and future solutions against these core American principles. We will specifically discuss fairness, opportunity, and, most importantly, negative rights or the government revoking a promise. The next chapter illustrates how the violation of American principles causes division.

2

IT IS FAIR TO ACCOMMODATE FAIRNESS

Among the numerous advantages promised by a well-constructed union, none deserves to be more accurately developed than its tendency to break and control the violence of faction.

— Alexander Hamilton, The Federalist Papers

Many years ago, when discussing public policy, Americans talked about the three-legged stool of issues: fiscal, foreign, and social policy. The balance of the stool shifted situationally depending on the headlines in the news. Was America at war or just preparing for the threat of war? Was the federal government actively engaged in rectifying social and moral issues, such as gun control and abortion? Were there critical cases before the Supreme Court? Were taxes, spending, rising interest rates, inflation, unemployment, shortages, or foreign trade causing shocks in the economy or the stock market?

Within each end of the political spectrum, there is very little consensus on fiscal, foreign, or social policy, yet hopefully most Americans believe in American principles. Because they are subject to human emotion and political expediency, the principles are violated from time to time to move priorities forward, but we gain unity or consensus when a solution feels right.

Much of this book is devoted to policy, but great policy must be referenced to American principles to entice potential voters to engage. As an organization, the Republican Party acts as though they are intentionally trying to lose with a resoundingly poor message on many issues to reach noncore voters. The Republican message on key issues is clearly directed at the true conservative base, but does it have to be this way in not just communication but in action? The progressive message is directed at building a coalition around voters perceived to be disenfranchised. When the principle of fairness is removed from the policy discussion or the term "fairness" is used for political advantage only, people default to a position of self-interest. Here are some examples.

One of the inspirations to write this book was listening to Republican politicians and conservative analysts defend the Georgia Voting Law. Of course, most Americans believe that voting should be available only to those who are legally able to vote and that identification cards are readily accessible in our society. Identification is required to fly, enter many public buildings, cash checks, and for many more aspects of life. The bill eliminated many potential abuses to ensure fair elections, and clear progress was made between the 2020 and 2022 elections, although voting itself became less convenient and arguments on voter suppression remain.

But instead of just saying there is nothing wrong with the bill and that it is equivalent to other states' bills, would it have hurt for the Republicans to simply say, "Obtaining legal identification is available to everyone. We will help anyone, even Democrats, who does not have an ID obtain one before the next primary so everyone has an equal and fair opportunity to vote as they choose"? In addition to good messaging, it would have been an opportunity to engage people who are not Republican to build unity across party lines and work with Democrats on voting processes. The position many people take is "If I can obtain a license and figure out how to clearly fill out and sign an absentee ballot or make it to the polling center on election day, why can't everyone?" By applying American principles, helping people vote legally, because it is the right thing to do, causes harm to no one, but allowing people to cast ballots outside of established law gives a perception of unequal treatment and potentially harms most voters regardless of election outcomes.

The Georgia Voting Law turned a technical correction to run better elections, exacerbated by the pandemic, into a major social issue focused on human rights and equality. When it comes to government involvement in the three pillars of policy—fiscal, foreign, and social—the one that is the most emotional is social issues. It has impacted every aspect of our lives, from abortion to LGBTQ rights to free speech to religious liberty. Republicans have lost many potential voters over the years because of a perceived lack of compassion, and Democrats have lost many potential voters based on identity politics and favoring certain groups over others, violating American principles.

What is a good message that blends policy and principle, and how can it be communicated in the context of societal issues? Besides defining your audience, which each party needs to do to expand beyond core constituency to build unity, good messaging contains basic elements of policy positions and must align with American principles. The policy must be communicated as fair and reasonable to both the majority and the minority, it must provide for equal opportunity and protection under the law, and its implementation must not incur negative rights by providing benefit to one at the expense of another.

Any change is difficult, but for people to cross political party lines, the Republicans must be more persuasive and the Democrats must recognize that pocketbook issues are divisive when policies that violate American principles are proposed (for example, eliminating student debt). We cannot just rely on charismatic leaders or absolute political control to enact change, but rather we need to make policy and messaging institutional first, and our elected officials must be able to unite on solutions that cross the political aisle and explain why they are fair and provide reasonable accommodation. Politics is emotional, but people will accept change if policy can articulate why change is needed, especially monumental change, and messaging is critical to the process. If the message is not clear and does not resonate, then a deeper look at the policy and the institution behind the policy is not probable regardless of the candidate or politician du jour. We will review these elements in order.

What is fair? Paraphrasing the famous Supreme Court ruling on pornography, we know fair when we see it. We can use car insurance as a simple example, since approval ratings for insurance companies are almost as low as for politicians. For instance, you are a loyal customer and have never had a claim, yet every year your car insurance premium goes up a few percent. You just chalk it up to inflation until one day you realize that new customers can get much cheaper premiums than old, loyal customers. The car insurance company assumes the inconvenience of change is worse than staying put even if you pay higher premiums. All other things being equal, you will reward the existing relationship. But at some point, that balance shifts and you shop for alternatives. In the back of your mind, you know your insurance premium hikes are subsidizing new policy holders, so you want to be "new" as well to get what you deserve. Insurance companies have low approval ratings because they are not perceived as fair and equal in transactions, leaving claims aside, because they treat one group, new customers, better than existing customers. We are loyal when we perceive we are being treated fairly and disloyal when we think we are not.

The concept of fairness breaks down at scale. In societies, we apply fairness at the personal level exceptionally well, especially when applied to human rights and helping our fellow citizens. Socialism works well in a family or small group where people give freely of their time, experience, and money to help one another, but this concept does not scale well to cities, states, and especially federal bureaucracies. This is a fundamental flaw of socialism that fairness, defined as equality of outcome, can be achieved across disparate groups with different needs over large distances. As the size of the group increases, the probability of positive and fair outcomes is reduced. The more separation between personal contact, or what I will call "custodian" or "sponsorship," the wider the fairness gap grows as competing groups vie for their "fair share" of the larger pie.

For example, do cities turn to other alternatives when the service in public schools is poor or costs are excessively high? In fact, the opposite is true—they double down on their commitment to public schools. In addition to spending more money, the government heavily taxes and regulates rival private education businesses, thereby making them affordable only to the wealthy. Is it fair that only the wealthy can send their children to better performing schools? Is it fair that a middle-class citizen must pay taxes to support poorly performing public schools while still spending money on a private education and potentially going into debt to give their kids an advantage later in life? The concept of fairness can be applied to almost every policy solution, and Americans inherently understand this concept as a foundational principle.

In Communism, the central tenant is "from each according to his ability, to each according to his needs." To Communists, this is fair because we cannot control to whom we are born but we can make everyone equal after birth. In reality, the outcome often is that everyone is equally miserable except for those in political power. Communist governments can control the supply of wealth through confiscation and redistribution. So why are there rich people in Communist countries? Why are commoners not of equal wealth to the rich and powerful? Should the American politicians who propose equality of outcome round up a few hundred of their closest supporters, pool their money, and distribute it equally? Should we not experiment with smaller groups of true believers before we try it on 330 million people?

What about the demand side of the equation? Who decides the needs and desires of each human? Are needs only monetary—to provide the basics of food, clothing, shelter, transportation, and energy? Apparently, the rich in Communist countries need to consume more based on their heredity or position of power.

Communism and socialism will never have a valid argument against capitalism's principle of free-market supply and demand because free economies are more fair than centrally planned bureaucracies despite the latter's perceived good intentions. Capitalism simply produces better results, even if the process is messy. All progressives know we will never have true equality of outcome because supply and demand will never be in balance. The question is true fairness.

Ironically, most people accept inequality of outcome if, and only if, they perceive the playing field as fair. Equality of opportunity can only be achieved through capitalism, where millions of people conduct billions of individual transactions that each party considers fair and equitable. When capitalism is not perceived as fair, such as what is commonly called "crony capitalism" or when governments give privilege to one person or group over another via tax code or regulation, division occurs. The problem with the Republican Party is that many support an uneven playing field, just not at the scale of the Democrats. "We're not as bad as the other guys" is not a strategy for long-term success. This is an opening for authoritarian rule. It is time to fight both parties with principled policy and messaging.

Simple fairness is a unifying theme for Americans. Is it fair for someone to have their student debt relieved when others worked through school to pay for college? Fairness and the concept of equality under the law must go arm in arm in any solution to ensure groups do not revolt. Is it fair that someone pays different federal taxes because of how many children they raised, the state in which they live, the returns on their investment portfolio, and many more "none of your business" items on a tax form? Is it fair that some receive more in Social Security than others when each may have similar living needs in advanced age? Or that each receives the same Medicare benefit when one worked harder at a lifetime of proper diet and fitness than the other?

For many Americans, one of the more appealing solutions to the issue of fairness is universal basic income. UBI is perceived as fair to many, and it would be if everyone who paid into the system would receive the exact same benefits. But politics is about power and control, and any implementation of UBI as proposed today would of course be means tested, or some other scheme, to ensure the government would be in control of the purse or certain groups were given advantage over others. The point is that rather than argue the proposals for something like UBI, we need to cross political aisles and have new policies defining not only the policy but also the philosophical messaging that is a litmus test for fairness in legislation.

One of the tenants of American principles is preserving the rights of the minority. But this concept of fairness must be paired with equal accommodation to ensure no rights, liberties, or benefits are taken from one group or person while implementing solutions that benefit another. This is the concept of negative rights and liberties some have espoused when discussing American culture and the philosophy of a limited government. It focuses on natural rights that preexist government and holds that a government's only role is to protect our rights and freedoms, not to give one group rights or advantages over another. When politicians try to "right wrongs" by providing material benefits such as education, lifestyle incentives, healthcare, admissions, and more to one group over another, they invariably confer negative rights. They get it wrong, and generational court battles result. Traditionally, we focused negative rights on only the wealthy via the tax code, but now that has changed to encompass all areas of society.

The idea of "do no harm" is the central issue. So long as there is no perceived harm, people can be persuaded with coherent policy. For example, not even the most ardent religious fundamentalist could argue that the marriage of two same-sex people harms anyone else. They may be morally outraged or believe they are doing good to help others avoid eternal damnation, but from a policy point of view, and from a legal point of view, others are not involved nor harmed. There are very few issues where the potential for harm is national and involves everyone, with national security being paramount. Policy in the context of fairness and harm or negative rights is best evaluated locally when possible.

The smallest minority group is *you*. The individual. Our founders feared majorities and giving power to political elites to represent the majority. This would lead to getting the protection of minority rights wrong. This is why the concept of human rights as enshrined in the Constitution is so important. Rights are granted to the individual, not groups, as groups are as transient as culture changes. We believe as a society that everyone is granted equal rights and that the sole role of government is to protect your rights. We, as a society, accommodate minority rights, even down to a single person, so long as this accommodation does not confer negative rights on others. In law, this is called "reasonable accommodation" and aligns with fairness.

However, it is also up to the people being accommodated to ensure their accommodation does not create negative rights for others. Several years ago, a clerk who was a government employee in Kentucky refused to issue a marriage license to a gay couple because of her religious beliefs. In this case, she was preventing the couple from being reasonably accommodated because they could not be legally married in the county where they lived and paid taxes. It would have certainly been easier to accommodate the clerk, as she could simply get another job that supported her religious beliefs without conferring negative rights on others. On the other hand, the baker who refused to make a cake for a gay wedding should have every right not to provide a service he does not want to offer (force of his labor without his consent) because the gay couple could easily be accommodated by other bakeries that are willing and able to perform the service.

To build unity in America, accommodation and fairness must be incorporated into our arguments. Both conservatives and progressives sound equally unprincipled when they support or attack the clerk and the baker. If you stand behind the fairness and accommodation principle, the message of protecting human rights through reasonable accommodation is primary and resonates to all without even discussing religious liberty or same-sex marriage.

In a larger-scope example of protecting minority rights, we now accommodate people with physical disabilities through the

Americans with Disabilities Act (ADA). Most would say this is reasonable accommodation without adversely impacting those who do not directly benefit. The ADA is part of our building codes and can be designed from the beginning of new construction with relatively minor cost to most projects. Since all new projects competing for capital and customers are designed to the same standard, there is no competitive advantage to implementing ADA guidelines and everyone is treated equally. The ADA was good law and policy supported by everyone, with maybe the exception of a few building owners who saw only cost. Buildings are owned by conservatives and progressives alike. Unity often occurs when both sides love or hate a law!

The laws around transgender participation in sports is another opportunity for us to revert to American principles as defined by fairness and equal accommodation. Clearly, transgender athletes should be able to participate in sports. But what is the best way? By allowing biological males to participate against females, it clearly removes rights from the biological females in basic competition and esteem, the ability to win scholarships, and social issues involving dressing rooms, bathrooms, etc. Could transgender athletes be accommodated another way without violating the rights of others? Have Republicans offered a solution, or are they messaging to the public that they are antitransgender? This is an opportunity to work on practical solutions, so long as those solutions meet the guidelines of fair and reasonable accommodation to everyone affected.

This issue comes on the heels of the North Carolina "bathroom bill," an example of bad legislation associated with the Republican establishment, albeit at the state level. Could they not have modeled a solution based on the success of the ADA? New unisex bathroom construction or converting existing bathroom facilities to unisex when the cost is minor accommodates everyone. Most establishments provide unisex facilities anyway as common sense. However, existing establishments should not be forced into compliance when construction is not feasible or costs are excessive. It is reasonable to ask the people who would benefit greatly to not create negative rights for others by forcing accommodation when it is not practical and there are public and private alternatives.

The point is to have a strong policy position and apply principled messaging. I once watched an interview of two Libertarian Party candidates for president and vice-president. The candidates were given what the interviewer called "the libertarian test." He asked them if people in Utah should be able to have polygamous marriages. The politicians answered no because they thought it would be the politically correct answer and would appeal to some religious voters. A true libertarian would have said something like this:

> "It is not up to the federal government to limit what consenting adults do, so long as it does no harm to anyone else. It is up to each state to decide what laws are right for them based on the concept of federalism in the Constitution. If the people of Utah want polygamy, or the people of Nevada want prostitution, or the people of New York want legalized gambling, or the people of Colorado want legal marijuana, it is up to them to decide. This is not a

federal issue. Although it may go against my moral and religious beliefs to act accordingly, I'm sure there are things I want to legally do that others may disagree with. We have a representative republic founded in federalism, and people in each state are elected to represent the views of their constituents. Accordingly, this degree of freedom comes with responsibility, and each consulting adult must be responsible for their own actions, not harming their fellow citizens."

Now we can argue, and have argued, about the dangers of marijuana, alcohol consumption, cigarettes, payday loans, and other products and services that may harm society. There are ongoing policy disputes, at both the state and federal levels, about guns, prescription drugs, gambling, driving after midnight, sugary soft drinks, fatty foods, plastic straws, and of course abortion. Where does it stop, and who decides? We cannot take different approaches to create policy based on the whims of politicians seeking to score political points with their base. Our elected politicians must follow a standard, just as we want judges to decide cases based solely on the law versus their own values or biases. Lack of standards and principles causes divide.

The concepts of fairness, reasonable accommodation, and protection of rights are applied in equal protection under the law, and that in and of itself provides for equal opportunity over time for more people than any other policy. Republicans seem to pay so much attention to the First and Second Amendments of the Constitution but pay limited attention to the Tenth Amendment (federalism) and the Fourteenth Amendment (equal protection). Democrats want to make everything a federal issue, as if one-size-fits-all legislation for 330 million people would ever build any resemblance of unity.

The equal protection clause is part of the first section of the Fourteenth Amendment to the United States Constitution. The clause, which took effect in 1868, provides "nor shall any state. . . deny to any person within its jurisdiction the equal protection of the laws." It mandates that individuals in similar situations be treated equally by the law. This essentially codifies the moral concept of fairness, but it does not say that states cannot pass different laws where federal authority is not applicable.

The meaning of the equal protection clause has been the subject of much debate and inspired the well-known phrase "equal justice under the law." This clause was the basis for many major Supreme Court decisions, including dismantling racial segregation, legalizing same-sex marriages, and other issues that made many discriminatory policies of the private sector illegal. However, protecting the rights of the individual or small groups of people is not the same as giving them advantages. We cannot confuse minority rights, the hallmark of America and our Constitution, with minority control.

We can, however, apply these concepts and messaging to one of the primary issues of the day—cancel culture. Conservatives complain about cancel culture and the new alignment between "woke" technology companies and the Democratic Party, and now its expansion to seemingly most of corporate America and the military. Here is a message for Republicans and conservatives in particular:

Technology companies have every right not to do business with you, just as the baker has a right not to bake a cake for a gay couple. What they should *not* be granted are protections under the law that no other company has, nor should they be able to collude with the government on policy that gives advantage to some over others.

All Americans should be against punishing any organization simply because it is too big or because we hate their politics. Speech is protected by the First Amendment, but conduct is not. We punish individuals and corporations alike when they break the law! Conservatives are being canceled by businesses at an alarming speed and not just by technology companies. Now, in response, woke companies are being boycotted by conservatives. The divide is widening.

So how do we apply this logic to create unifying law around big technology? First, the law does need to be modified, but rarely do we hear a single principled proposal. Simply breaking up the large technology companies for whatever reason is contrary to American principles. The answer is simple and constitutional: define companies with censors, editors, fact-checkers, and the like as not protected from lawsuits. They are publishers, so submit them to the exact same laws as the *New York Times*, Fox News, or any other media outlet regarding publishing false and defamatory statements and violating the right to privacy.

If they do not censor or willingly violate the law, they are effectively a public utility operating a business, like the phone, power, and gas companies. When we turn on the power or talk on our phone, we are not subjected to worrying about being deplatformed, and the wireless company cannot be sued because a terrorist used their platform for communications.

But what about child pornography and other materials deemed inappropriate? This is governed by law. If someone posts child porn on Facebook (assuming they are a public utility and not a publisher), we hope that our law enforcement would issue a warrant to Facebook for the identity of the violator and issue arrest warrants following due process. As with any public safety issue, we know with proper enforcement, these acts stop over time. It is not up to public platform corporations to enforce the law, but it is within the realm of publishers to block or omit any content on their physical or intellectual property, so long as they are subject to the same laws as all publishers. We need a level playing field established for companies to exist that have different views and business models.

But what about the competitive advantage or head start the big technology companies have gained? That stifles competition! But exactly what business has not had government assistance at some point (and now) with tax policy and regulation? No, big tech apparently is just more skilled at exploitation than energy, automotive and EV manufacturers, banking, pharmaceutical, defense, insurance, farmers, and anyone engaged in foreign trade. As an industry, technology companies crave freedom to innovate and competition more than protection. The large technology companies now want regulation because of the simple fact that all large companies want regulation. Regulation, applied equally across an industry, hurts small, nimble, disruptive, and undercapitalized startups more than large companies with huge liquid assets.

Remember, the only entity that can legally maintain a monopoly is the government. The public education system is a prime example. Under current law, a monopoly cannot exist unless crony capitalism and unequal laws give it an advantage. Dominant market share in the free market is gained through providing better service, convenience, quality, and value for the consumer. The product or service is irrelevant, whether it is software, steel, phones, education, or healthcare. The government, however, gave big technology companies an advantage to dominate by giving them the power to eliminate their competition and insulating them from lawsuits. The government can take the immunity away but avoid legislating the size and scale of their business. If you believe in the free market, competition will arise. Once, we thought Walmart, ExxonMobil, General Motors, and IBM were invincible to market competition. Why would we not think that the free market cannot create competitors to Google and Facebook?

Breaking up big technology companies is not a solution aligned with American principles. Should we now break up big pharma, major healthcare systems, and the insurance industry because they have been subsidized through Medicare? How about big defense, which has been subsidized through government contracting? We must believe in free-market capitalism 100 percent to succeed, so long as we have true, fair competition and laws and regulations applied equally to all. This provides the greatest opportunity and outcome for America.

Fundamentally, Americans believe in human rights at the individual level, private property (physical and intellectual), freedom of speech and religion, and equality under the law. Where we have differed is in the solution. Progressives want big government solutions, and most libertarians want extremely limited government. Conservatives want big government for national defense and nothing else, on the surface. Our common ground is our American principles. It is un-American to believe in government owner-ship of the means of production rather than private property. It is un-American to believe in controlling speech that is offensive to you. It is inherently un-American to believe in equality of outcome, not of opportunity, despite the wrongs of history. Many Americans can align on these principles with solid policy and communication focused on the rights of the individual and offer bold solutions that solve long-term systemic problems.

As a preview of the American Unity Plan, what if, as one of our core elements of policy messaging, we adopted the "Fairness Litmus Test" for taxes and benefits, which goes something like this?

> We believe that any federal benefits be applied equally to all and only to American citizens who have already contributed. We support policies whereby all federal taxes be collected based on the voluntary consumption of goods and services. We recognize the current policies of tax collection and benefit distribution are inherently unfair, pitting Americans against each other, and are intrusive to our personal lives and freedom. We also recognize the current system has evolved over many generations and believe it is fair that during the implementa-tion of these policies, no American will receive fewer benefits or pay more in taxes than they currently do throughout their lifetime, as America must keep its promises.

Specific policies will be discussed later in this book, but if you read the above message, would you not want to hear more, regardless of how you currently vote? You might be thinking, "Let me get this straight: All Americans receive the same amount, and no one gets less than they were promised? Only Americans citizens who have already contributed by paying into the system will receive these federal benefits?"

Many progressives would hate the above message because they want regressive policies. Many conservatives would hate the above message because, to some degree, it violates their focus on personal responsibility. But that is the point. We need to disengage from traditional party extremes and appeal to more Americans with principle-based solutions. American policy must have a supporting and unifying message that resonates with core principles, including a doctrine of inherent fairness.

3

THE GREAT POLITICAL COMPROMISE
– POLICY AND PRINCIPLE

Equality before the law is probably forever unattainable.
It is a noble ideal, but it can never be realized, for what
men value in this world is not rights but privileges.

       – H. L. Mencken, American journalist

When principles are violated, factions are created. There are factions within the conservative movement and within the Republican Party. There are factions within the progressive movement and within the Democratic Party. However, these factions within each party are becoming more uncommon. The party-line vote is now the standard. So, how can we unite across party lines without one party simply abandoning their own ideology?

American principles are clearly different than political party principles. Democrat principles co-opt the term fairness, but most proposals favor core constituents, while making Republicans the evil and uncaring populace. Republican principles focus on limited and smaller government, but the party is clearly ineffectual in governing to their voter mandate. As a result, Democrats compromise their party principles much less than Republicans do, as they have a longer-term view of society as their ideology.

Parties seek power through popular movements. Once politicians perceive a movement's popularity, they will abandon party position to legislate and seek to win elections. To show why speaking in terms of policy and principle is important, here is an example of public policy and the potential conflict written from a Republican perspective.

Should America increase defense spending even if it means larger deficits? Most Republicans and all true conservatives would argue for both stronger defense and less spending, but they are capable of compromise. Two potential answers are:

- Yes, we need to increase defense spending even if we are not at active war because we need to be prepared against threats from Russia, China, Iran, radical Islamists, cyberterrorists, and many others, even if this means increasing the deficit. This is so important that, to secure Democrat votes, we would vote for increases across the board in social spending and increase the debt ceiling, as without a strong defense, everything else is meaningless.

- No, we need a balanced budget, or we are mortgaging our future and will incur rampant inflation leading to stagflation. The threat of war will always be present, but the wars of the future can be won with a more modern and streamlined defense. Every government agency, including the military, can reduce expenditures, and we can reduce defense spending now to gain fiscal control.

Are Republican politicians who take one view or the other any less Republican? I would argue they are not, because they rarely legislate on principle. They believe they are moving their priorities forward within the ideology of their party. But are either of these solutions violating what attracted many voters to the Republican Party? When they increase social spending and apply it unevenly, even if it means stronger national defense, do they violate their stated policy principles? Yes. When they sacrifice defense and compromise the fundamental role of government in the protection of our freedom and liberty, do they violate their stated principles? Yes.

We now will apply American, rather than party, principles. Do progressives violate American principles? Yes, because they argue specifically for an unfair system based in progressive ideology, with class, gender, race, and sexual orientation being primary in policymaking to right historical wrongs. Many do so for humanitarian reasons, as they promote equality of outcome to overcome life being inherently unfair to some, whether due to their choice or life's circumstance. Many argue for unfairness for political reasons to accumulate more votes and power by transferring resources from the fewer with more resources to the majority of voters with less.

Do Republicans articulate American principles of fairness, equal opportunity, and the American dream? I would argue they do, more so than the Democrats. But certainly these principles are not applied well in policy solutions and legislation, even when Republicans are in control of the government. Their solutions are lacking in broad appeal and rarely resonate beyond their political base.

However, if we assume both parties all well-intentioned, Republicans seem to lean toward the status quo and reducing advances of the Democrats. They build on tested free-market principles when they can. Democrats have bolder solutions, albeit mostly untested or proven to fail historically in America or in other parts of the world. They believe historical failures can be corrected within the modern American system with smart people making more decisions, elected or unelected, who are given more control at the federal level.

Clearly, the point is not to persuade progressives to become conservatives, or vice versa. The point is to build common ground, where voters in both parties find something to like. People, rather than parties, are more accustomed to compromise when they see their own principles incorporated into policy. The ideological extremes compromise less often.

Many of you may be asking whether the Republican or Democratic Party could ever be the home to American principles. Why not a third party? Like it or not, we have a two-party system. The infrastructure is in place and will remain in place. It has been proven many times since World War II that voters will cross party lines if practical solutions are presented with real leadership and conviction by articulate candidates. Recent third-party candidates have been ineffectual. In addition, we cannot and should not wait for changes in party leadership simply because one party fails.

On the other hand, the number of people who identify as independent is growing rapidly. Recent polls show independents approaching 50 percent of Americans. This is reflective of the dissatisfaction with both parties. The American Unity Plan is designed to be a platform for this electorate. If a third party is formed, the American Unity Plan could be the basis for a party platform.

The table below illustrates what happens every election cycle.

Election Results	Democrats Win	Republicans Win or Divided Government
Republican Focus	Minimize the Damage • Hold down tax increases • Spend less than Democrats want • Maintain military funding • Point out hypocrisies • Complain about the media	Do Nothing or Temporary Wins • Tax cuts that can be repealed • Focus on improved security and trade • Ignore social issues and hope to get additional court seats • Complain about the media
Democrat Focus	Bold Ideas and Transformation • Major tax increases everywhere possible • Introduce new government programs and direct payments to constituents • Cede global power to foreign governments and increase regulations • Expand doctrine to education, corporations, military, etc. • Change laws and government rules to maintain power	Incrementalism • Maintain the size of the federal government plus inflation • Use crises for political gains • Focus on inequality and injustice to gain support for the next election • Call Republicans names and the party of no

When Democrats are in power, they focus on their bold ideas and transformations, while Republicans try to maintain the status quo. When Republicans are in control, they seem stagnant and satisfied with temporary or transient wins, such as tax cuts. When either party compromises American principles, we all lose in the long run.

Both parties violate American principles regardless of who is in office. Progressives are happy with incremental change. Conservatives and libertarians are generally happy with divided government, as gridlock achieves their goal of limiting the power of the federal government as much as possible. Ideological progressives within the Democratic Party have been playing the long game for over one hundred years and are satisfied with making incremental improvements because they have a clear vision of their desired utopian future and have bold policies of their own. Republicans seem content to slow the progressive movement but not permanently reverse it. The Republican Party has been branded the party of "No," and rightly so. If you believe in limited government, *not* doing something is a winning strategy most of the time. But most people who vote want to vote *for* something—anything that moves their agenda forward. They want real-world solutions that benefit them. Doing nothing may result in better policy than most things the federal government does, but it is not a strategy to unify the country and certainly not to solve generational problems.

Each party has a current message and a brand based on their respective ideologies. At the ends of the political spectrum, almost all progressives are Democrats, but not all Democratic Party voters are progressives. Almost all conservatives are Republican, but not all Republican Party voters are conservatives. This distinction is important to drive unifying solutions and win elections. Many independents, moderates, classical liberals, and libertarians vote across party lines but have some ideological belief in American principles or simply want a balanced approach.

In past elections, voters have changed party affiliation. Usually, it was because the country was perceived to be in crisis, and it was a referendum against the incumbent party as opposed to voting for the long-term direction of the winner. These voters could easily swing back in the other direction. To unify Americans, albeit for different reasons, Americans need a policy to vote for (not just a person to vote against) with a clear message, and they need to be invited to participate in the solutions.

Americans have heard the same talking points from each major party for decades, therefore a conversion to the other side only occurs when a dynamic leader emerges, one party oversteps, or a party runs a toxic candidate. This can and does happen, seemingly more often now, but this approach cannot be counted on to reverse our divide. No, a unified public platform must be created that addresses America's biggest and most pressing long-term issues. This platform must be delivered with a unifying message that is direct, honest, and fair and addresses the problems voters want solved. And most of all, it must show compassion in both policy and messaging, ensuring American principles are the foundation for change.

So how do we build common ground or unity around bold solutions that solve the critical issues of today? It certainly will not be generated by the current class of Washington politicians, in either party. These politicians, most of whom have outlasted any reasonable proposal for term limits, need to be mandated by the People to implement bold solutions, as they are incapable of creating long-term American policy on their own. The problems need to be specifically defined, and clear solutions need to be presented and communicated out of compassion rather than ideology.

Incrementalism is ineffectual for long-term improvement unless it is part of a broader policy. Progressives get this concept and live it. They have principles. They are just not necessarily unifying American principles. Rather than discussing long-term solutions, we are arguing and compromising with one another on short-term situational ethics. This is dividing us. I would argue there does not currently exist a meaningful political coalition across party lines proposing solutions that align to a long-term strategy based on American principles.

Democrats, led by the progressives, typically have bolder plans, as they want more government to remedy inequities. Republicans, led by the conservatives, have strict ideology focused on the size and control of government but rarely offer bold solutions or implement any of their ideas. The failure of the Republican Party is that rather than proposing solutions themselves, they spend 95 percent of the time saying no to Democrats. Republicans have lost their ability to engage and communicate with many potential voters, and Democrats propose solutions that have historically failed, and Americans know it, as many live through the resulting ramifications. Americans want generational solutions based on rational ideas they believe will work, not simply stopping the other side.

Incrementalism from both parties moves elections temporarily but results in chaos in the long term. The national debt, the pending Social Security and Medicare bankruptcies, immigration, and the failing education system are prime examples. The basic problem is situational morality and expediency. We address each issue individually as the next crisis or political opportunity arises, as opposed to holistically as a multigenerational platform that is bold and solves problems with a long-term, American-principle-centered mindset. In other words, we need systems-level thinking with a clear vision of the end goal in mind. We must envision solutions that do not violate what unifies Americans.

This book will present a bold policy platform, but clearly, whatever solution is delivered cannot be ambiguous with platitudes like reduce taxes, maintain a strong national defense, and fix social security. The American people deserve to know exactly what the government and its representatives will do. The American people want their representatives to be committed to policy and principle for the long run.

4

BOLD SOLUTIONS REVISITED

The curious task of economics is to demonstrate to men how little they really know about what they imagine they can design.

— Friedrich August von Hayek, economist

Americans are innovators, entrepreneurs, and risk-takers. We applaud and reward the big, bold, visionary ideas and celebrate those who risk their own money. Americans also, for some reason beyond comprehension, still look to politicians for big ideas. When politicians talk boldly, we rarely agree with them, but they get our attention.

Progressives have big, bold ideas. Progressives are credited for implementing the New Deal, the Great Society, and the Affordable Care Act. Now on the horizon is Medicare for All, the Green New

Deal, a national minimum wage, free college, and the elimination of student debt.

The progressive initiatives currently in place all have two things in common. First, they were years in the making and persisted beyond their initial defeat until legislation passed. Their sponsors never gave up the fight. Second, every one of these programs violated American principles. Over time, the inherent issues resulting from providing benefits to some at the expense of others created many of our divisions, despite their positive intentions and the fact that they did help millions of Americans.

Going back one hundred years, the only equivalent bold ideas from Republicans, led by the conservative wing, were the Contract with America and the Fair Tax. The Tea Party was more of a movement within the Republican Party that focused on reduced spending, smaller government, and other conservative agenda items rather than passing specific legislation. Legislation is different than, say, the leadership and resolve necessary to defeat Communism and win wars. Where are the big ideas like the Contract with America and the Fair Tax today? And, unlike the progressives, why did the conservatives within the Republican Party just give up when they promised sweeping tax reform, balanced budgets, term limits, and dramatically reduced regulation? Do Republicans have any new bold solutions that rival progressive ideas like the Green New Deal or Medicare for All?

Republicans seem to have abandoned the big ideas they once had. As much as we can follow leaders who espouse principles we agree with, Republicans do not have the unifying theme that continues the idea without the individual leader. Is there any doubt that when the progressives of today are gone, a new breed will not be espousing increased government spending, reduction in fossil fuel production, more government-subsidized healthcare and social services, free education, minimum wage increases, and more? The ideas and specific policy proposals must transcend any leader, Republican or Democrat, and be part of a generational platform. Republicans abandon the fight more than the Democrats.

Let us use the Contract with America as an example of how policy, messaging, and generational persistence is needed for lasting change. Although admired by many on the political right, the Contract with America was not bold enough and did not transcend time as a principled position. Much of it focused on the problems of the day and not the future. It focused on things that were "doable." Do progressives worry that the Green New Deal is doable within the next few election cycles? Did the progressives abandon climate change initiatives when energy security and the threat of war with Russia emerged? Why would conservatives ever give up on a balanced budget, and what does this say about their ability to lead and attract the majority of American voters who could be unified around fiscal discipline?

America needs a bold plan that makes good policy sense and appeals to many progressives and conservatives alike, albeit for vastly different reasons. Yes, Republicans believe that free-market capitalism and limited government are what produce both wealth and happiness for the most people, but something is lacking in both their policy platform and message to win elections and implement lasting legislation. Many progressives also want fiscal discipline but want guardrails to avoid crony capitalism and assurance that the social safety net is in place.

For example, we recall that the Contract with America worked to win an election, but it was only modestly implemented in 1995, and it has never been mentioned again other than for nostalgia. According to the Heritage Foundation:

> The Contract itself emerged publicly with the staging of the mass signing of the Contract on the steps of the U.S. Capitol by 367 candidates for office on September 27, 1994. On that day, all of these candidates publicly pledged: "If we break this Contract, throw us out." The Republicans who were already Members of the House of Representatives organized themselves into 11 working groups that eventually drafted ten bills that made up the Contract.
>
> The items in the Contract were carefully selected in terms of issues that were of fundamental policy importance but also were "doable," that could be accomplished rather quickly because of the broad support they engendered. Extensive public opinion polling revealed that at least 60 percent of Americans supported all ten of the specific items in the Contract. By dealing initially with popular items, such as the Congress being governed by the same rules as all Americans, and broad philosophical concepts, such as balancing the federal budget, the Contract engendered popular momentum that could eventually lead to confronting more contentious issues, such

as environmental regulations and Medicare and
Medicaid reforms.

Politically, the Contract found a particularly
receptive audience in the elections in the fall of
1994 because of a combined disenchantment with
the existing Congress and the widespread view of a
lack of leadership being provided by President Bill
Clinton in the White House. The Clinton cam-
paign in 1992 had generated the expectation of
great changes being made to deal with domestic
problems. Moreover, the fact that Democrats in
1993 controlled both branches of the Congress together with the White House seemed to create the
means for changes to take place by breaking the
so-called partisan gridlock in Washington. But the
failure to make substantive policy changes in 1993
and 1994 clearly facilitated the political changes in
November 1994. Thus, the concept of the Contract
found a particularly receptive audience.

Does this sound like today? What was passed as legislation
and what has become of the ideas in the Contract with America
that were so popular but not passed? More from the Heritage
Foundation:

The ten items in the Contract were all acted upon
in the first 100 days of the new Congress, which is
what the signatories had pledged. Nine of the ten

items in the Contract passed the House: Only the constitutional amendment on term limits (which required a two-thirds vote) was defeated. Out of a total of 302 roll call votes on issues related to the Contract With America, the conservatives prevailed on 299 of them. A balanced budget amendment passed in the House by a 300-123 margin but was subsequently defeated as it fell one vote short of the two-thirds needed for passage in the U.S. Senate. The overall margin by which the items in the Contract were passed averaged about 70 percent despite the fact that the Republicans only held a 12-seat margin over the Democrats (52-48 percent, the smallest House majority margin in 40 years). Given the notorious lack of party discipline in the American Congress, the passage by a large majority of nearly all of the items in the Contract was a remarkable achievement.

One vote away from a balanced budget amendment, term limits, and the line-item veto, and the Republicans gave up the fight? The point is not to denigrate the Contract with America but to learn from history. Some of the points in the Contract were timeless and are just as applicable today. In addition, the Contract proved bold solutions are politically popular even if one party has a slim majority. However, the majority of the points were transient or situational to the needs of mid-1990s but were effective in winning an election because the Contract made the problems "less worse." It would be like getting a tax-rate reduction without changing the actual process of how we are taxed and reducing federal spending. Tax-rate reductions, as we know, can be reversed, but systemic changes, such as elimination of the inheritance tax, would be almost impossible to reinstate. Conservatives want to enhance, reduce, cut, invest, and make other incremental changes without an end plan in mind. In other words, Republican establishment politicians espousing conservative solutions focus on what is "doable," and the Democratic Party focuses on their ultimate prize even if that means not achieving as much today. Conservatives in the Republican Party negotiate and compromise with the Democrats toward the progressive endgame, but the Democrats simply block Republican proposals when in power and only compromise when necessary to preserve political power. Republicans are generally weak politicians because they do not stand on long-term policy and principle and lack policies that are popular, visionary, and consistent over time.

Three Contract with America proposals became law. The Congressional Accountability Act of 1995 required Congress to follow eleven workplace laws. The Unfunded Mandates Reform Act of 1995 restricted Congress from imposing mandates on states that are not adequately funded. The Paperwork Reduction Act of 1995 reduced federal paperwork requirements. Notice anything? These were probably the most situational or relevant to the politics of 1995, and none were very bold.

Other than the Fiscal Responsibility Act, which specifically addressed a balanced budget, the line-item veto to curb spending in the future, and the Citizen Legislature Act, which proposed term limits, the other acts focused on blending tax policy and federal funding with personal responsibility and social issues, such as crime, good-faith sentencing, discouraging illegitimacy and teen pregnancy, cuts to welfare programs, child support enforcement, adoption, reduction in the marriage penalty, senior citizens earnings limits, small business tax incentives, legal liability reform, and more. The point is not to debate the legislative merits but to note that they were not structural and irreversible changes such as the New Deal. The proposals were situational to the times. They were not carried forward strategically as a movement.

Similarly, the Fair Tax of 2005 was bolder than the Contract with America around tax policy but very narrow in focus. Some of the ideas of the Fair Tax will be presented in this book and would be perfectly applicable today as a foundational solution to collect government tax receipts. At the time, however, the Fair Tax was too hard to explain and applied only to those who felt overly and unfairly taxed. According to data from the Tax Policy Center, in 2022, about 40 percent of US households were estimated to have no or negative federal income tax liability. This means they either have no taxable income, or they have enough tax credits and deductions to eliminate their federal income tax liability. Note that even though these households may not pay federal income tax, they still may pay other taxes such as payroll taxes, state and local taxes, and excise taxes. It is hard to build a coalition at the federal level when many are not directly impacted.

Compare the Fair Tax to recent and major Democratic Party legislation, such as the Affordable Care Act (ACA). The ACA built on the popularity of Medicare. Of course, *popularity* in this case means simply implemented as law and has nothing to do with quality of care or cost of the program. Building on Medicare, a form of the ACA was introduced in the 1990s as soon as the Democrats had a perceived mandate to move forward with healthcare legislation. That failed, but then the ACA was introduced and implemented twenty years later. Was there much difference, other than repackaging, over the next twenty years? In fact, the ACA was a much bolder reform when passed than the 1990s version. Structural change is never abandoned by the progressives or the Democratic Party. Is the ACA the end or just the beginning of the path to a completely socialized, single-payer healthcare system?

Besides policy and messaging to win one election, America needs a consistent approach that exceeds the abilities or charisma of any one leader. Whatever bold policy is adopted to win one election, such as in 1994, must be made permanent and cannot be undone easily by extremes in either party. Rather than untangle the unsustainability of Social Security and Medicare in their current form, many progressives are building on them to achieve even greater centralized government control. Alternative solutions, promoted by either party, must be guided by American principles.

Progressives are playing the long game. Marxism goes back to 1847, when Karl Marx and Friedrich Engels began writing *The Communist Manifesto*. Woodrow Wilson took the ideology to the national stage in 1914. Every thirty or forty years, progressives make a bold move and usually settle for something that moves their ideology forward, many times moving the country further away from American principles. The Republicans have systematically lost control of education, culture, the tax code, energy policy, and immigration, and are slowly ceding the military and big business.

When progressives implement their policies, the long-term effects are not understood at the time by most people but over decades become apparent, when it is then difficult to reverse course.

Indeed, progressives have always had bold solutions. Are we implementing their solutions systematically over time? Consider Karl Marx's "10 Planks" (in italics) and the current state of affairs in America (in roman):

1. *Abolition of Property in Land and Application of all Rents of Land to Public Purpose.* The federal government owns around 640 million acres of land (about 28 percent) of the 2.27 billion acres of land in the United States. Rather than private ownership, industries such as farming, ranching, oil and gas production, and more must lease from the federal government, and these lands are heavily regulated and used as political weapons.

2. *A Heavy Progressive or Graduated Income Tax.* According to data from the Tax Policy Center, the top 1 percent of earners in the United States (those with an income of about $540,000 or more) are estimated to pay an average adjusted federal income tax rate of over 22 percent and contribute over 40 percent of all federal income tax receipts.

3. *Abolition of All Rights of Inheritance.* Inheritance is heavily taxed, and as such, an entire industry has evolved in estate planning to minimize the impact on future generations, needlessly adding costs to many American families.

4. *Confiscation of the Property of All Emigrants and Rebels.* The government may have begun classifying people who

disagree with their social agenda as domestic terrorists, and this will result in fines and imprisonment for merely voicing or publishing an opinion. The government tried to create a Disinformation Governance Board but withdrew the proposal due to political backlash.

5. *Centralization of Credit in the Hands of the State, by Means of a National Bank with State Capital and an Exclusive Monopoly.* The Federal Reserve is an early twentieth-century creation effectively governing the cost of capital. Now the federal government regulates almost all lending, from homes to education, and decides how much risk private banks may take. It is not difficult to imagine that crypto currencies such as Bitcoin will be highly regulated beyond the legislation recommended by the industry and that the government will create their own digital currencies to compete with the private issuers.

6. *Centralization of the Means of Communication and Transport in the Hands of the State.* The government has traditionally regulated public utilities, as the only service provider at scale to communities, albeit at the state level, except for nuclear power. Now the collaboration with the social media giants has escalated the initiative to the point that freedom of press and speech is challenged daily. Transportation is still a free-market endeavor, but infrastructure is highly regulated, especially in terms of foreign trade, aviation, ports, road construction, and more.

7. *Extension of Factories and Instruments of Production Owned by the State, the Bringing Into Cultivation of Waste Lands, and the*

Improvement of the Soil Generally in Accordance with a Common Plan. The power of the Environmental Protection Agency is growing exponentially to regulate and control many businesses. The government owns vast lands with no current strategic purpose other than control, taxation, fees, and limiting free enterprise.

8. *Equal Liability of All to Labor. Establishment of Industrial Armies, Especially for Agriculture.* The federal government takes an active and aggressive position to promote labor unions and preferred industries, picking winners and losers. As the government grows, unions in particular gain more power, even with their reduced membership. In 1847, agriculture was the primary means of production, but the concept has expanded to industrial production, retail, technology, and services such as education and healthcare.

9. *Combination of Agriculture with Manufacturing Industries; Gradual Abolition of the Distinction Between Town and Country by a More Equable Distribution of the Population over the Country.* The federal government is now attempting to influence suburban and even rural zoning to exercise more control over private property and land under an affordable housing initiative.

10. *Free Education for All Children in Public Schools. Abolition of Children's Factory Labor in its Present Form. Combination of Education with Industrial Production.* Over 90 percent of K-12 education is delivered in the public sector, and many progressives are actively working on subsidizing college, daycare, family leave, and more.

The language of 1847 may be different, but would any progressive today disagree with these points? In fact, they may not think Marx was visionary enough, since his hope was that these points would be realized in the nineteenth century. After so many failures of Marxist policies, are progressives still determined to realize Marx's vision? Failure has not deterred Communism and socialism in many parts of the world. Compared to the Contract with America, each of Marx's points are not situational to the times but are fundamental to ideology. Do many care that inflation is rampant, so long as they save the planet by controlling or regulating the means of energy production?

What is the Republican or conservative equivalent of Marxism? As Speaker of the House Newt Gingrich wrote in his book *To Renew America*: "We must replace our centralized, micro-managed, Washington-based bureaucracy with a dramatically decentralized system more appropriate to a continent-wide country. . . 'Closer is better' would be the rule of thumb for our decision making; less power in Washington and more back home, our consistent theme." Many Republicans and others such as libertarians agree with federalism, but what does the policy endgame look like? Or stated another way, what problems would the ideal solution solve in modern and future America, and would this solution stand the test of time?

To specifically contrast Marx, here are ten competing points based on American principles noting that not all of today's biggest issues were originally identified by Marx.

1. <u>Marx</u>: Abolition of property in land and application of all rents of land to public purpose.

American Principle: The federal government will only own property and land necessary for national defense and government operations to ensure no landowners operating private enterprise are treated unfairly or differently than others through taxation or regulation.

2. Marx: A heavy progressive or graduated income tax.
   American Principle: All Americans are taxed at an equal rate without government intrusion into our personal lives.

3. Marx: Abolition of all rights of inheritance.
   American Principle: After paying taxes, we have the right to invest, save, and distribute any wealth accumulated as we wish.

4. Marx: Confiscation of the property of all emigrants and rebels.
   American Principle: We believe in the unwavering support of human rights and constitutional freedoms, including private property rights.

5. Marx: Centralization of credit in the hands of the State, by means of a National Bank with State capital and an exclusive monopoly.
   American Principle: We have the right to legally transact with anyone we chose, with government taxation, credit, and regulation applied equally to all and only as necessary to ensure a transparent and free market.

6. <u>Marx</u>: Centralization of the means of communication and transport in the hands of the State.

   <u>American Principle</u>: We have the freedom to engage in free speech and commerce as we wish, with laws and regulations applied equally to all.

7. <u>Marx</u>: Extension of factories and instruments of production owned by the State, the bringing into cultivation of waste lands, and the improvement of the soil generally, in accordance with a common plan.

   <u>American Principle</u>: Private property ownership of all means of production is central to American life, with businesses complying to only those regulations specifically passed by Congress into law and applied equally to all.

8. <u>Marx</u>: Equal liability of all to labor. Establishment of industrial armies, especially for agriculture.

   <u>American Principle</u>: We believe in freedom of association and equality under the law.

9. <u>Marx</u>: Combination of agriculture with manufacturing industries; gradual abolition of the distinction between town and country by a more equable distribution of the population over the country.

   <u>American Principle</u>: Those items not enumerated in the Constitution are governed by state and local jurisdictions.

10. <u>Marx</u>: Free education for all children in public schools. Abolition of children's factory labor in its present form.

<u>American Principle</u>: Parents have the right to choose what is best for their children, subject to laws and benefits applied equally to all.

Marx's ten points are not complete in the context of our modern society, but many of the concepts have transcended time and geography. Clearly, as we revisit and envision new policies, we must take ideas from both conservativism and progressivism to build a unifying coalition. Changes—rather, dramatic improvements—to the social safety net, tax policy, immigration, and many other issues must be timeless and have permanence that cannot be undone easily by extremes in either party.

Putting aside the messaging and the politics of the day, policy solutions must address the following issues, or they simply will not be transformative toward maintaining American principles and values. Here might be a starting policy position focused on the ideal solution first instead of the tactics of passing incremental change:

- Social Security – All Americans agree there should be a retirement social safety net. The magic of compound interest over time is the best way to build retirement wealth for all Americans to eliminate the generational transfer of wealth from young to old. The rate of return of publicly funded, private accounts, with proper guardrails, far exceeds the return on Social Security taxes paid, and these accounts can be passed on to heirs to build generational wealth and close the wealth gap in a fair way. Both taxes and savings restrictions on personally funded, private retirement accounts would be eliminated.

• Healthcare – Equal federal public funding of private healthcare accounts is paid only to American citizens, and each American would receive the exact same benefit. This benefit would allow Americans to buy the healthcare policies that fit their needs and save for higher expenses later in life. The delivery of healthcare services would solely be the purview of the private sector, with payments made directly from consumer to service provider to create transparent pricing, reduce administrative costs, and provide an incentive to shop for competitive services. The cost of healthcare services would be dramatically reduced by eliminating third-party bureaucracy and opaque and controlled pricing to mandate each consumer is treated equally. Highly customized plans and services would cater to consumer needs across states and without restrictions. Government regulation of the private insurance and healthcare service delivery industry would be focused solely on safety, fraud, criminality, and transparency, allowing consumers to shop for services the way they do any consumer product.

• Education – Similar to healthcare, to grow the social safety net to help many disadvantaged Americans, education will be publicly funded and private delivery will be significantly increased. Money for education will be provided directly and equally in savings and investment accounts to every American. This will be used by the student, parents, or custodians to fund all education and related needs as they see fit. Private delivery of education services will produce better educational outcomes at a lower cost, resulting in the best education free market in the world. The federal government will have no role in education other than to fund education accounts as a social safety net to ensure all Americans have an equal opportunity to succeed.

- Taxes – The tax code is an abomination requiring the government to be intrusive to our lives just to pay taxes, and the cost of tax compliance on both the payment and collection side is staggering. The current tax code must be repealed in its entirety, with no exceptions, and replaced with a consumption tax on all retail goods and services that are paid equally and voluntarily by anonymous consumers, all but eliminating tax cheats, fraud, crony capitalism, and the cost of compliance. The role of the IRS would be only to enforce collection of taxes at the retail level, as most state and local governments do today. The elimination of all individual and corporate taxes on labor and capital would return industry, spur investment in the United States, and eliminate much of the risk and cost of global supply chains as well as many national security concerns in key industries. The United States would be the fairest taxed country on the planet, with retail taxes paid by American citizens, immigrants, and visitors alike. The elimination of the embedded cost of taxes and compliance would reduce the cost of goods and services before the federal retail tax is applied.

- Entitlements and Universal Income – All American citizens would receive the exact same monthly federal distribution, similar to universal basic income, to ensure lower-income earners or those who are incapable of working are better off than in the current tax system while increasing the incentive to work. Noncitizens would not be eligible for federal benefits, thereby making their net tax contribution to America higher than American citizens.

- Federal Budget – Over time, the collection of taxes must be in equilibrium with the distribution of funds, including social safety net payments, to operate the federal government. Any increases in government spending would have to be offset by an increase in the federal sales tax, incentivizing all politicians to work together to avoid unduly taxing the poor.

- Immigration – There must be significant increases in the number of legal immigrants to America, as governed by both free-market principles and true sponsorship by non-government entities including schools, businesses, investors, families, nonprofits, and charitable organization. We will eliminate centrally planned and arbitrary government immigration quotas. We recognize talent is global, and America will attract the best, brightest, and hardest working people in the world, including those seeking freedom from repressive governments. As immigration is legal, voluntary, and sponsored, immigrants will receive no supplemental assistance from the federal government and while living in the United States will pay the federal retail tax when buying goods and services. We will eliminate any regulations on length of stay and reporting so long as the immigrant or visitor arrives through legal means, maintains proper identification and sponsorship, and follows US laws.

For every one of these major issues, there is not a single cohesive Republican policy statement in existence today. We hear about, for example, the need to reduce taxes, but reduce them to what? And what taxes specifically? The above major issues have been discussed ad nauseam for decades, but the Republicans have never produced a bold solution because there is no vision. The default direction for America today is based on a progressive vision for the country focused on the social safety net and equality of outcome, which violates American principles and, by definition, will never unify the country. We cannot continue with the policies of either party. An alternative approach is required, one that will unite Americans from across the political landscape.

The next chapters will present both the policies and the message that will appeal to most Americans by adhering to American principles. Progressives and conservatives will both hate and love elements of this platform.

Introducing the American Unity Plan.

PART II
THE PLAN

5

THE AMERICAN UNITY PLAN

We shall tax and tax, and spend and spend, and elect and elect.

— Harry Hopkins, head of the Works Progress
Administration under FDR

I t is okay to lose a few battles but win the war. Our politicians have already compromised on the idea of individual responsibility. In a perfect world, parents would take care of all the needs of their children from birth to adulthood, and children would take care of the basic needs of their elderly parents to the grave. Where the family could not do so, neighbors, local communities, churches, and charities would assist. The federal government would have no role in your care. We all know help is much more compassionate when it is provided within your own social influence and directed by family and others who care. Help is much more than money—it is love, advice, guidance, and compassion. We as Americans are more compassionate—rather than our government benefits—than most others on the planet, as demonstrated by our personal global giving and how we mobilize to meet any emergency.

But many people today confuse compassion with taxation and wealth redistribution. Republicans, conservatives, and libertarians have lost the argument that the government should not be involved in the social contract. They have accepted it and now fight with the Democratic Party, as led by the progressives, over how much and to whom it goes. There is no argument that Social Security is flawed as a concept on several levels, including people giving money involuntarily to people they never met, the inefficiency of the system, and the minimal financial return when and if you fully get your share in the future. The only argument from Republicans seems to be that the Social Security system is bankrupt, and Democrats easily agree and counter with more taxes, rather than promoting savings and investment. The same is true for welfare, food stamps, healthcare, education, and more.

If this battle is lost, what war is being fought? More importantly, what war should be fought? The battle must be waged not over public funding of the social contract but public delivery. We collectively need to refocus on the concept of public funding coupled with fully privatizing the delivery mechanism of all publicly funded social contract endeavors, with the proper guardrails in place. Once privatization is achieved, services and outcomes will improve, costs will decrease, and most importantly, American citizens will be more incentivized and motivated to be much more self-reliant and even more generous.

The solutions about to be presented will be based on the model of privatization of the industries of the social contract, yet the implementation will be painful, especially to budget hawks such as this author. Any solution must be fair and compassionate, as presented in previous chapters. It must be considered that current beneficiaries have already contributed to the system and should receive what the government promised. The vision is grounded in American principles, but the journey assumes the short-term battles are already lost and will be for the foreseeable future. We can debate the details of any solution. Any plan will have flaws and will become more flawed over time in response to societal needs. But it is better to argue what degree of American principles we want and when it will be fully achieved rather than how much government centralized planning and control will be thrust upon us year after year, which is divisive in and of itself. Let us argue about the degree of freedom and the best way to allow people to prosper to eliminate misery with minimal interference and loss of freedoms from the federal government rather than argue about the next problem we want the government to solve for us.

The heart of the American Unity Plan is based on two concepts addressing taxes and social safety net spending.

1. Building on the brilliance of the Fair Tax, taxes will be based on retail sales of goods and services, and all other federal taxes and withholdings will be eliminated to make cheating extremely difficult, and payment of taxes will be voluntary and nonintrusive to the individual. Payroll (Social Security and Medicare for both the employee and employer),

self-employment, capital gains, corporate, inventory, excise, inheritance, and all the other taxes will be eliminated at the federal level. This lowers the burden and cost of government itself and reduces the cost of compliance for individuals and businesses alike. The embedded tax cost in every product and service would be replaced by a federal retail tax so that the price paid by the consumer is only modestly higher than now. Unlike the Fair Tax and other proposals, there would be no product or services exemptions or modifications to the federal retail tax rate to ensure that politicians stop picking winners and losers for us rather than letting the free market work its magic. This also reduces crony capitalism and lobbying for tax credits and incentives by businesses. It is the ultimate achievement in fairness and equality under the law. Without withholdings of any type, Americans would have more money in their pockets. Individuals, nonprofits, small businesses, and corporations would no longer need to prepare federal income returns, seek tax deductions and credits, shift revenue and expenses between reporting periods, move money offshore, and be audited by the IRS. The focus of business would be on serving their stakeholders, not on minimizing their tax burden. Additionally, although noncitizens would also pay no personal taxes and have no withholdings from their pay, they would be paying a greater percentage of taxes when they buy goods and services, as explained below. Those who report less income than they are required to by law would also pay more in taxes, using the systems already in place at every retail sales counter or e-commerce site. Federal tax payments would flow at the same pace of retail goods and services sales, without artificial deadlines such as April 15. For purposes of streamlining explanation from here forward, we will call this retail tax on all goods and services the "American Unity Tax," or the "Unity Tax."

2. All current federal benefits, including Social Security, Medicare, Medicaid, welfare and food programs, government pensions, education assistance, and all other federal government social safety net programs would be replaced by a single monthly payment and paid only to American citizens. With the exception of children who have not yet graduated high school, this payment is the same to every American regardless of age, location, income, marital status, and dependents, and this payment will begin at birth. For Americans, this payment, along with eliminating tax withholdings, offsets any potential increase in the cost of goods and services, but since non-US citizens are ineligible for payments, they would effectively carry a higher tax burden. This is their toll or repayment to the taxes paid by generations of Americans over many years to create our economy. In addition, since this payment is the same for wealthy and poor alike, the rich will be taxed more fairly and progressively because they simply buy more. This social safety net system is fair, cost-effective, and simple to administer. During the transition from the current system, which might take a generation or two, no American citizen currently receiving benefits from the federal government would

receive less than they receive today, and many recipients will receive more, helping the most vulnerable in society. The money follows the individual and is deposited directly into individual accounts, just like Social Security and stimulus checks are deposited today. However, Social Security payments and 401(k) and IRA distributions will not have taxes withheld. From this monthly payment, which we will call "American Unity Income" or "Unity Income," a portion would be required to fund our own responsibilities:

a. Retirement – Personal retirement accounts, similar to 401(k)s and IRAs, would be owned and directed by the individual (or their parents or custodian).

b. Healthcare – Personal healthcare accounts would also be owned by the individual and used for any healthcare needs, including buying healthcare insurance, disability income insurance, and long-term care. Unused funds could be saved for later in life when expenses are higher. Government guardrails will require that everyone must have noncancelable catastrophic health insurance covering 100 percent of all healthcare needs after the individual out-of-pocket maximum is met. This would replace the current Medicare trust, as well as Medicaid, CHIP, and other federal healthcare programs. Unlike the ACA, the new system would provide a greater and more affordable opportunity to purchase insurance for the 28 million uninsured Americans. It would incentivize healthcare consumer competition, thereby improving services and lowering costs, reduce the cost of compliance by healthcare service providers, and encourage savings for the later stages of life.

c. Education – Parents and students would have direct funding to support their preferred education opportunities, including existing government-run schools, private schools, homeschooling, daycare, tutoring, private classes, and other education needs (internet access, computers, books, etc.) starting at the child's birth. Public funding coupled with expanding private delivery of education will allow students to receive a more customized education experience, shifting the power from the one-size-fits-all approach of school boards and teachers unions to parents and students, and at a much lower cost. States, counties, and local jurisdictions will likely shift their funding from the public schools to the individuals as well, all but eliminating the current abysmal delivery of public education from birth to high school, which affects a much higher percentage of the poor and contributes to generational poverty.

Each of these ideas will be explained in greater detail in subsequent chapters. First, we start with a conceptual overview of the end state, which is that Americans control their own retirement, healthcare, and education with proper federal government guardrails, and the value they build contributes to their wealth and security over time. The issue is and always will be exactly how we get there from here to avoid the ever-increasing government control of all aspects of our lives.

Using prepandemic spending as a baseline to eliminate one-time emergency spending, the total annual mandatory and discretionary spend by the federal government for Social Security, healthcare, education, and other social benefits is approximately $3.1 trillion of the $4.4 trillion in total government spending. Both rose significantly during the pandemic and will continue to rise for the foreseeable future given the current levels of inflation and proposed new programs. To privatize these programs, the same $3.1 trillion must be distributed to individuals who currently receive payments and new money must be paid to new recipients. This change is required to implement the American principle of fairness and equality under the law relative to our tax and safety net systems and to ensure no negative rights are incurred on the American population who have already paid into the system and expect their current benefits to continue for life.

However, for those currently receiving benefits, the social safety net programs could be reduced on day one and replaced by the new Unity Income. For example, for those receiving Social Security or Disability Income, including currently eligible survivors and children, if the new Unity Income payment is more than their current gross Social Security payment, Social Security would be eliminated and replaced in its entirety by Unity Income. These recipients are typically less affluent Americans or spouses who earned less during their working lives. These recipients would receive more retirement distributions from the federal government. After implementation, the current Social Security system would spend less federal money every year, offsetting some of the new spending. Essentially, this transfers federal funding from the Social Security system to the new Unity Income payment system as part of annual Congressional budgeting, as it should be. The difference is that the less affluent Social Security recipient would be better off not only receiving a larger payment, but also not having to worry about withholdings and tax filings. In addition, since Unity Income is the same for every individual, there is no need to worry about adjustments based on family status, and all Americans are eligible without worrying about government qualifications, dividends or interest received, or additional income from working beyond retirement.

On the other hand, if Unity Income is less than the current Social Security benefit, Social Security will be reduced by the Unity Income payment. This is the same concept as when a higher-earning spouse dies and the surviving spouse receives their benefit. Recipients would receive the same Unity Income payment as every other American plus a smaller Social Security payment, but once again, there are no withholdings, so they are better off than under Social Security alone. In addition, distributions from private retirement plans are no longer taxed. The concept works the same whether a retiree is married or living alone, since the payments follow the individual and the government does not get to ask about your personal life when collecting taxes!

For Americans who are not retired, this is simply new money. We will discuss messaging later, but the plan is similar to the progressive's concept of Universal Basic Income (UBI) except for a few key differences.

1. Every adult American gets the exact same benefit, and every child gets the same benefit, with no qualifications whatsoever other than you are a legal American citizen living in the US. This is equality and fairness at its core.

2. The money is used to end all other federal entitlements once and for all and culminates with a permanent balanced budget in a generation or two.

3. The plan reduces the size, scope, and control of the federal government, reduces the actual cost of critical services through free-market competition, reduces federal regulations, and improves outcomes.

We pause here. After being critical of Republicans for abandoning a balanced budget, you must be thinking, "Huh?" Trillions in additional annual spending will destroy the budget. Yes, in the very near term, but not nearly as bad as many current proposals for new spending. How much will they spend on UBI, free education, debt relief, the Green New Deal, and increased government regulations and control without solving the entitlement issues that have plagued us for generations and are mounting annually? Under the American Unity Plan, the budget deficit gets less each year until it is in balance, as opposed to growing for the foreseeable future.

To recap, we are talking about transforming 75 percent of federal government spending from government control to free-market capitalism, with proper guardrails, while leaving a social safety net in place for all American citizens. This entitlement spending is roughly 14 percent of the US GDP but controls or influences roughly 40 percent of the economy when you consider healthcare and education. On the surface, in the short-term, this violates the spending debate conservatives and libertarians have championed, but the Republican Party has failed precisely because they have no plan other than to spend less than the Democrats. The American Unity Plan is an admirable end state that solves a one-hundred-year-old crisis in the making in just a generation of two.

Simply stated, the problem is too large to fix without a long-term strategy that is short-term painful. We have tried incrementalism (tax cuts, regulation reform, etc.) and it will not work, as any gains are eliminated by the next politicians in office with a different agenda. The problem expands each year due to simple demographics. We need a plan that is extremely difficult to change once in place, as we have learned from history.

The key point is this concept is "doable" because some form of UBI will appeal to many progressives, classical liberals, and moderates. Libertarians and conservatives will focus on a long-term balanced budget and privatization that cannot be repealed easily like a temporary tax or spending cut. In other words, it will be bold and have great messaging to win elections and get votes to implement. How many Democrats will be opposed to some form of UBI to benefit the 28 million uninsured in this country and close the wealth gap? We will get UBI one way or another from the progressives in the Democratic Party. The movement is gaining steam. America needs a unified approach to implement privatization of government-controlled industries and a balanced budget in return!

Here is the big picture leading to a balanced budget. GDP and investments typically grow faster than inflation over time, and privatization will cut the cost of social program delivery. In effect,

wealth (Unity Income and work to accelerate savings and investments) will grow as fast or faster than the economy when viewed
generationally. As people grow wealthier and retain more of their income, they spend more and therefore will pay more tax voluntarily.
Over time, as individual accounts rise faster than inflation, the
current system of government benefits is reduced. Even with current
federal benefits indexed to inflation, every year entitlement spending
will decrease. A child or a young worker receiving Unity Income on
day one will never see a penny from the current Social Security or
Medicare systems. They will not care because their wealth will far
exceed any future Social Security benefit, they will have insurance
to protect against catastrophic health costs, and Unity Income will
be there as a safety net for their entire lives. Also, since they own
their accounts, this wealth can be passed to their children or any
beneficiary they choose, further eliminating reliance on the current
entitlement system for the next generation.

Another key reason why the budget will be reduced annually
after a one-time investment is simply demographics. As we all
know, the current Social Security and entitlement systems assume
that workers will transfer payments to older Americans, but that
only works if the pool of workers is growing as fast or faster than
the retired population. We are living longer, and the birthrate has
dropped below the 2.1 births per biological woman rate needed to
sustain the population. As the older generation leaves us, current
entitlements are reduced under the American Unity Plan.

This is also why immigration (to be discussed later) is so important to not only national security but the implementation of the
American Unity Plan, leading to a balanced budget. In effect, under

the current entitlement system, we need more young people with jobs paying into the system to sustain the older Americans living longer. Under the American Unity Plan, legal immigration would be vastly increased over today's levels, with immigrants unable by law to receive Unity Income until they become naturalized citizens. Any social benefits to immigrants would be strictly voluntary by the private sectors and the states if they choose. In effect, we need more skilled, legal talent voluntarily coming to the United States, paying taxes through their retail buying, and paying down the national debt in exchange for the opportunity to live, work, and raise a family in America.

The elimination of the current income tax system will incentivize many companies to relocate back to the US. This will have major implications with China, and coupled with their own shrinking population demographics, will slow their growth, as well as improve efforts to solve the climate crisis, as China is a major violator of climate deals. This will also have a profound impact on our balance of trade and help to reduce inflation and the debt.

As an implementation strategy under the Unity Plan, no one is worse off than today or worse off in their retirement years than promised. In addition, there are no preset government regulations on retirement age or withdrawals from privately held retirement accounts as income, savings, and investment are not taxed. Unity Income is there as security for life. Therefore, the Unity Income budget changes only in relation to changes in legal US citizenship, and government across the board Unity Income increases or reductions applied equally to all American citizens. The $3.1 trillion in current government social program spending, after a one-time increase when implemented, will reduce each year until it reaches zero! In addition, eliminating tax cheats, increasing legal immigration, the repatriation of American business to invest on these shores, and the additional spending from the wealth created by putting more money in individual pockets will dramatically increase GDP and the tax base.

The messaging focus to unite Americans and implement change over time needs to be on the Unity Income side of the equation rather than the elimination of the current federal tax system, a major flaw of the Fair Tax proposal. We need to shift from a discussion on future entitlement benefits to one on savings and investments in the here and now. The message of the American Unity Plan is quite simple and will appeal across the political landscape:

We believe every American should have a social safety net that includes retirement, education, and healthcare, from cradle to grave. The cost of healthcare and education will be more affordable to Americans, primarily helping the poor. We will permanently fix the soon to be bankrupt Social Security and Medicare trust funds. We will ensure every American can invest in their own retirement to close the wealth gap and build generational wealth. No American will receive less money from the federal government than they do now, and many will receive much more. We will reduce the cost, size, and intrusiveness of the government by eliminating the current federal income tax system and replacing it with a simple federal retail tax, as many states have now. Taxes will be fair and voluntary based on the consumption of goods and services, with no exceptions, to eliminate government lobbying and crony capitalism primarily benefiting corporations and the wealthy. We will subsidize the poorest Americans proportionately more. We will balance the federal budget while ensuring social safety net payments and other federal spending are matched to retail taxes collected to create a stronger and more prosperous America. Our plan treats every American fairly, compassionately, and equally under the law and ensures no one currently receiving government benefits as promised is harmed financially.

There is something to like and something to hate for everyone. It is not about bringing Democrats over to the Republican side or vice versa. It is about voting for something bold and positive across ideologies, which is absent in the current political environment. Someone could remain progressive and still want the American Unity Plan because it is a means to UBI, maintaining a highly progressive tax system, encouraging more immigration, securing the social safety net from imminent disaster, providing the path to healthcare for all Americans, helping the poor save, promoting family wealth and opportunity, and increasing federal funding for education. Republicans could support the American Unity Plan because they want a simpler and more equitable tax system that reduces the size of the government, a path to a balanced budget and lower national debt, privatization of key industries, repatriation of jobs, and improved national security. Libertarians and classical liberals want to reduce the intrusiveness of government in our lives and promote self-reliance.

We first need a bold plan or framework with broad appeal that solves problems. Once that is on the table, we can debate specific Unity Income tax rates, Unity Income payments, and more. The American Unity Plan as explained in the following chapters dives into these details.

6

PAYING YOUR FAIR SHARE

Income tax returns are the most imaginative fiction being
written today.

— Herman Wouk, American author

Conservatives, progressives, classical liberals, independents, and moderates alike would probably agree everyone should pay their fair share of taxes. The problem is what is the definition of "fair"? Americans have no problem paying taxes, so long as the practice is perceived to be fairly applied to all, easy and cost-effective to pay, and minimally intrusive to our lives. Our current federal tax system meets none of these objectives.

Our tax system is a perfect example of why it is difficult to build unity in America. Is it fair that a couple with two children gets a tax deduction and pays less taxes compared to a childless couple with the same combined income? A progressive might argue the family of four needs more resources to make ends meet. An environmentalist, who might align mostly with progressives, might argue the family of four consumes more resources, robbing the planet, and therefore the tax code should not incentivize reproduction. They would argue within the Democratic Party. A social conservative might want a larger tax deduction for the children to promote families or simply because they like tax deductions. A fiscal conservative would argue against any deductions and call for a flat tax. They would argue within the Republican Party. A libertarian might be offended by the question and not support any policy requiring the government to take a position on the size of your family.

Tax policy, when applied in isolation, is a difficult means to unify the country. This relates back to the issue of "fair" and trade-offs that cross social and economic issues, better known as compromises. This is where people from across the political spectrum can agree on a policy issue, but for totally different reasons. This requires the message of the policy to be presented differently to different ideological groups.

Let us start with personal freedom and intrusiveness. Besides knowing if someone is working or living in the United States, to pay taxes, does any government need to know if we are married and to whom, how many children we have and whether they are what the government classifies as "dependents," whether we pay tuition or child support, what vehicle we drive, how we power our home, what stocks we invest in and how long they have been owned, where we bank or what brokerage we use, if we own a home and how it was financed, how much interest we pay, if we own crypto, if anyone died and left us money, how many medical bills we paid, what charities we give to and whether it's cash or goods, and frankly, how much money we make and how we make it (so long as the money was made legally)? Soon they will be asking how much wealth (to be taxed) and total debt (to be relieved for some) we have. We have come to accept this, but in the age of ever-increasing government intrusion on our lives, many believe the less the government knows about us the better.

The original amendments to the Constitution permit the federal government to count us, but that is all. They promoted our freedom from government intrusion into our lives. The Sixteenth Amendment, passed in 1913, instituted the income tax but did not provide guidance as to how "income" would be calculated. Given the intrusiveness of the IRS and the federal government today, many would claim the Sixteenth Amendment conflicts with our freedoms, especially privacy.

The Congress shall have the power to lay and collect taxes on incomes, from whatever source derived, without apportionment among the several states, and without regard to any census of enumeration. Clearly, the question is "what is income and how do we calculate income fairly?" To many, any earnings or profit are fair game, but is it fair to tax invested wealth after taxes have already been collected once? Is it fair for the government to pry into your personal life and make compliance expensive to calculate income?

Why are there deductions if all income should be taxed, especially for state and local taxes (SALT), which violates apportionment, giving citizens in one state preferential treatment over another? It is interesting that many political leaders in blue states, who vote for a "progressive" income tax, complain about their unfair tax treatment when they pay higher income taxes because deductions for state and local taxes are limited. If blue state residents earn more, should there not be a transfer of wealth and benefits to red states who earn less?

No one challenges the need for taxes. However, the issue as to the best way to collect taxes needs to be revisited. *Constitutional* and *fair* are different. Many would prefer to pay all the taxes we legally owe totally anonymously and in a manner that makes for easy compliance and makes it almost impossible to cheat out of basic fairness. This is the foundation for the American Unity Tax based on the consumption of goods and services. At the retail store, if we pay in cash, it is anonymous. The whole concept of money laundering exists to hide revenue gained from illegal means and avoid paying taxes while keeping personal transactions anonymous. Maybe these should be two different issues—is what you do legal and, regardless of whether it is legal or not, were taxes paid because you reside, work, or visit the United States? Unfortunately, drug cartels and clergy both use the same roads.

If we give our names to the person at the retail counter because we choose to finance purchases or sign up for their mailing lists, it is our voluntary choice and not mandated by some government entity uninvolved in the transaction. The retailer should have zero obligation to report to the government exactly who bought what goods and services. As done now, with every state that charges a sales tax, the only reporting is gross receipts. If a government entity needs to know who bought what because they suspect illegality, they can get a warrant. To build unity, we need to focus on the freedom aspect of paying taxes in a modern, efficient, transparent, confidential way.

Many tax proposals have been presented that tweak the current tax code, but only one meets the standard of American principles. Many proposals have suggested reducing the number of tax brackets, lowering tax rates, creating a flat tax, and modifying deductions, credits, and exemptions. But, as discussed previously, any proposal that works around the edges of the problem can be changed when the next group of politicians is in office. Is it fair to change tax structure every two, four, or eight years when Americans are planning retirements a generation or two from now? Is it fair to hire CPAs and lawyers for the privilege of paying your fair share or to preserve wealth for your children? No, the only proposal that meets the standard of bold and permanent change based on American principles is the Fair Tax as proposed by Neal Boortz and Congressman John Linder in the early 2000s, which unfortunately did not become legislation. The American Unity Tax builds on the Fair Tax, with only minor changes to the tax side of the equation but major changes to the "stipend" side. On the tax side, Fair Tax was bold and made sense, and if it had passed, America would be in a better position today in all aspects of society, from fiscal responsibility to government intrusion in our lives to immigration.

So why did it not pass? Before discussing the policy details, we return to messaging. As outlined in Boortz and Linder's book *The Fair Tax Book: Saying Goodbye to the Income Tax and the IRS*, the message of the Fair Tax completely missed the mark.

1. The Fair Tax's main point was to eliminate the complexity of the federal tax code and make April 15 "just another Spring Day." Only people who pay substantial federal taxes

and use CPAs to do their taxes care about the complexity of the tax code. For most people, taxes are simple and can be completed with the "easy" form. Almost half of American households pay no net federal income tax. In addition, unfortunately, Americans have become used to living on net income and do not realize their withholdings, including Social Security and Medicare taxes, are a low-interest loan to the government. Since the national savings rate is so low, many like to receive money back from the government after filing taxes, as if it were a gift. The Fair Tax was sold mostly as a tax replacement system as opposed to a holistic proposal to return to federalism, balance the budget, preserve freedom, and unify Americans.

2. The Fair Tax was bold, but it was not bold enough. It was presented as tax neutral as opposed to an opportunity to either balance the budget or increase social spending from the savings of government inefficiency, waste, and fraud.

3. The Fair Tax missed the mark on rampant federal government intrusion into our lives. The book did not mention creeping government control, which would have appealed to an entire generation. The central point could have been a message of freedom. In fact, *The Fair Tax Book* produced a table of who qualifies for the "prebate" requiring Americans to report their income, family size, and other intrusions. It opened the plan to Congressional manipulation of the prebate for political gain. It also exempted many products from the tax, which would have made lobbying worse. It violates equality under the law on both the tax and prebate.

4. The book got too technical and did not appeal to personal greed. By focusing on whether the sales tax rate was "inclusive" or "exclusive," they handed their opponents a hammer to wield. The authors were concerned about the perception of a high exclusive tax, but that is exactly how state and local sales taxes are applied, and it is the easiest concept for the public to understand.

5. The stipend was the key. Rather than focusing on the tax side of the equation, the focus should have been on the stipend paid to every American and sold as a giveaway that secured a social safety net and the opportunity to build wealth. Everyone knew then, as everyone knows now, that Social Security and Medicare are going bankrupt. But instead, the stipend was mentioned in just a few pages of one section. The reason is that the authors claimed that prices would not go up, as the reduction of embedded taxes would offset the sales tax. As explained later, the convoluted current tax code makes this statement hard to believe for many people, and it would be situational to the specific products sold. Whether true or not, to middle-income Americans, the prebate to people who pay no tax would seem unfair and further divide the country.

Once again, the purpose here is not to criticize the Fair Tax. As stated, it was probably one of the best proposals of our lifetime, and we would be much better off if it had been implemented. The purpose here is to show how solving problems in isolation does not build broad enough support and how effective messaging is needed to promote good policies to legislate when they align with American principles.

The Fair Tax and the American Unity Plan are very similar in their concepts of elimination of all taxes on income, capital, and wealth whether applied to businesses or individuals. Here are the details:

1. All federal paycheck taxes and withholdings are eliminated, including income, Social Security, and Medicare taxes, for both the employee and the employer.

2. All corporate and business income taxes are eliminated, as are all tax credits, deductions, incentives, and exemptions.

3. All personal federal income taxes are eliminated, including the alternative minimum tax (AMT), short- and long-term capital gains (applied to stocks, real estate, gold, crypto, etc.), self-employment, estate and gifts taxes, and many more.

4. All special taxes focused on products and services are eliminated, including tariffs (if reciprocal with trade partners) and excise taxes on such items as gasoline and energy, wireless communications, and all the other hidden taxes rarely noticed by the consumer.

5. All special business taxes and exemptions, such as the carried interest provision applied by hedge funds, are eliminated.

In both the Unity Tax and Fair Tax, these taxes are replaced by a retail or consumption tax, but under the Unity Tax, it is an "exclusive" tax. This means the tax is added to the final retail sales bill to make collection simpler and fully transparent, just as state and local sales taxes are already collected. Also, it is applied to all new retail sales of goods and services, including real estate, but resales of any type are exempt, as taxes on the same asset have been paid once already.

The adding of tax to the end retail bill will make the tax rate look higher, as the opponents of the Fair Tax pointed out, but so what? The actual sales price is the same whether exclusive or inclusive and whether higher or the same as the sales price today after eliminating embedded taxes. The opponents to ceding government control of the tax code will balk no matter what. They want to maintain its complexity as a way to wield control. The message is not about the tax rate or trying to justify how much prices will increase, if at all. It is about removing most of the control from Washington bureaucrats, reducing the cost of the government managing and enforcing the tax code, reducing fraud and criminal activity, eliminating much of the lobbying in Washington, and collecting more taxes from visitors, immigrants, and the tax cheats. It is also about making the tax system 100 percent voluntary, as the only time taxes are collected is if and when we choose to purchase a good or service.

The financial impact of the current tax code on all taxpaying Americans is obvious, but less obvious is the massive compliance costs for both businesses and individuals alike. These costs include time to prepare taxes, salaries and payments to accountants and lawyers, excess recordkeeping and accounting, establishing alternative legal entities, audits and litigation, tax penalties resulting from complex laws, tax planning for wills and estates, payments to lobbyists to change tax law, and lost interest and investment growth on withholdings. Maybe the biggest cost is the poor business decisions resulting from focusing on tax reduction, avoidance, and compliance instead of on stakeholders and the economics of managing a business.

Without corporate taxes, the entire concept of a corporate structure refocuses from reduction of tax liability to limits of legal liability, as well as the operating needs of the business for shareholder reporting or simply managing disparate businesses. Financial reporting will still be required for transparency to investors and creditors, but the focus will shift to free cash flow generated by business operations and away from financial engineering to reduce taxes. Business decisions will no longer be made for tax credits and avoidance. Business costs will be reduced by having decision-making simplified and compliance costs eliminated. Accountants and lawyers will be redeployed to more productive uses (insert your own joke here).

With the elimination of corporate and personal income taxes, combined with any stimulus where direct payments are made to Americans, GDP will grow, and therefore more total taxes will be paid, especially by the highest earners. This will be a bonus to reduce the deficit even faster, but the American Unity Plan is presented with no assumption for GDP growth. However, imagine the impact on the global economy when:

- Jobs are repatriated to the United States because of the elimination of corporate income taxes, and foreign companies increase investment in the United States to access our markets at a lower cost.

- More money is in consumers' pockets to spend with no tax withholdings.
- The costs of education and healthcare are reduced, placing more money in consumers' pockets to spend elsewhere in the economy.
- More legal immigrants come to the United States and buy goods and services, and therefore pay proportionately more in taxes.
- The number of people who avoid taxes by underreporting income and outright tax fraud is greatly reduced.
- Regulations and the cost of compliance are eliminated (for example, paying an accountant or purchasing software to prepare your taxes).

Corporate taxes, and the associated big business lobbying for tax breaks, is a major reason for crony capitalism. American principles mandate a level playing field, with the federal government solely playing the role of the law enforcement official, not selecting business winners and losers. Many would unite under the goal of eliminating crony capitalism and "too big to fail." If the corporate tax code were eliminated, including regulations that benefit only the largest corporations, many would perceive the concept as truly aligning to free-market principles.

In a postpandemic world, the elimination of this complex tax code would be a huge competitive advantage to American businesses or foreign businesses that operate in America to sell into our markets as well as export. It would solve a major national security issue through business repatriation and ensuring we are not dependent on foreign entities for critical products, such as oil and gas, semiconductors, pharmaceuticals, and much more. Besides pure price pressures, this reduces supply chain risks and product shortages without any government handouts or incentives.

The Unity Tax will be applied to all products and services, both domestic and foreign made, giving US manufactured goods a competitive advantage. Goods made in the United States but sold overseas could be sold at a much lower retail cost, since the Unity Tax is only applied to retail purchases in the US. Foreign governments will want to tax "cheap imports" from America. Key to this concept is reciprocal trade agreements that start at a baseline of zero tariffs. Rather than protecting certain industries and skewing markets, US trade policy should shift to zero tariffs, if our trading partners will do the same. We will tax foreign-made products into the US at the same rate our trading partners tax our products into their countries, assuming no currency manipulation or intellectual capital theft.

Foreign governments will want to tax lower-cost American goods at higher rates. America needs to be prepared with trade policy that aligns with American principles. Ideally, there would be no tariffs at all, and all nations would have a consumption tax at the point of sale. However, we know many nations, especially in Europe, love all taxes—tariffs, income, value-added, and much more—to fund their version of the social safety net. Ironically, the value-added tax is rebated to the producer when European and Latin American countries export products to the US, making some foreign-made goods cheaper. By implementing the Unity Tax on foreign products sold in the US, we give American products a greater advantage.

Our policy needs to drive our trading partners toward Americanism, not drive America toward their versions of free-market socialism. The ideal policy would simply be for the US to add a tariff to all foreign goods from a country at the rate of the highest single tax applied to any of our products imported to their country. Essentially, we let our trading partners set the tax rate! Why are we allowing foreign governments to pick winners and losers within a global free market? Because of the size of the US market, the US could influence other countries to lower their taxes to be competitive in US markets, and this benefits everyone. Conversely, foreign governments could subsidize their products, which will only strengthen the US dollar. For countries that want a tariff (for example, France protecting the wine industry), the US policy could be this simple: the US will tax all foreign products imported to the US at the rate of the highest single tariff on US products. Over time, nations will compete on who reduces their version of the value-added tax the most, the same way our fifty states compete for business.

The American Unity Tax is much different than any global value-added taxes (VAT) that many countries use. In the Western Hemisphere, with the exception of the US, the VAT can be over 20 percent and is applied to every step in the production process or services delivery. The Unity Tax is only applied at the final point of sale and paid only by the consumer, which makes it voluntary, simple, transparent, and cost-efficient. The Unity Tax will make American-made products less expensive than products made in countries with comparable or even slightly lower wage rates. All products sold in the US, domestic and imported, will have the Unity Tax applied.

For example, wines are produced, marketed, and sold globally, and every country has their own tariff on imported wine. Recently, the US taxed French wine in response to France's subsidies on aircraft. Wine and aircraft—does this make sense? And worse yet, why are we asking the World Trade Organization to be involved with US tariffs, subsidies, and quotas? Since France adheres to EU trade policy, imports from the US are taxed at various rates up to 17 percent. We can tax all products from France at 17 percent until France and the EU lower all tariffs, hopefully to zero. The UK, in the post-Brexit world, would be a great starting point for zero-tariff reciprocal trade. Quotas will die a natural death if US products wanted by French consumers are suddenly not available. As for subsidies? Let the French government explain to their citizens how they are taxing everyone in their country to give preferred tax status to certain companies and industries that apparently cannot compete globally without government support.

The Unity Tax will give America a competitive advantage by only taxing all products and services at the point of sale. The EU would certainly add taxes to American products at their point of sale in country. Fair. But what happens when a European company builds a plant in the US and exports back to the EU to take advantage of our best-in-class business environment and lack of any tax on capital and labor?

Capital crosses borders relatively quickly and seamlessly. We need to prioritize reciprocal trade with our strategic partners who operate under democratic systems. In contrast, reciprocal tariffs with China are mostly worthless when issues such as in-country business ownership, intellectual property theft, data security, and currency manipulation are present. Reciprocity includes all trade issues.

By far the most compelling reason to institute reciprocal trade agreements after implementing the Unity Tax is our relationship with China. Our true allies, such as the UK, Canada, and Australia, will likely match the US over time on tax and trade. But what would China do? Because of the balance of trade, they would have to reduce taxes and tariffs, or US companies operating in China would shift production to the US. The only remaining US assets in China would be specific to selling in the Asian markets, where taxes are offset by lower labor and transportation costs.

Assuming all tariffs were eliminated, foreign goods from these countries would only be taxed in the US at the point of sale, thereby making their products more competitive. But if other countries still retained their corporate and payroll taxes, VAT, and all the rest, and add their energy and transportation costs to the equation, the US would only be noncompetitive on mass-produced commodities with extremely high labor content and limited intellectual capital value. So many products, from pharmaceuticals to automotive components to semiconductors, currently made in countries like China, would soon be made in the US, improving not only our economy but our national security. This is the opposite of a trade war. This is a global trade peace initiative!

Later in the book, we will discuss why increasing the number of legal immigrants and visitors to the United States is so vital to the federal tax base and reducing the deficit. Even if prices increase, many foreigners are willing to pay the tax price to live here although, under the American Unity Plan, they will receive no Unity Income benefits whatsoever at the federal level until they become citizens. More importantly, regardless of one's position on immigration, illegal immigrants would pay their share of taxes through their purchases of goods and services.

Many illegal immigrants would be faced with harder economics than US citizens and might even self-deport, although living in the higher-cost US may be preferable to many of their home countries. Conversely, some US workers who receive Unity Income may choose not to work, thereby reducing the supply of workers and increasing wages for many people, skilled or unskilled. The point is that work, not federal benefits, should be the primary factor for arriving in the United States. Illegal immigrants, as well as lawful US residents, could elect to be paid in cash from employers (assuming no state income taxes) but still would be taxed at the point of purchase of any goods and services, including housing, education, healthcare, and more.

The burden of collecting taxes in a consumption-based tax system falls to three entities in addition to the IRS—retailers, importers and immigration services, and businesses that buy under the guise of business-to-business for personal consumption. First, most retailers are already set up to collect taxes (forty-five states collect statewide sales tax), but many other businesses that will collect the Unity Tax are not. It is likely that businesses will incur an additional cost to act as collections agencies for the federal government, as well as states, and will pass this cost on to the consumer. This is fair, since it impacts all competitors in the same industry equally. In addition, each retailer could be required to do an annual sales tax audit with an independent, licensed accountant. This would catch both simple mistakes and fraud, such as collusion with buyers, buying goods or using trade discounts for personal use, or simply not paying taxes collected. Audits ensure transparency. The penalties and fines should be stiff, including federal prison for repeat and flagrant offenders.

The Unity Tax may also create more incentives than there are today for someone to buy a product overseas and transport it across the border. This will increase the importance of detection defenses of a system already in place at our borders, but which many times is not enforced. Today, many illegal products are seized and sold at auction, and the proceeds of these sales would be taxed, of course.

Finally, undervaluing assets to avoid federal taxes needs to be eliminated by ensuring the original tax on the new asset sale is paid in full by the original seller or the buyer. If the intent is tax fraud, as opposed to, for example, day-trading a stock in a transparent stock market, then federal authorities should intervene. We enforce this concept of transacting to manipulate taxes now with "wash sale rules" where stocks are sold to realize a tax loss and then purchased again shortly after selling.

Our message is not eliminating taxes but focusing on growth, jobs, and national security.

> The American Unity Tax will repatriate jobs to America. It will eliminate our foreign dependance on supplying the goods and services America needs to reduce inflation, create jobs, and improve national security. More money will be in the hands of Americans by eliminating crony capitalism and lobbying to ensure everyone pays their fair share.

Next are the details of the American Unity Tax, such as what exactly is taxed at the point of sale and why!

7

THERE IS NO UNITY LIKE INFLATION

The way to crush the bourgeoisie is to grind them between
the millstones of taxation and inflation.

— Vladimir Lenin, former head
of Soviet Russia and Soviet Union

U nfunded liabilities—including Social Security, Medicare, state
and private pension plans, and the growing corporate and
private debt—are, in addition to the over $31 trillion and
counting in national debt, a tremendous burden on the American
taxpayer. In recent recessions, modern monetary theory (MMT)
has been the basis for using debt to stimulate the economy. In
economic growth periods, we never seem to reduce the debt, and
spending continues because "we can afford it." Many think we are in
unchartered waters with the amount of carbon being released into

the atmosphere. We are also in uncharted waters with both high inflation and record high levels of debt. Using additional debt to stimulate the economy to grow GDP no matter the economic cycle may no longer be feasible and might lead to even higher inflation, resulting in both spiking unemployment and recession, which some call stagflation.

Eliminating the debt will require substantially increasing GDP, which is almost impossible with high inflation and disproportionately hurts the poor. In reality, our leaders have no idea how to accelerate GDP given the current tax code, debt levels, and inflation. Simply cutting interest rates to spur economic demand and grow GDP is contrary to fighting inflation. In contrast, interest rates must increase to curb inflation, which works directly against fiscal priorities.

The argument against the Unity Tax, like for the Fair Tax, will be that it will accelerate inflation. However, it will free the economy to increase GDP without raising interest rates, thereby increasing the tax base through consumption, leading to lower debt and lower inflation. Even if politicians raise Unity Income too quickly (increased government spending on the social safety net) and fail to balance the budget, at least simplification and streamlining the tax collection system will be stimulative. But will it also increase inflation, thereby eliminating any gains to personal wealth?

We have no idea how GDP will accelerate when the US economy is freed from the current tax code and the associated cost of compliance. If GDP grew by 5–6 percent, and even if an extremely high 30–35 percent was used as the Unity Tax rate, it is conceivable the budget could be balanced almost immediately if there were no additional spending on the proposed Unity Income payments, new spending on wasteful federal programs, or even new initiatives to combat climate change.

What about the effects of higher retail prices after applying the Unity Tax on consumption and therefore GDP? As we have seen during the pandemic and throughout 2022, excess government spending and years of loose monetary policy by the Federal Reserve can eventually cause inflationary pressures on the economy. The old definition of inflation is too much money chasing too few goods. This supply and demand imbalance means businesses cannot supply enough products and services to meet market demand, and therefore raise prices to stifle demand. However, with the Unity Tax, prices of goods and services will decrease before the tax is applied to raise the final product cost. The issue regarding inflation and balancing the budget is not the Unity Tax, but the rate of Unity Income and other government spending. How might these balance out?

On the demand side, the Unity Tax will increase consumer prices and stifle demand. On the other hand, Unity Income and the elimination of taxes and withholdings from employees' pay will stimulate demand by placing more money in the pockets of consumers and businesses. Demand will also increase by reducing the cost of healthcare and education, freeing the consumer to save, invest, and spend. On the supply side, businesses will have more money to invest in capacity, and new capital will come to the United States.

What will be the net impact on demand, productive supply capacity, consumer prices, and tax receipts by the federal government? No one knows, and all forecasts will be exactly wrong. The point is to let the free market work, with the proper guardrails, without artificial stimuli from the federal government pumping money into the economy and an arcane tax code that stifles competition and capital creation. Supply and demand will reach their natural equilibrium soon enough.

There is no question the transition to the Unity Tax will have an enormous positive impact on GDP and tax receipts. Of the over $4 trillion in total taxes collected by the federal government, the largest tax receipt is paid by individuals through payroll. Corporate income taxes are only about 7 percent of the federal taxes collected but have the most profound impact on the supply side of our economy and prices before taxation. Once corporate taxes are eliminated, existing businesses and new businesses operating in America will drive the cost of goods and services down to their optimal levels. In particular, the costs of healthcare and education, two industries in which costs have grown much faster than general inflation, will see the biggest decreases, not only from tax elimination but from privatizing the delivery of education and moving healthcare to a consumer pay model versus the third-party payment system we have today.

The Fair Tax proponents studied the embedded cost of the current federal tax code and concluded the embedded tax rate is between 15 percent and 26 percent of the final retail price, without even considering the cost of compliance. This varies greatly by industry because our current tax code and resulting crony capitalism promote industry preference. Whether we tax based on income or consumption, the free market always drives prices down through competition (e.g., Amazon versus Walmart). For retail goods and services where there is competition, prices eventually settle to the lowest point of capital return, including paying taxes. More importantly, because of its transparency, the American Unity Plan better protects the poor against inflation than the current tax code and social welfare system by incentivizing the federal government to lower the Unity Income tax rate and reduce federal expenses. Also, Unity Income progressively benefits the poorest Americans because the social safety net will be financed primarily by the purchases of middle-income and wealthy taxpayers. This is true unity when the Democratic Party wants to reduce taxes!

It is evident in California and Hawaii that state government taxes on gasoline increase prices more than lower-tax states. Under federalism, that is fine if Californians think taxing gasoline will save the planet despite hurting consumers, but at the national level, the debate on balancing climate against an inflation tax on the poor is intense. The retail cost of some products and services may increase when the Unity Tax is applied. Therefore, there will be pressure on legislators to keep prices lower by lowering the Unity Tax rate applied to goods and services.

Another argument that could be made against any consumption tax is that, even with only a slight increase in prices, demand for products and services could go down. This will not happen, because there are only three things you can do with money—save, invest, or spend. The savings rate in the United States is very low, and interest on savings paid was almost nothing until we started raising interest rates to cool the economy and fight inflation. Hopefully this is temporary, but there is concern inflation may be permanently at a higher level than the 2 percent Federal Reserve target. The only reason to save is risk avoidance, and Unity Income alleviates some of that risk with a social safety net benefiting the poorest Americans the most. In addition, Unity Income forces investment, so any new money from eliminating withholdings will either be spent or invested, adding liquidity to the economy. We are a retail economy. The more money we have in our pockets available to finance purchases, the more we spend, and a slight increase in retail costs will have minimal impact against the increased spending power of the consumer. We will not have to worry about hedge fund managers getting tax breaks by paying only carried interest, as this will be eliminated along with all corporate taxes. They will pay huge taxes on their purchases!

Therefore, it is more important to shift to a consumption tax, regardless of the tax rate, than to maintain the current tax code. The US GDP is over $23 trillion, and it is estimated 70 percent of the economy is consumer spending on products and services. We have a huge deficit. The deficit will increase in the future as new spending is passed in Congress and makes its way into the economy. It will increase substantially more with any spending targeting climate change and if UBI is passed. Assuming the goal of the Unity Tax is simply to replace current receipts, it would need to be approximately 25 percent, which is near the rate suggested by the Fair Tax authors.

The point is we need to be strategic, not tactical. Strategically, if we want to balance the budget faster, we can raise the Unity Tax or cut spending, including the Unity Income. Again, the tax is paid by everyone proportionate to their wealth and spending habits, not their income and use of accountants and lawyers.

The question to be answered is which products and services have the Unity Tax applied. Some people would want to exempt certain items, such as prescription medicines, food, gasoline, electricity, medical services, education, daycare, and more, to keep prices on "essentials" lower. Once we start exempting products, though, the result will be the reemergence of crony capitalism, excessive regulation, and politicians picking winners and losers. In addition, if we exempt certain products and services, then others will have to be taxed at a higher rate to create the same tax base. This would violate the American principle of fairness and equal treatment, as some would benefit more than others, including visitors and immigrants who use the same services as American citizens. We must apply the Unity Tax to all retail products and services.

Once the federal government starts exempting certain industries, products, and services, then government bureaucracies (increased spending) and loss of freedom return. We need to stop pitting brick-and-mortar stores against internet retailers, renting personal residences against hotels, rideshare against taxis, EVs against gasoline-powered vehicles, and most importantly, public provided services against private sector delivery. Here are some examples and guidance.

First, the Unity Tax is applied only to operating businesses that benefit from the elimination of taxes on corporations, payroll, and capital and where no further value is added. The Unity Tax avoids double taxation, which is inherent in the current corporate tax system, by exempting assets that are resold between consumers or traded between businesses. The Unity Tax does not apply to the resale or trading of any personal goods, such as cars, boats, jewelry, guns, stocks, and bonds.

In another example, payments made to a nanny or babysitter would not be taxed because they are not operating as business entities and get no benefit from the elimination of corporate and payroll taxes beyond what any other worker receives. However, a daycare operator with dozens of children in their care would collect the Unity Tax from their customers, as their costs of doing business will shrink immediately when the embedded costs of paying caregivers and teachers and buying diapers, books, toys, cleaning supplies, power, insurance, and more all are reduced.

Business-to-business trade is not taxed, as is done in much of the world, but retail purchases are. For example, Amazon Prime purchases and subscriptions are taxable, but Amazon Web Services sold to internet retailers and corporations are not.

Similarly, energy must be taxed equally at the point of consumer consumption. A business buying power to make steel or automobiles, mine crypto, or produce solar panels is not federally taxed, but power and gas coming into personal homes are. Gas at the pump and chargers for electric vehicles are taxed on the consumer end. The federal government must be agnostic to the product and service. If someone buys a solar panel to place on their roof or an electric vehicle charger for their garage, these products are taxed the same as a new home or car that runs on conventional power sources.

Every industry will benefit from eliminating corporate, payroll, and capital taxes. The biggest beneficiaries are also the most emotional. These include real estate, education, and healthcare. We want these costs to be as low as possible to make them affordable to more people and lower the perception of inflation caused by the Unity Tax alone. But has government intrusion and regulation produced higher or lower prices in these industries? If you believe in American principles, then creating a level playing field with proper guardrails and letting free-market competition work its magic will produce the lowest cost to the consumer. No business that benefits from changing the federal tax code, including the industries of food, clothing, energy, and medicine, should be exempt.

The point is to eliminate government interference in free-market competition. The government has a miserable history of getting the tax rules exactly wrong over time and should focus on consumer safety and transparency. This transition lowers the cost of goods and services and is the remedy to inflation. Once the government starts exempting certain industries, then incremental government control and crony capitalism return and costs increase. Medical practices will benefit greatly from the elimination of company, payroll, and capital taxes, as well as professional practice profits. For example, malpractice insurance is a major medical service provider expense, and its cost will be reduced because insurance companies also benefit from reduced corporate and payroll taxes. The insurance purchased by the doctor will not be taxed, and savings will be passed on to patients through competition. The cost of medical equipment, healthcare professionals, administrative staff, and more will be reduced. In addition, healthcare is one of the biggest industry beneficiaries of the American Unity Plan, and costs for all will go down by privatization of payments, reducing administrative staff and eliminating burdensome insurance filing. This will be explained in detail later.

Financial markets and asset values are a prime target for many wishing to raise taxes. Assets that have appreciated over time are taxed heavily when sold or transferred and potentially hurt family businesses the most. Capital gains from business sales, stocks, bonds, digital assets, real estate, and more have been tax targets for years. Under the Unity Tax, the sale of assets is protected from tax until the proceeds are used to buy retail products and services. Arcane tax rules, such as wash sales, are eliminated forever. Year-end selling of stocks to realize tax losses will go away.

We have a once in a lifetime opportunity to build a cross-party coalition of protectors of wealth, creating assets for a new generation of young Americans who think the dollar will be worthless in their lifetimes due to rampant debt and inflation and will never see a dollar of Social Security. Hard assets are hedges against inflation, and their appreciation cannot be taxed until converted to cash and spent. Younger Americans are investing in homes, crypto, and stocks as a way to build wealth but have yet to feel the full impact of financial planning and taxation. A potential policy platform to build a coalition is:

> We will not tax any asset appreciation, including all digital assets, real estate, stocks, gold and silver, or any other investments, until the proceeds are used to buy retail products and services at the point of sale. We encourage innovation in these new technologies and stores of value as security against excessive government spending and the resulting inflation.

In a *Fortune* magazine interview in the April / May 2021 issue, Margrethe Vestager, the EU's "antitrust enforcer," when asked about antitrust and privacy, said "That is a reflection of the fact that the digital marketplace is unregulated compared to all the other markets that we're used to dealing in. We have a regulated financial market; we have a regulated energy market. So many markets regulated; only tech has not been. And because of that it has become increasingly clear that it is not a given that these markets will stay open and competitive." To her list of regulated markets, we can add healthcare and education. Scarier words could not be said. What many bureaucrats really want is power and increased taxation, not transparency, market performance, or freedom. Is it any wonder why there is so much interest in cryptocurrencies such as Bitcoin, which are decentralized and not under the control of a government or private issuer? We need to build unity with younger Americans around this issue, and the Unity Tax, which eliminates the taxation of digital assets, would be a great start. The premise of the Unity Tax is freedom and transparency, and regulations for new technologies should be consistent with this theme to protect consumers from fraud rather than a means to raise federal tax receipts.

Another asset that drives intense complexity in the tax code and is central to Americans' standard of living is real estate. It is one of the largest and most important asset classes in America. This includes not just personal homes but commercial real estate ranging from office buildings, retail stores, hospitals and medical office buildings, data centers, manufacturing plants, and distribution centers. After the implementation of the Unity Tax and the increase of legal immigration, the rush of businesses to build in the US will send existing real estate prices soaring, benefiting those who made the decision to own hard assets and operate here in the first place. However, there is currently a significant embedded tax and compliance cost in new construction, which will reduce real estate costs over time.

Real estate is a source of controversary anytime a retail tax is suggested. When the current tax system is eliminated, the price of building a home or office will be dramatically reduced. Home builders will be able to buy lumber, shingles, concrete, and equipment less expensively because those are business-to-business transactions, so no taxes will be paid on these purchases until the home is sold to a consumer. As a result, after applying the Unity Tax to new homes, the end cost of a new home will not change significantly. As a side benefit, since most homes are financed, the new home seller will act like a retailer and pay the tax to the federal government on behalf of the consumer, but the home buyer will essentially be financing the tax as part of their mortgages, as is done today. The same will be true on any big-ticket item that may be financed, from cars and boats to art and appliances, medical procedures, and more.

What will be the impact on interest rates if banks and other financial services companies suddenly have their operating costs reduced? Financial services lenders compete for consumers with interest rates and will lower rates somewhat accordingly, though this impact will be dampened by the Federal Reserve. In addition, Unity Income will provide a guaranteed payment to consumers, thereby improving credit scores and making larger purchases more affordable to many Americans.

Existing homes (as with any asset that is resold) will not be subject to the Unity Tax because homes were taxed previously, and home valuations are local property tax issues. Homes built prior to the Unity Tax were taxed under the old tax code. Would a Unity Tax favor resales over new homes? No, because the cost of building a new home will decrease before the home is placed on the market. New home builders will have more room to innovate and compete against the resale market for new customers.

Similarly, apartments, online accommodation marketplaces, and hotels must have the Unity Tax applied to make the rent-versus-own decision based on nontax decisions and ensure no competitor for the same consumer has an advantage. All apartments would benefit from the reduced cost of new construction and upgrades, appliances, property management services, and more. All traditional and short-term rentals will have the Unity Tax applied to ensure fairness and keep markets free.

Another interesting point is whether the Unity Tax should be applied to education services. With Unity Income, many more private schools will compete for the consumer's Unity Income dollars, and the cost of education will be lower. But schools now are controlled by local governments and heavily regulated. Private delivery of education will be more cost-effective and deliver a better product than government delivery. Applying the Unity Tax to any public institution that competes with the private market, including education, is imperative to move as many services to the private sector as possible. Police and fire departments should not be taxed because these are provided as a municipal service with no private competition. However, public education benefits from lower costs of school construction and maintenance, payroll, books, supplies, and more. By being exempt from the federal Unity Tax, they would be given an advantage over private schools who compete for the same students. If we exempt all schools, do we do the same for homeschoolers, religious schools, trade schools, and daycare? What is the definition of education? The point is to not exempt any entity that benefits from the Unity Tax and competes for consumers because the old tax system would reemerge over time. Let them focus on educating our children!

What happens when corporations subsidize healthcare, life insurance, and other benefits for their employees? At this point, they are competing with private markets and enabling employee dependency. If the consumer would pay the Unity Tax on insurance purchases, then the corporation should pay the Unity Tax on the subsidized portion of the insurance policy. The employee's insurance cost would also have the Unity Tax applied. Over time, consumers and employers will move to private insurance to give employees more freedom of mobility and reduce employer operating expenses.

One previous criticism of the Fair Tax was that it was punishing retirees. Since retirees already receive Social Security and Medicare, would they be better off under the American Unity Plan? First, many retirees will receive more money under the Unity Income than they receive today under Social Security, and Medicare remains unchanged for current retirees. For those seniors who will be receiving Social Security as well as Unity Income, almost all will be much better off. There are no withholdings on their Social Security checks, distributions of their private retirement accounts, and pensions. Seniors have the most savings and investments of any group in America, and an overwhelming majority will benefit enough to offset the slightly higher cost of goods and services. Examples will be provided in the Unity healthcare chapter.

The biggest benefits of the shift to a consumption tax are the inherent fairness and the increase of tax revenue from tax cheats. There is a sizable under-the-table-payments economy in this country, estimated at 10–15 percent of GDP, due to unreported cash payments for services, and it may be much higher. Increasing tax burden, regulation, and complexity promotes the underground economy.

With the American Unity Plan, many retailers will benefit from a reduction in theft. Rather than simply being a local law enforcement issue, shoplifting would become a federal crime—tax evasion by the thief. Not only would the justice department need to be concerned about retailer theft (not paying the Unity taxes they collect on behalf of the government), it would also have to worry about merchandise theft, either isolated instances or collusion between retailers and thieves. In general, the underground economy, whether supporting illegal activities or avoiding taxes with cash receipts, must be made inconsequential and the Unity Tax does just that. Remember, Al Capone went to jail for tax evasion!

Will underground retailers appear? Maybe. An underground retailer would have to allow someone to buy their products at less than the retail cost. Would people risk federal prosecution just to save a few dollars? Some will always skirt the law. Unless housing, medical care, energy, food, and other products go underground, there would not be many illegal markets. The largest portions of the economy, dominated by very large and mostly public companies, have no incentive to commit fraud on the Unity Tax.

Many governors, especially Republicans, will leverage the Unity Tax to more efficiently raise tax receipts for healthcare, education, and other services. Some states already have no state income tax, and many more states would follow the federal Unity Tax model for both efficiency and privacy issues. They would eliminate their state income taxes accordingly and implement their own state sales tax. In addition, they will seek to eliminate the burden and cost of local tax collection and move toward private delivery of many government-run services. By shifting to a consistent federal and state tax model, tax cheats, visitors, and immigrants will pay more state sales tax for goods and services, but most citizens will dramatically reduce their net financial burden after Unity Income payments. Also, as more states move to a state sales tax model, businesses would all but stop chasing tax incentives when deciding where to locate and focus on more important issues like attracting and retaining the best workforce or minimizing other operating costs like energy and real estate. In contrast, states will compete for larger populations, both living in and visiting the state, to increase the tax base as more of the social safety net funding (not delivery) is shifted to the federal government.

The idea of the Unity Tax is truly unity. What we lack with our current tax system is the political cover to keep taxes and inflation low on all constituencies. The Unity Tax politically incentivizes a lower tax rate, even if motivations are different across political viewpoints. Inflation is the biggest tax on the poor, and progressives, operating under a system of one tax fits all, would be loath to raise the Unity Tax. They would be more focused on raising Unity Income, even if that means higher deficits. This makes a balanced budget discussion critical.

Beside the unification of Congress, one of the wonderful things about the Unity Tax is that it also shifts the growing power of the Federal Reserve back to Congress. Say for example, in the next recession, we want to stimulate the economy. What better way to do that than to lower the Unity Tax by a percent or two, or even raise Unity Income? Both are fast and incredibly efficient without artificially inflating the Federal Reserve's balance sheet or changing interest rates and distorting capital markets.

The final point of this chapter is implementation. The Fair Tax suggested an exemption to inventory of $1 million, since the tax was already paid. Again, this is arbitrary and contrary to the concept of fairness. If necessary, we can implement the Unity Tax gradually to allow supply chains to adapt. As witnessed during the pandemic, supply chains need time to adjust to new economic realities. There would be a major shift to US production, which would vary greatly by industry. One suggestion would be to implement change incrementally over twelve to twenty-four months. Income, payroll, and corporate taxes under the old system would still be paid for the year following the elimination of the current tax code, but the Unity Tax would start immediately, potentially increasing federal tax receipts. The trailing impact of issues like inventory would be minimized. By the end of the first or second year, all previous taxes under the old system would be collected and the new system fully implemented.

The Unity Tax is firmly grounded in American principles. It is inherently fair, and Unity Income accommodates the poor who may be burdened the most. It provides for equality under the law by not forcing Americans to pay different tax rates based on decisions they make in their personal lives. However, the messaging of the

American Unity Plan clearly needs to be focused on Unity Income, not tax policy. The Unity Tax rate should be a side argument.

The transition from the current tax code and its compliance costs will free the US economy to grow and create jobs by bringing business back to our shores. The new Unity Tax is based on the voluntary consumption of goods and services. It will be paid by every citizen and noncitizen in the US. This will result in a larger social safety net for Americans, young and old, so the poor can increase their buying power. The plan will provide opportunities for the poorest Americans to succeed, while creating a clear pathway to reduce the debt and balance the federal budget.

Under the American Unity Plan, there are only two levers politicians can pull. They can raise or lower Unity Income payments, and they can raise or lower Unity Tax rates. The real beauty of the American Unity Plan is that this will align politicians across the ideological spectrum. To raise taxes, Congress must increase the Unity Tax rate, and this proportionately hurts the poor. There will be universal pressure to reduce tax rates from across the Democratic Party, something not seen since the Kennedy administration. On the other hand, there will be pressure from the progressives to increase Unity Income payments in the guise of both increasing the safety net and stimulating the economy in times of recession (or pandemic). Both parties will likely accept a lower Unity Tax initially and accept larger deficits, because that is what politicians do. This would stretch out balancing the budget.

The Unity Tax provides transparency and focuses federal economic decisions on GDP growth, inflation, and balancing spending with tax receipts. The issue is how fast we move to a balanced budget and how much deficit we can afford in the interim. At some point, though, the current entitlement costs will go away, and the Unity Tax will achieve political and economic equilibrium, as no one will want to raise taxes. Conservatives and libertarians will push for a balanced budget over time. Progressives and many centrist Democrats and Republicans will want to increase the budget deficit to "manageable levels" but will no longer be able to do it by "taxing the rich" to give the impression of trying to be fiscally responsible. The rich will be taxed more fairly and progressively because they simply buy more!

Americans want a balanced budget but have given up hope. With a secure social safety net that is adequate and rationalizes the reduction of government spending over time, Americans will overwhelmingly support moving to a balanced budget. The bottom-line question is simple and direct: Do you support a balanced budget by ensuring Unity Income payments are aligned to Unity Tax receipts?

8

AMERICAN UNITY INCOME – UBI WITHOUT GOING BROKE

*Mark my words: A Universal Basic Income is coming,
as artificial intelligence and robots eat away good jobs.*
– Robert Reich, former US secretary of labor

One of the reasons Universal Basic Income (UBI) has not been front and center recently is because pandemic stimulus checks and rent elimination essentially accomplished what federal UBI legislation could not. However, as these "temporary" government programs subside, UBI will once again be promoted. Most petitions promote $1,000 per person per month, but of course that will be the starting point. The movement is also gaining traction around the world. Many countries, including the US, have pilot programs. Alaska has UBI, and some states and cities have pilot programs.

The difference between Unity Income and UBI is that no current programs will be eliminated under UBI. UBI is new federal spending. Given progressives' history of incremental gains, unless an alternative is presented, UBI will be implemented nationally at some point. Once implemented, the price tag will only go up over time, especially because UBI may be granted to noncitizens, legal and illegal alike.

The bigger point is that we are playing with fire. We are currently over 130 percent of GDP in national debt, not including unfunded liabilities such as Social Security and Medicare. The parallel to the climate crisis is hard to miss, and they are interrelated. Will the next year's or the next ten years' emissions be the tipping point for global catastrophe? Who knows. Will adding $2 trillion, $5 trillion, or $10 trillion more to the debt cause a monetary crisis the likes of which we have never seen? Who knows. But there is currently no acceptable plan from either political party to solve the budget deficit and avoid this crisis, as there are plans to address climate change regardless of the cost. However, if, while fighting climate change, dramatic spending increases and UBI are implemented in parallel, then the debt crisis is much more likely to occur. The debt crisis must be solved to have the wealth to fight climate change, but fighting climate change without addressing debt increases the probability of the debt crisis happening first, which will effectively end spending on the climate.

If the US wants to remain an economic leader, with its biggest advantage being its global currency and low cost of borrowing, we must have a plan to reduce the public debt. We have time but probably not much, not when Social Security and Medicare will go into crisis mode within the next decade. We need to show the debt is on a path to reduction, even if the debt increases slightly in the short term. Unlike UBI, the American Unity Plan proposes replacements for the current social safety net programs that are going bankrupt. Unity Income aligns with American principles of fairness, accommodation, and equality and has a resounding message to legislate around the "third rail" of politics.

Currently, the social safety net is over 70 percent of federal spending. Conversely, the long-term goal of Unity Income is to minimize long-term government dependency while ensuring an adequate and fair safety net and opportunities for all current and future American citizens. These goals include:

1. Saving Social Security through lifetime funding and mandatory investment of Unity Income funds in the financial markets, directed by the recipient, not the government, and allowing wealth to accumulate and be passed down generationally.

2. Saving Medicare through funding private healthcare accounts early in life to eliminate third-party payments and promote free-market competition for healthcare dollars without rationing the supply of healthcare services.

3. Privatizing education to increase the quality of service and outcomes for our children and young adults through education accounts directed by families and custodians based on their individual needs.

4. Ensuring the social safety net is in place, compassionately, for generations, targeted proportionately to the poorest Americans while shielding Americans from inflation, excess regulations, and work eligibility compliance.

5. Providing the means for individuals and nongovernmental entities to solve problems relating to affordable housing, nutrition, childcare, homelessness, drug addiction, and other social issues where government programs have failed.

6. Balancing the federal budget in our lifetime!

Using recent numbers, the total annual spend by the federal government for retirement, healthcare, education, and other social benefits is approximately $3.1 trillion of the $4.4 trillion in total government spending prepandemic. To privatize these programs, we must fix the insolvency and performance problems of these programs through free-market capitalism, with proper guardrails, while maintaining the concept of fairness and equality under the law relative to our tax and safety net systems. The allocation of Unity Income contributions per month per American citizen would be:

Birth to high school graduation:

- Retirement: $100 per month
- Healthcare: $200 per month
- Education: $500 per month
- Flexible: $0 per month

High school graduation to end of life:

- Retirement: $300 per month
- Healthcare: $400 per month
- Education: $0 per month
- Flexible: $400 per month

Compared to recent UBI proposals, these amounts may seem low. The goals of Unity Income and UBI are quite different. The goal of Unity Income is to focus on poverty, not envy and wealth inequality. Wealth inequality will not be solved with a higher social safety net, including education. However, education provides the best chance to move the most people to middle class. The middle class does not envy the rich who achieved because they are productive, smart, and innovative. We all despise people who attained wealth through political means and connections, and providing government subsidies to some but not all Americans continues to divide the country.

Before discussing how each amount was determined, demographics need to be discussed to understand the initial bill to taxpayers without considering tax receipts. The US population is now over 330 million people, with over 95 percent being legal American citizens through birth or naturalization. Only citizens are eligible for Unity Income. Approximately 78 percent of the American citizens would receive the adult portion of the Unity Income payment. The total Unity Income bill would be $3.8 trillion annually, without offsets to current spending. The plan would immediately reduce social security, healthcare, education, and other government spending by roughly $1.4 trillion, leaving a net increase of government spending of $2.4 trillion. Of course, these savings are only at the federal level and do not include potentially huge savings at the state and local levels, especially on education and healthcare. This also does not include personal benefits from lowering the cost of a significant portion of our economy—private health insurance, education, and more.

To be practical in approach, and in fact pessimistic, assume this is not "paid for" by increased GDP and tax receipts and the typical Washington accounting gimmicks. This is new federal spending of $2.4 trillion in year one, or about an 8 percent increase in the national debt. People who oppose new ideas will always challenge numbers and estimates. How many times in our life have the so-called experts in the Congressional Budget Office or White House economists been right on their forecasts? No, we will be exactly wrong, as they are with every forecast and time horizon, but our goal is to be approximately and strategically right and avoid arcane arguments about whether the budget will be balanced in twenty versus forty years or what retail tax rate will be needed to replace the current income tax.

There are so many assumptions and politics in play that Americans who support the American Unity Plan do not want to be sucked in to playing the forecast game. We need to focus on policy and message with the goal of favorable, long-term, systemic change by returning to free-market capitalism, increasing our freedoms, and improving the social safety net in areas that Americans care about deeply. So, please do not get hung up on making the numbers exact, as good approximations will suffice. Good approximations will be more accurate than the so-called experts and bureaucrats residing throughout government who never get fired for being consistently wrong!

Unity Income pays the individual. First, a child receiving $800 would be allocated $100 per month for their retirement, $200 per month for their healthcare-related expenses (including insurance, prescriptions, etc.), and $500 per month for their education-related expenses, including daycare. The American citizen is free to spend on these goods and services or to save and invest what is not spent in individually controlled accounts. A newborn may not need $500 per month for education (daycare), and that money can be saved and invested for pre-K education, or even college, 100 percent tax-free.

An adult receiving $1,100 per month would be allocated $300 per month for their retirement, $400 for their healthcare, and the remaining $400 for whatever they see fit, including college tuition, loan repayment, additional education spending for their children of any age, additional retirement savings, food, rent and mortgage, local taxes, or whatever they need versus what the government dictates.

Looking at the big picture, the wealth accumulation for retirement starting at birth with just $100 per month and increasing to just $300 per month as an adult would create generational wealth beyond the dreams of most Americans. Seniors, years from now, will not need Social Security, which supports the means testing many progressives seek. The spending on healthcare would allow for a family or any group of like-minded people to pool insurance for catastrophic events and long-term care while saving for later in life through Unity Healthcare Accounts. The spending on education will allow private education for everyone, not just the rich, especially if states, cities, and counties also contribute to personal Unity Education Accounts. The specifics of these accounts and their guardrails will be discussed in detail later.

Unlike many UBI proposals, Unity Income is not intended to pay for 100 percent of a person's living expenses. A family of four American citizens (two adults and two children) would receive $3,800 per month with the flexibility to direct money as they choose so long as their individual retirement, health, and education needs are met. Most importantly, this is not enough money for most people to stop working! Children would have nothing left over after their mandatory social investments, and adults would have only $400 until they were no longer eligible for Social Security and Medicare later in life. Under federalism, left-leaning states are free to provide whatever additional funds they wish, and right-leaning states are free to not provide anything if they choose, but no federal money or benefits beyond Unity Income can be provided to individuals. Therefore, there would be no federal regulations placed on the individual governing the distribution and use of the funds other than to ensure social safety net needs are met (as the DMV ensures you have car insurance or identification cards needed for many services in life). The incentive must be to work, and by not withholding any federal taxes, workers keep all their earnings.

The exact contributions and allocations of Unity Income are not as important as implementing the conceptual goals of fixing three of our biggest societal problems in parallel. Republicans have historically argued with Democrats on their turf. They discuss the amount of new spending instead of where spending can be reduced.

Republicans have no new ideas of their own. With Unity Income, we will all engage based on American principles. Progressives will want to increase Unity Income payments, and conservatives, under federalism, can respond that the high-cost-of-living states are free to provide whatever additional funds they wish and that other states are free to not provide anything if they choose. Many progressives will want means testing and regulations, and others can counter that anything that is not equal and fair treatment for all American citizens is an assault on our freedom and an intrusion on our lives. We want to provide all American citizens with an equal opportunity to participate in the American dream to improve their lives and their financial positions. Some will want to provide Unity Income to anyone living in the United States, legal or illegal, citizen or not. We must stand firm that Unity Income is a privilege, not a right, reserved for US citizens. This becomes an incentive for visitors and immigrants to follow our laws, assimilate into American society, and become American citizens.

The federal government has an abusive history of overregulating. Before getting into the details, we first need to establish policies that align with core American values and principles to build unity across America. These are:

1. There must be an incentive to work for those who are able.
2. No American can lose benefits during the transition to Unity Income. We cannot incur negative rights on those Americans to whom the federal government made promises.
3. There must be a social safety net that ensures families are securely above the poverty line for basic needs. The federal government can provide the safety net stability for the long

term, and local charities and governments can supplement shortfalls for short-term needs.

4. Foreigners living in the United States, legal or illegal, have protections under the Constitution but do not have the same benefit of Unity Income as American citizens.

5. All must contribute to funding the federal government fairly and equally relative to their earning power (Unity Tax). Americans living abroad, except for those serving in the Armed Forces, are not eligible for Unity Income since they do not contribute to the Unity Tax.

6. We must eliminate waste, fraud, and bureaucracy while increasing transparency. We must simplify taxes and benefits to make them understandable and easily auditable.

7. Time is both your friend and your enemy. Start early and invest consistently.

8. Avoid assumptions, models, and accounting gimmicks. Provide processes and systems that can adapt easily and quickly to societal changes such as demographics.

9. Provide solutions that are acceptable to and unify the majority of Americans.

Of all the American values, the incentive to work was listed first for a reason. The achievement of personal self-sufficiency is a core American value and helps the individual more than any government program ever could. We must carefully balance this incentive to work with our commitment to basic security.

Unlike UBI, Unity Income, as part of the American Unity Plan, provides the incentive to work; however, there is no work requirement to be a recipient. Instead of the money being wasted in Washington through fraud, inefficiency, and bureaucracy, the money is given directly to the American people and will stimulate the economy, as we have seen during the pandemic. Some people may choose not to work, but Unity Income is not enough to live a comfortable life—it is truly a safety net for funding education, healthcare, and retirement. In fact, it incentivizes people to work more because all withholdings are eliminated! No need to wait for spring to get your money back!

Because the Unity Income safety net is in place, and by not withholding any federal taxes, participants who choose to work keep 100 percent of their income except for state and local taxes. Some recipients of Unity Income will simply not work, but the number of people who choose not to work will be far less than today. There are certainly people who are unable to work, and then there are others who choose not to work to their full capacity, capability, or at all. Human nature does not change. However, the social safety net benefits to all Americans will be standardized and fair, and the choice of working or subsisting on a minimal cash allowance for adults after retirement, healthcare, and education needs are met becomes only a personal issue, with no federal monitoring except to ensure Unity Income accounts are in place and withdrawals are consistent with federal law. Unity Income benefits are much less than current benefits and provide less immediate cash. It is a long-term safety net intended to transition people while they pursue their dreams and ensure the federal government is solvent to provide funding over time.

To summarize again, for adults who have graduated high school, while grandfathering in those past the age who have not yet graduated, every American will receive $1,100 per month. There are no exceptions based on wealth or income tests or anything else. For those who have not graduated high school, Unity Income will be $800 per month. This applies to future children who choose not to graduate or get a GED. Why distinguish between adults and children? Because graduating high school vastly improves the ability to get a job and become more productive in life. This is an incentive to finish school, and the "raise" would be a graduation present. From a fairness perspective, US law already distinguishes between citizens at many stages of life—for example, voting, alcohol consumption, and joining the military.

The poverty threshold in the United States is about $26,000 for a family of four. Unity Income is slightly below the poverty level for individuals and well above the poverty level for a family of four ($45,600). But much of Unity Income is directed toward retirement and healthcare for adults and education for children. Unity Income is not meant as a federal safety net for all basic needs, such as food, clothing, shelter, transportation, and energy. It provides for some security but does not replace work, saving and investing, state and local assistance, and charities. It is just enough for now, but it will be a lot in the future.

Unity Income promotes families and work, without mandates, while providing a reasonable, guaranteed safety net for life. To put this in perspective, a full-time $10 per hour job equates to $1,600 per month ($19,200 annually) take-home pay, in addition to the Unity Income, as there are no deductions for Social Security taxes, which disproportionately hurt the working poor. With Unity Income, it would not require much part-time work to be well above the poverty line for all American citizens while providing for a secure future. It is not unreasonable to suggest that if US residents and visitors provide the means for your retirement years, healthcare, and education, you are responsible for becoming self-sufficient for other needs and rely on custodians (such as family), local charities, or state governments if needed. Unity Income is not intended to solve all societal problems immediately, but it does increase the odds that an educated and prepared child will succeed!

Relative to the budget and the national debt, Unity Income also does not need to be indexed automatically to inflation. Unity Income is transitioned in to replace the existing programs, and specific funding levels can be voted on each year in Congress. The existing programs will continue to be indexed, but Unity Income funds, directed by individuals, will grow over time at a rate exceeding inflation. The decision to raise Unity Income levels would be for reasons other than just keeping up with inflation. As part of the budget, not the so-called "trust funds, Unity Income must be viewed against the national debt.

The message of the American Unity Plan is quite simple and appealing:

> We believe every American should have a new social safety net that substantially improves lives for generations. Unity Income allows every American to fund their retirement, provides a means for healthcare for all, and ensures quality education. Unity Income provides guaranteed funds to ensure no American citizen lives in poverty. Unity Income proportionately benefits the poor and provides for a more comfortable

retirement while meeting our healthcare needs and ensuring wealth can be passed on to families or charities of choice. Unity Income and the Unity Tax, working in concert, provide a pathway to a balanced federal budget.

Progressives in the Democratic Party will get a version of UBI with no work eligibility or requirements, minimal constraints on how the money is spent by individuals, and increased spending in healthcare and education. These will be new programs. Conservatives in the Republican Party will accept the incentive to work, a plan to balance the budget, save the unfunded entitlements with political cover, no rationing of care as happens in single-payer programs, and a focus on privatization and cost reduction affecting a major portion of the economy. Once again, there is something for everyone to like and hate while achieving compromise with the final numbers.

The next chapter will assess how Unity Income affects the American family.

9

WHAT'S IN IT FOR ME?

The problem with socialism is that you eventually run out of other people's money.

> — Margaret Thatcher,
> former British prime minister

A sk any young person which of these alternatives they would choose:

A) Keep all work wages, pay no federal income or payroll taxes, receive a guaranteed government payment now, and invest and save to pay for your own retirement, or

B) Rely on a promise to pay you Social Security and Medicare forty or fifty years from now.

We know the answer.

On the tax side, the elimination of all taxes will reduce the cost of every product and service purchased before applying the Unity Tax at the retail level only. Studies supporting the Fair Tax have shown the embedded cost of taxes varies between 15 percent and 25percent of products and services costs depending on the industry. This does not include non-value-added compliance costs placed on businesses and individuals, which add huge costs to society. These costs are much higher for heavily regulated and subsidized businesses, such as healthcare and education.

This percentage of embedded tax is controversial because some believe that only employer expenses before profit (payroll costs, healthcare contributions, 401(k) matches, supplies, inventory purchases, debt interest, etc.) are included in products and services retail costs. To this camp, tax expenses are not included in business costs. Some believe that corporate taxes apply to profits only and, if eliminated, would not impact products and services costs (except of course for the cost of all the accountants, offshore accounts, and lawyers required to reduce tax costs and comply with tax laws and regulations). This is obviously true for the many corporations that pay no or little federal income taxes due to operating losses, tax credits and incentives, depreciation, and other accounting gymnastics. In other words, if business taxes were increased, businesses would just absorb it and there would be no impact on product cost. So, why not tax businesses 50 percent, 75 percent, or even 100 percent to balance the budget and create more "government revenue" to be given to constituents? This debate is with people who recognize that taxes are passed on to the consumer one way or another and that the current mechanisms for taxing businesses, large and small, add unnecessary expenses just to avoid excessive taxation.

The large range of embedded tax cost is significant. Some industries are capital-intensive and take huge depreciation expenses. Again, the point is to debate strategy, not tactics, so we will use only 15 percent as an example of very conservative embedded tax cost.

Because we want to avoid the federal government picking winners and losers, subsidizing pet industries, and creating even more lobbyists, the retail Unity Tax will be applied equally to all products and services without exception. The Unity Tax will be applied in the same manner as states and municipalities apply their sales taxes. Congress will set the tax rate, but we will assume it is a whopping 35 percent. Again, this is an extremely high number, as we shall see. So, costs go down by our conservative 15 percent estimate, retail taxes go up by 35 percent, and we are just as well off? No, we are actually better off, and here is how.

First, we start with a simple illustration to show the impacts on purchasing power regardless of income level, family situation, or specific items sold.

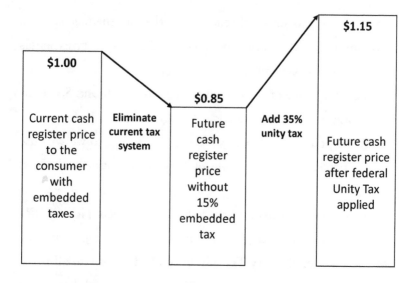

The actual cost of the product at the retail level will increase by about 15 percent from the current baseline. This includes both a low reduction in the embedded tax and a high Unity Tax rate. However, this is not the entire story. If prices went up 15 percent but you were given (yes, gifted) Unity Income, would you be better or worse off in purchasing power? Would you have paid more federal taxes or less? What would be the impact on federal tax receipts?

Assume an average American family of four, who are all American citizens, currently spends every after-tax dollar they take home from work. If this average American family has an income of $6,600 per month, or $79,200 per year, slightly above the median in the United States, they will pay 7.65 percent in Social Security and Medicare taxes and maybe 10 percent in federal income taxes, which are withheld from pay. If they are self-employed, the tax would be higher. This amounts to 17.65 percent extra take-home money, or $14,000, of tax savings this family may spend, save, or invest. However, we are not done. How much does this family currently spend on education, healthcare insurance and medical out-of-pocket expenses, and retirement? Unity Income provides another $45,600 annually for our family of four, which reduces their current expense burden.

Most of the Unity Income is required to be invested in their future to become self-sufficient and not rely on the solvency of Social Security and Medicare. However, there is still $800 per month, or $9,600 annually, to be used any way they see fit. This is equivalent to over 12 percent of their annual gross salary. Adding this all together, this family of four is subsidized to the tune of 30 percent of their annual gross salary. If the family currently spends 18 percent of their gross income on retirement savings, health, and education-related expenses, including daycare, this money would also be freed to use as purchasing power. We will not include these benefits to finish the illustration.

If we assume this average family of four had no savings (not an uncommon assumption) and spent every last take-home dollar on purchases under the current system, they will have $65,600 of purchasing power. With the Unity Tax, and given our very conservative assumptions, they would have to spend $75,440 (15 percent price increase) to buy the exact same goods and services as with the current tax system. However, they are keeping $14,000 of their own money by not paying payroll and federal income taxes and are receiving an additional $9,600 in cash in Unity Income. This results in $89,200 of purchasing power for the same $75,440 of products and services, or an 18 percent increase in money they can use to buy more products for their family or invest and save.

Current tax system for an average American citizen family of four:

- Annual income: $79,600
- Taxes and withholdings from pay: ($14,000)
- Net purchasing power with take-home pay: $65,600

Unity Tax and Unity Income for an average American citizen family of four:

- Annual income: $79,600
- Taxes and withholdings from pay: ($0)
- Net purchasing power with take-home pay: $79,600
- Unity Income cash (after funding retirement, healthcare): $9,600
- Total purchasing power with American Unity Plan: $89,200
- Retail purchases cost ($65,600 plus 15 percent increase): $75,400
- **Net purchasing power improvement:**   **$13,800**

As we know, there is no such thing as a free lunch. To determine how this might impact federal tax receipts and the deficit, we return to our retail price example. The equivalent $65,600 in purchasing power would first be reduced to $55,800 by eliminating all corporate income, payroll, and other embedded taxes and compliance costs. In our example, the 35 percent Unity Tax would collect $19,600 for the federal government, or an increase of $5,600 over the original personal income and payroll taxes collected through

Social Security, Medicare, and federal income taxes. So how is this not a tax on the middle class? Because Unity Income provides $9,600 in cash to this family of four, resulting in a net increase of $4,000 in their pockets!

How is this miracle possible? The family has more purchasing power and more cash in their pocket yet pays more in total federal taxes? Yes, because the tax burden is being transferred from businesses to individuals, the myriad of "other taxes" are eliminated, and there are incredible savings in compliance and administrative costs. The plan itself may or may not be tax neutral depending on changes to spending habits, GDP growth, elimination of tax fraud, increasing the population that pay federal taxes, and more.

Additionally, we are spending over $2 trillion more in year one to fund the transition without assuming any increase in tax receipts. The taxes collected will likely increase, but so will government spending. Currently, this family is funding the retirements and healthcare costs of others through their payroll taxes and are funding government programs for others who pay zero in federal income taxes, as well as paying for fraud, government waste, and tax cheats. Tax receipts and spending will increase, but taxes are paid transparently, anonymously, and voluntarily, and this family will receive Unity Income cash to assist with the higher product cost after federal income taxes are paid at the retail level. Wealthier families will pay more in taxes because they buy more!

In addition, this example assumed that the family was employed by others. The savings accrue even more for the self-employed and small business owners who pay proportionately more in taxes, hire more employees, and assume the burden of compliance costs to minimize their tax bills without triggering an audit. Of course, there is a myriad of assumptions.

- If consumers saw their federal tax bill on every purchase, would they cut down on spending, thereby hurting GDP, or would they spend their additional cash?

- If the price of the product went down at the retail level before applying the Unity Tax, would state and local municipalities increase their local tax rates to make up for the lost tax revenue?

- Would businesses really reduce their prices by a modest 15 percent, or would they grow profits? Or would they invest more in supply capacity knowing consumer spending would increase with more money in their pockets?

- If a very high 35 percent was used as the Unity Tax rate, would the government reduce spending and pay down the debt, or would they use the increase in tax receipts to spend even more and accelerate inflation, causing a downward spiral of the economy?

By the way, the same family of four who are not American citizens would also benefit, but so would the American taxpayer. Understanding the current tax system for legal foreign nationals working in the US is very complex. The tax rates are based on treaties between the US and their home country, types of visa, exemptions, and much more. The tax compliance costs are higher for foreign national citizens and their employers. However, using the same basic assumptions, from an income perspective, a family of foreign nationals making the same wages and paying the same or greater tax rate than an equivalent family of American citizens receives a slight increase benefit in net income compared to the current tax code, despite receiving no Unity Income.

However, this is very deceiving. If we assess the impact of their spending on goods and services in the US, under the American Unity Plan, their net contribution to the US Treasury is much higher than the citizen family. Rather than having a net increase after taxes, their purchasing power is reduced because they receive no Unity Income. This is why we need a dramatic increase in sponsored legal immigration to fight the deficit and pay down the national debt.

There must be a catch, right? Many progressives in the Democratic Party would argue, as they did with the Fair Tax, that despite the fact that this helps the middle class and provides a mechanism to save the social safety net and reduce the debt, it would disproportionately benefit the more affluent in America. To build unity across the political aisle, the American Unity Plan must have a progressive tax system built in to garner Democrats' support.

Suppose another American family of four makes $30,000 per month, or $360,000 annually. We will call this family affluent, although in many American cities, this is a stretch. Under the current federal tax system, using the 2021 tax year, Social Security was capped at $142,800 in income, resulting in a tax of $8,850. For Medicare, the first $250,000 of income is taxed at 1.45 percent, and this family's remaining income is taxed at an additional 0.9 percent (ACA), for a total of 2.35 percent. The total Medicare tax is $6,200. This results in total payroll taxes of $15,000. In addition, the family has a federal income tax liability of about 25 percent, or $93,000, per year. Under the American Unity Plan, this family saves $108,000 per year in taxes and receives only $9,600 in Unity Income cash, which amounts to $117,600 in total new cash available to spend. This results in a 15 percent increase in purchasing power compared to an 18 percent increase for the average family.

Assessing the politics, both families are better off in their purchasing power, and the average family is 3 percent better off than the affluent family due to the higher impact of Unity Income on their lives. Who can argue this is unfair? Well, compared to the current tax system, the affluent family received much more in real purchasing power dollars than the average family. That is not fair if, and only if, you assume the affluent family will not spend the money!

This is where we need to return to our goals. It is impossible to build unity if we are focused solely on wealth redistribution. Wealth redistribution may be popular to many Americans who do not pay federal income taxes or receive a net tax benefit. However, if our goal is to create a fair system of taxation where the wealthy pay proportionately more in taxes while we save the social safety net, reduce fraud and theft, eliminate crony capitalism, reduce government intrusion in our lives, reduce the debt, and curb inflation, then the American Unity Plan meets these objectives. We can argue and come to a compromise on the Unity Tax rate and Unity Income payments, so long as they are applied equally to all, but when we start to argue that some Americans receive more benefits or pay disproportionately more taxes than others, then unity is impossible because it violates American principles. The government has been proven to get this wrong every time, and we create generational fighting, so core problems only get worse. The affluent family will keep more of *their* money because their tax rate is 25 percent now compared to 10 percent for a middle-income family.

Purchasing power is only one side of the equation. Would the affluent family pay much more than the average family in taxes? Of course. The increase in purchasing power will likely result in more spending, although they could increase savings and investment, which would not be taxed until spent. Both would benefit the economy and their fellow citizens.

In our examples, the affluent family will pay about four times more in federal taxes than the middle-income family. Both will pay about the same percentage of their income in federal taxes, and both will have more cash to spend and save than before. Unless we tax people at different rates at the retail counter, there is absolutely no way to make what we now call the effective tax rate equal, and certainly no way to make the tax rate itself progressive. We want the payment of taxes to be simple, cost-effective, voluntary, and anonymous. The American Unity Plan is a progressive tax system but simply cannot be compared to how we currently pay taxes. The affluent will always benefit in nominal dollars more than others because they simply pay much more taxes now.

Rather than being withheld at every paycheck, each family will pay taxes daily as they voluntarily and anonymously live their lives. Every time they spend on products and services, they will see a tax bill that looks massive (for example, $35 in tax on a $100 item), but the end price of the product is only 15 percent more than before. The affluent family pays much more in nominal taxes on its increased spending. Each family funds the federal government relative to their earning power, and each receives the exact same government benefit. No tax system is perfect, but this is as fair as it gets!

Finally, we need to address the social safety net. How does this impact the working poor and the elderly? We know those with no income will receive Unity Income and pay taxes only on their purchases. They will be supplemented at state and local levels, where care and benefits are more compassionate. Many states, however, will provide no supplemental benefits to those employed, even those working at minimum wage standards. The American Unity Plan has a goal to balance the incentive to work with a social safety net that improves lives over time. If for example, a young adult is working full-time and earning minimum wage, they would earn approximately $30,000 per year. We will use $20,000 per year in our example to understand the impact of the American Unity Plan on their lives.

Someone earning $20,000 must pay payroll taxes. Likely, if they have federal income taxes withheld, they will be fully refunded after filing taxes. In addition, we can assume they will receive the earned income credit. This varies by the number of children they have. For someone earning $20,000, Unity Income would increase their cash availability by about 50 percent! This is real money, considering Unity Income also provides healthcare and retirement benefits, which would improve their lives over time compared to traditional government subsidies.

More importantly, Unity Income increases their purchasing power by about 33 percent. This is the highest rate of any demographic modeled. The combination of payroll tax elimination and Unity Income of $6,600 in net increased spending capability is meaningful to their lives.

Please do not be fooled by the argument that "tax cuts only help the rich." The American Unity Plan is not a tax cut. It is a new tax system based on American principles that promotes unity. The impact on every American will be different because of our current convoluted tax and government assistance system. The American Unity Plan meets the goal of a better social safety net system while addressing our fiscal responsibilities. Unlike the current system, will the working poor pay federal taxes? Yes, and that should make us all proud that everyone living here will be contributing what they are able.

Finally, the voting group in America that has the most participation are senior citizens. To recap, if current seniors receive less in Social Security than the Unity Income amount, Social Security would be replaced by Unity Income. These are the poorest of the seniors, and they would effectively receive a higher social safety net. Remember, they are of the age where the retirement and healthcare amounts of Unity Income are available as immediate cash. If a current senior receives more in Social Security than Unity Income, there would be no impact on their income. However, each senior is treated individually, not as part of a household. This particularly benefits married seniors where the lower-earning spouse may be penalized in our current system.

Every demographic was analyzed, and only one group stands out as receiving less purchasing power and potentially paying more taxes than others. A senior who is single, receives only one Social

Security check that is higher than the Unity Income rate, and has very high expenses (for example, assisted living, additional care, high out-of-pocket medications, etc.) but does not qualify for Medicaid will be part of the group that benefits the least. These seniors have modest retirement accounts and pay very little in federal income taxes.

We need to analyze this group to ensure no negative rights are incurred. How are they impacted by the American Unity Plan? There are no changes in income except that there are no withholdings on retirement distributions or income from investment accounts, but both are modest for this group. Because this group pays so little in federal income taxes compared to spending, this group only benefits if spending in the key category of healthcare is reduced by the assumed 15 percent (which will probably be much more).

For example, if the cost of an assisted living center goes down by only 15 percent before the American Unity Tax of our assumed 35 percent is applied, she will receive no benefit compared to other Americans but will be no worse off. Healthcare will be one of the biggest beneficiaries of the American Unity Plan, and it is likely their costs will be greater reduced, but we will stay with our assumption of 15 percent. We also cannot assume that all savings will be passed on to the residents of an assisted living center.

The reason these seniors will see their purchasing power potentially decrease is because they will pay substantially more than before, since under the current tax system, the young and working effectively pay the tax bill as their generational promise. Our social safety net is called the third rail of politics for a reason. Imagine the political demagoguing on a potential increase in federal taxes paid for any senior, even if for just a small percentage. Of course, seniors pay, on average, very little in federal income taxes compared to those collected during their lifetime. The whole idea of these entitlements is wealth transfers from young to old. However, these entitlements generate miserable returns on a lifetime of Social Security and Medicare taxes but receive a huge medical and care benefit. The time has come to address the problem and provide the means for future generations to care for themselves, but we need a humane approach to implementation aligned with American principles.

The current system of taxation and wealth redistribution is unsustainable without significant pain. The American Unity Plan proposes the pain be focused on short-term additional debt. Most proposals that have failed to become legislation have involved raising the retirement age, increasing payroll taxes, reducing benefits, increasing premiums, or implementing single-payer healthcare, which will result in rationing services. Without a remedy and even with some additional national debt, the American Unity Plan effectively suggests potentially raising taxes for only a small group of seniors and only if healthcare costs remain inflated. Are there alternatives to ensure these seniors do not incur negative benefits?

We can brainstorm some solutions. Could we lower the Unity Tax rate on senior care facilities? Maybe we could allow seniors to opt out if they are in senior care? These solutions violate American principles and open the door for many other exemptions. Lobbyists and voter group pandering would reappear. Could we provide higher Unity Income for seniors who are worse off than before? Those who are worse off will vary greatly by state, where living expenses vary widely, requiring additional reporting and compliance costs and many other government controls we want to eliminate. At the federal level, we need to apply Unity Income equally to all Americans.

We must do something since Social Security and Medicare are going bankrupt. The American Unity Plan is a better way to keep our promises to seniors than taxing the next generations more, raising the retirement age, or cutting healthcare for seniors. It will be hard to predict, but less than 5 percent of senior Americans may potentially be negatively impacted. The fairest way to solve the problem is for the states to subsidize those negatively impacted, including seniors and any other American citizen that falls into a tax and income trap. The states are much better positioned to remedy issues, as the cost of living is radically different between state and local communities.

For example, the cost of assisted living in Atlanta is 17 percent lower than the national average, while New York is 42 percent higher than the national average. Maybe New York should subsidize their seniors more than Georgia? There are many forms of subsidies available. Could state and local governments exempt seniors from state and local taxes, as many do now with seniors above eighty-five? Could states subsidize the assisted living centers directly? In sum, the states are better at solving problems, and federal involvement must be limited to setting the Unity Income and Unity Tax rates. The federal government needs to focus more on inflation and balancing the budget to fight climate change and protect our nation.

Would states be able to fund new spending? In an ironic twist, if businesses pass on all the embedded tax and compliance cost savings to their customers in the form of lower prices, then states and local governments will receive less tax receipts than today because they are taxing a smaller base amount. They might have to raise their local and state sales taxes to make their budgets balance, thereby increasing the total cost to consumers. On the other hand, states could tax products and services that are currently exempted to increase revenue.

In some aspects of the social safety net, the states will spend more, but in others, they will spend less. The education portion of Unity Income will reduce the education expenses at the state and local level. The federal government will fund more education with Unity Education Accounts, allowing local jurisdictions to reduce their budgets accordingly while still educating our youth. In return, some seniors and potentially others negatively impacted by the higher cost of goods and services could be assisted more compassionately than the federal government does now.

We have provided many examples of how the American Unity Plan has positive benefits for most. Specific to some gap seniors, if this group was less fortunate and had lower Social Security, they would receive greater benefits and would be better off in purchasing power. If they were married or not living in assisted living, where expenses are higher, they would also be better off than today. If they were wealthier and paid more in federal taxes, they would incur no negative impact. The point is that there will always be some exceptions, but the current tax system is unfair to many more people, and we need to be sensitive to that. If we apply American principles, we need to maintain the same Unity Income benefit to all, and all those living, working, and visiting the United States need to pay the same income tax rate. Over time, this issue will go away. Every year, fewer seniors will need Social Security and Medicare, and more Americans will have their own accounts and not rely on the federal government. The full transition will take a generation or two, but we must keep our promises in the interim.

In all, the American Unity plan recognizes that no plan is perfect, but this plan is better than every other proposal. The plan must return more power to the states to ensure American principles are fully applied at the federal level.

We know entitlements cannot be slashed. We should not run from exceptions but include in the solution proposals that overcome objections. The goal is not to create a perfect program but one that is superior to our current system that is collapsing under its own weight of bureaucracy, inefficiency, and demography.

In sum, all working income levels do better under the American Unity Plan. The poor do much better because of the Unity Income payment. Some seniors, but relatively few, may do slightly worse. The middle class does slightly worse than the poor and the affluent on the surface in nominal dollars. However, the middle-class family will gain the most from the healthcare, education, and retirement benefits of Unity Income.

Some would argue the rich do not need Unity Income and it should be means tested. Wrong. The concept of equality and fairness must be driven into everything we do to eliminate divisions in our culture. All Americans must be treated equally. We need to get out of our collective heads that it is currently government money that is allocated to us. The only source of "government money" is the taxpayer—i.e., taxes on money you and I and everyone else who works in the private sector earns. It is our money to spend as we wish. Then, and only then, will we meet our collective obligation to support the government fairly among us.

If the rich want to pay more in taxes, here is a simple idea: They can buy more stuff, especially American made, and give the products they buy to the poor. It is like double giving. They can pay the retail tax to fund Unity Income for all Americans to benefit the poor and middle class and give real products and services to the less fortunate so they can keep more of their Unity Income and earned wages. Or, better yet, they can donate their Unity Income to the charity of their choice or opt out so the savings could pay down the national debt.

The elimination of the federal income tax transfers money from the wealthy to the less fortunate in society without having to worry about the tax deductibility of the contributions, offshore accounts, charitable trusts, estate taxes, and more. Money can be given to your children at any time without any consequences, except for perhaps spoiling them.

Many people will donate more money to charity, even though it is not tax deductible, because they will have more disposable income! All tax deductions, credits, and exemptions will be eliminated, and everyone living or working in the United States, citizen or not, legal or illegal, will pay the exact same tax rate based on their total spending. But, more importantly, it is our money, and taxes need to be voluntary and anonymous. You will not need to show a photo ID or give your Social Security card to a clerk to pay taxes!

Unity Income ensures that, proportionate to earned income, the people who earn less are subsidized a much greater amount but in a fair and equitable way. There are no negative rights incurred. Other than the politics of controlling the purse, this should appeal even to the most ardent progressives. The poor are much better off under Unity Income than traditional government subsidies. We cannot continue to argue the merits of the current tax system. We are not eliminating federal taxes. We are changing the way they are paid to ensure taxes are paid fairly by many more people while maintaining a social safety net from cradle to grave. This is a fundamental American principle.

To gain unity, the analyses must be centered on how much Unity Income each American will receive, the exact Unity Tax each person buying goods and services in the US will pay, and how each of these factors will affect our tax collections to pay down the debt and fight inflation. The above examples used very conservative assumptions. We can easily run the math with a Unity Tax rate of only 25 percent to further stimulate the economy but collect less in taxes. Or maybe the embedded tax will be much higher than the assumed 15 percent, reducing the pretax cost of goods and services and allowing us to raise the Unity Tax rate even more to pay down the debt faster without prices spiking out of control. The natural equilibrium will be reached just a few years after implementation.

To build unity, we need to create a framework for agreement across the political landscape. The Unity Tax supported by Unity Income, under the American Unity plan, does just that. The messaging should resonate:

The American Unity Plan transfers the responsibility for paying taxes solely to individuals residing in the United States to ensure we repatriate jobs, provide the framework to attract more legal immigration, and allow for America to be competitive and secure. The American Unity Plan increases purchasing power and the social safety net while raising more tax money by eliminating the cost of compliance and fraud, minimizing tax cheats, and taxing non-Americans proportionately more.

We have discussed in detail the impact of taxes and the cash portion of Unity Income benefits. Next, we will address some guardrails, or rules of the road, regarding retirement, healthcare, and education accounts under the Unity Income umbrella.

PART III
THE UNIFIERS

10

SOCIAL SAFETY WITHOUT DEPENDENCY

In social policy, when we provide a safety net, it should be designed to help people take more entrepreneurial risks, not to turn them into dependents. This doesn't mean that we should be callous to the underprivileged.

— Nassim Nicholas Taleb,
author and mathematician

Retirement, healthcare, and education are the foundation of the social safety net. As a society, these programs are a massive part of both the annual budget and our unfunded liabilities. No plan can be complete unless we develop a way to ensure we continue to provide for the most vulnerable while ensuring we have the wealth to avoid crises and fight other major problems, such as climate change.

As discussed in the previous section, Unity Income provides modest cash, benefiting the poor proportionately more. It ensures the slightly higher prices due to the Unity Tax do not create inflation and make energy, food, medicine, and shelter unaffordable. The Unity Tax provides the funding for the social safety net programs while decreasing the debt over time and is a means for American financial solvency. The cost that is bigger than the cash portion is the funding of personal accounts for the three programs.

The American Unity Plan addresses these programs head-on. As always, we start with some basic rules of the road. These are the guardrails to ensure true market capitalism, not crony capitalization, fraud, and waste, are incorporated from the onset. Some of these guardrails are:

1. Funds are distributed exactly in the same manner as Social Security and unemployment checks are today, whether by direct deposit or debit cards. There is no argument whether the government can efficiently distribute money, whether that is stimulus or Social Security checks. Distributing money seems to be one of the few federal core competencies!

2. Parents, of course, would be the default custodians of their children's funds. For those who are unable to manage their own accounts due to health or living conditions, others can be custodians, as is done quite often today. Children of the elderly, guardians, caretakers, attorneys, or court-appointed

nonprofits can provide not only financial management but also compassion and life guidance, something lacking in many government systems. We will call any individual who manages an account for someone else a custodian. The key is no government agency (federal, state, or local) would be allowed to manage Unity Income on behalf of any American citizen. The role of any government in the American Unity Plan is to ensure the law is followed by both the recipient and the custodian.

3. Recipients would only have to prove they have active and managed accounts. Unity Income has minimal regulations to eliminate "one-size-fits-all" government requirements that make no sense for large segments of Americans and add unnecessary compliance costs. All accounts are in the name of the recipient. Attesting to an active account is no different than proving to the DMV that you have automobile insurance before obtaining or renewing a legal driver's license. There is rampant fraud in our current retirement, disability, survivors, and supplemental benefits programs that must be eliminated with strict fines and penalties for abuse either by the recipient or the custodian.

Every American citizen will have Unity Income accounts in his or her name, and the management of that account would transfer from parent or custodian to able recipient at high school graduation. Setting this transfer date as high school graduation, rather than an artificial age, incentivizes all children and young adults to graduate high school and manage their own money. Some may graduate before the age of 18, and some may do so later in life after obtaining a GED. The parents' or custodians' responsibilities are:

- Open the appropriate accounts for retirement, healthcare, and education and select the specific investments.
- Select the insurance plans and appropriate education services.
- Pay all service providers.

The custodians would receive no money from the Unity Income recipient. This would discourage "harvesting" for profit, and many organizations would volunteer their time and money to give children and others who need guidance and a chance to succeed.

Besides parents, custodians could be volunteers or charitable organizations that provide guidance and mentorship. Any funds to manage accounts on behalf of others would be raised through charitable giving. As a reminder, the concept of distinguishing between charitable and for-profit organizations goes away when the current federal tax system is replaced with the Unity Tax!

Unity Income replaces all federal benefit programs over time, including Social Security and Medicare. There are over eighty federal programs that provide cash (welfare), food, housing, medical care, social services, training, education, and much more. Besides the inefficiency of so many programs administered by government bureaucrats, and the inherent fraud that comes with complexity and government largesse, the programs lack the flexibility to meet individual needs. These programs force recipients to become experts in playing the assistance game as opposed to focusing on improving their life circumstances. Much of the money provided by the federal government is in the form of grants to the states, and this transition to Unity Income would provide the states even more flexibility to serve the needs of their citizens without federal strings attached.

Combining Unity Income with the Unity Tax eliminates government manipulation of both markets and personal choice through mechanisms such as the earned income tax credit and directed tax deductions based on behavior the current administration values. The current government programs provide the incentive to work for some but not for others, which violates the principle of fairness and equality under the law. The choice of whether to work and how much to work will be personal and driven by the cost of living and personal lifestyle choices. People living in high-cost states will have more incentive to work. That is, unless those states continue to spend more than the federal safety net by supplementing Unity Income with state and local funding. Federalism will allow the states to experiment with additional social safety net benefits as they choose. Many states will eliminate all supplemental benefits, and others will deem Unity Income as too low and provide funding. Federalism promotes experimentation and innovation.

The dream of many on the left is to have both UBI and a federal minimum wage. This puts the burden on the employer. From the beginning of the agricultural revolution twelve thousand years ago, there has been an investment war between labor and capital. When the cost of labor goes up, spending capital on mechanical automation becomes a good return on investment compared to spending on people. We see this when inflation is high, unemployment is low, and capital is cheap. In the services industry, artificial intelligence and machine learning provide the same equation for businesses. The minimum wage artificially raises the cost of labor, eliminates jobs through capital investment, and results in making more people dependent on the government for support. Unity Income without a minimum wage levels the playing field and lets the market decide the correct mix between labor and capital, as it should. Also, when investment is not focused on labor cost reduction, it becomes focused on the human experience and improved services, which helps every consumer.

Many left-leaning states complain about the balance of tax payments originating from their states versus federal money returned. Ironically, they complain most about the cap on state and local tax deductions, which help only the upper middle class and the wealthy. They complain because they want to avoid the wealthy and their tax base leaving their states. Unity Income and Unity Tax eliminate this argument. When given an equal choice, consumers will choose lower cost and shop where the same products and services are less expensive, regardless of where they currently live. Under the American Unity Plan, there is no federal incentive to live in one state or another from a federal taxes and benefits point of view. However, the cost of goods and services, and therefore the Unity Tax, will be greater in higher-tax and higher-spend states. Higher-tax states will continue to disproportionately pay more federal taxes not because of the federal tax code but because of the cost of their local economies.

Unity Income promotes federalism and provides a safety net while letting states compete for talent within their own balanced budgets or deficits as they choose. States are free to supplement the federal Unity Income with their own funding for healthcare, education, and retirement programs and are free to raise or lower state and local taxes. States with modest costs of living will need to provide minimal or no supplement to their citizens, while high-cost states may increase state supplements. If states and cities want to provide benefits, the assistance will be both more compassionate and more effective, as the supply is geographically closer to the demand, especially if it is provided by custodians in the private sector.

Some left-leaning states not only have higher costs, but these costs could lead to less savings and more debt for the poorest Americans without state subsidies. Besides inflation, debt is one of the worst impediments to financial health. Debt on a typically appreciating asset like real estate (without the periodic bubble) is American. Debt for depreciating assets or everyday expenses assigns many people to a permanent financial hole. Unity Income has a far-reaching social impact beyond saving Social Security and building a retirement nest egg. Knowing that Unity Income provides the means for critical needs in life, tax-free earnings can be used to pay down both credit card and education debt. In addition, the guarantee of federally backed income will improve credit scores, lower the cost of debt to many Americans, and allow for more people to obtain credit in the first place. Predatory practices such as payday lenders and high-interest credit cards will be dramatically reduced, helping young adults and the poor.

This idea of personal debt reduction and increasing credit availability has far-reaching implications. Many poor Americans do not have access to the credit markets and are subject to exceptionally high interest rates when credit is even available. A guaranteed federal income stream, supplemented by some states, can be part of the solution for homelessness and especially help the working poor. The free market may develop banking and housing alternatives for an entirely new consumer group that suddenly has guaranteed income and credit. Currently, federal, state, and local governments are trying to incentivize affordable housing, but rules and regulations requiring signed occupants prior to construction, local zoning, and massive regulations have hampered efforts. As always, people freely making buying decisions with their money, backed by a guaranteed income stream, would reduce the compliance burden on builders and eliminate archaic or political zoning rules and regulations.

In fact, if state and local governments want to subsidize affordable housing, they could pay the federal Unity Tax for real estate purchases or apartment rents on behalf of the recipient. However, the necessity to do so would be diminished. Fewer and fewer people will want or need this assistance over time. They will simply enter the housing market on their own.

With both debt reduction and Unity Income as a guarantee, Americans will feel more financially secure. Historically, when Americans feel finally secure, there has been an increase in charitable giving. Most Americans believe charity is personal, from person to person within your family, community, place of worship, or nonprofit organization of one's choice, and it should not be mandated or influenced by government. Americans respond to crises better than any nationality in the world. Unity Income and the elimination of federal taxes will put more money in people's hands. When Americans feel financially safe, we give more and will do so even when there is no federal tax deduction for charitable giving.

Another appeal is that Unity Income could continue to be collected by the incarcerated and managed by their custodians. The money in the account could only be used after a person exited prison and would build a nest egg, as inmates released from prison have a tough time gaining employment and transitioning into society. It could be used for education, and it could certainly be used for healthcare and later needs in life. In addition, the children of inmates often suffer, and the money could be used to assist with the care of children of the incarcerated or potentially could be paid as restitution to the victims of crime.

Unity Income would even have a far-reaching impact on marriage, custody, alimony, child support, and many more societal concerns. Many people stay in abusive relationships because of financial immobility. Since Unity Income goes directly to the recipient, including children via their custodians, there is a built-in safety net, so many more decisions are made for the right reasons. Some deadbeat fathers do not pay child support now, and Unity Income would dramatically help single mothers and children.

Unity Income is the key ingredient of the American Unity Plan to uniting America and implementing American principled solutions. Unity Income allows Republicans to engage Democrats in debates around affordable housing, nutrition, childcare, homelessness, and other social issues that the Democrats have historically owned. This replacement American social safety concept separates the focus many have on government dependency from a true, fair social safety net. There is no stigma to receiving funds that all Americans receive equally. The message of the American Unity Plan is quite appealing to the American family to build a unifying coalition:

Unity Income helps families build financial credit and repay student loans and other debts, assists single parents and children from broken homes, and ensures no one is stuck in a job because of its benefits. Unity Income provides new educational opportunities currently available only to the wealthy and supports working families. Unity Income is the foundation for solving many societal problems.

Except for the last sentence, reading the above out of context would certainly make every conservative shudder, and most Republicans and libertarians. That is the point! Republicans need to stop running from societal issues and face problems head-on with bold solutions based on American principles and the values of federalism, liberty from government intrusion in our lives, fairness, and equality. Simply saying we need to decrease government dependency, with no solution, is unacceptable. Democrats need to recognize that Social Security and Medicare are going bankrupt, public education has failed many, and it's time to transition to a realistic alternative that is fiscally sane.

The next three chapters discuss the details of how each of the three main American Unity Plan social safety net solutions would function and transition from the current broken systems.

11

★ ★ ★

GENERATIONAL WEALTH
FOR THE REST

*Compound interest is the eighth wonder of the world. He
who understands it, earns it. . . he who doesn't. . . pays it.*

— Albert Einstein

More than half of the US population has stock ownership, but
the numbers are skewed to the wealthy, as expected. Social
Security provides the safety net for those whose savings are
lacking, but investments that provide dividends and interest when
people can no longer work provide a much greater return. As we
live longer and retirement years become a greater percentage of the
human lifespan, passive income becomes critical.

In the future, demographics will not allow Social Security to be supported by generational transfers of wealth from the young to the old. The system is simply going bankrupt, and we are kicking the can down the road. Today, the impending crisis, which is plain for all to see, has been usurped by arguments over climate change and immigration. If we continue to delay the inevitable, the potential solutions available to us will be few and painful.

We need an innovative transition plan from Social Security to a new, modern system where all Americans join the investor class much earlier in life, allowing their personal wealth to make Social Security payments insignificant by the time they retire. It is critical to drive more and more people from debt and Social Security subsistence to personal investments they control. It would be better to have discussions about whether Amazon or Walmart is a better investment instead of fighting over government distributions between generations. Every investor wants the economy to grow. Too many now are focused on the government return on political capital instead of return on investment.

The Social Security trust fund is projected to go bankrupt around 2034. In 2020, about 3.6 million babies were born in the US, down 4 percent from 2019. Births are reducing every year, dropping an average of 2 percent per year since 2014. In 2021, the growth rate of the United States, not including illegal entry, has effectively dropped to zero. Due to advances in healthcare and fitness, the older population is living longer. The replacement fertility rate math is simply not working for Social Security to continue without significant change. The only levers that can be used to save the current system are to significantly raise payroll taxes, reduce benefits, or increase the retirement age to delay benefits for millions. There is an alternative that leverages what America does better than any country in the world. We innovate and invest!

Incomes typically grow as we age in our careers. Employees grow to be managers with experience. Entry-level waiters advance to upscale restaurants or become chefs and restauranteurs. Startup owners learn to scale enterprises and increase profits, and some become fortunate enough to be acquired by larger companies or investors.

Many, however, never fulfill their potential. With the pace of change, many of the jobs of today will not exist in ten or twenty years, and income progression may decline sooner. A critical question is job mobility. Will someone whose job is being outsourced or automated due to higher wages or changes in technology be willing and able to work for less money as they age? If so, what will happen to their savings and ability to invest? The free market has always had creative destruction, where inefficient businesses give way to new technologies and nimble startups.

In the future, we cannot assume accelerating income and may see a wider gap between peak earnings and retirement. This has huge ramifications on society. Will a pipeline worker really learn to program? What will truck and rideshare drivers do when autonomous vehicles reach their potential? Disruption, whether caused by free-market economics or government policy (for example, oil and gas production), displaces workers. It always has and always will, but the pace of change is accelerating.

In capitalist societies, the innovators and leaders in the private sector get rich. In socialist societies, politicians and government bureaucrats get rich. In either case, there will always be rich and poor in any society. Many call this the wealth gap, or wealth inequality, and have politicized this issue. It has been a successful strategy for more than one hundred years, as Communists have attempted class warfare since their first revolution. Americans accepted and grew accustomed to the concept of the social safety net without attempting to artificially close the wealth gap through redistribution of wealth. Progressives focused on government spending to increase the safety net but may have created a lifetime dependency for many. This has now become both a crisis and an opportunity.

The concept of risk mitigation through the social safety net, coupled with moving more people to investing, is a critical issue that needs to be addressed to unify the country. Social Security needs to transition, and real policy solutions not involving involuntary redistribution of generational wealth need to be part of any proposal. Unity Income provides every American with the social safety net to fund private retirement, healthcare, and education accounts.

We call the retirement portion Unity Retirement Accounts or URAs. URAs are like IRAs, as they are owned by the individual and can be transferred to others. However, they are very different in a few fundamental ways:

1. When the money is invested, grows, or is transferred to others, it is not taxed until the account holder or recipient spends money on goods and services thanks to the Unity Tax. The entire concept of before-tax and after-tax treatment of investments ends with the American Unity Plan. This eliminates much of the cost and complexity of tax

and estate planning. We do not penalize tax savings and investment, only spending.

2. Funding is provided by the federal government, and investing is up to the individual, with proper guardrails. Account holders are free to invest as they wish in any federally regulated investment account, including stocks, bonds, money markets, etc. Investment vehicles must be licensed, auditable, and report account status to the federal government to reduce fraud, as opposed to creating government policies that attempt to mitigate investment risk.

3. URAs cannot be combined with other assets. They can only be federally funded or added to by transference from other URAs. This means that the rest of the account holder's wealth is protected from the prying eyes of the federal government. Remember, with the implementation of the Unity Tax, Americans will no longer have to report income to the federal government. It is fair for the government to know your URA account exists, since taxpayers are funding the investment, but privacy is a constitutional right and should be protected wherever possible.

4. URA holders cannot borrow or withdraw any funds until they are no longer dependent on the current Social Security system. This means that Social Security is still in place should investors make poor personal decisions, even with investment guardrails in place. Using IRAs and 401(k)s as an example, the federal government demands a "required minimum distribution," mainly to ensure more taxes are paid in the present. Many financial planners advocate that if

only 4 percent of an account balance is withdrawn each year, this will usually ensure sufficient funds for life through both up and down markets. Similarly, once 4 percent of a URA exceeds what a recipient would have received under Social Security, future Social Security payments are eliminated. In other words, the federal government kept its promise of retirement income in exchange for paying for the retirement of someone else earlier in life. This is how we transition away from Social Security over time. As a reminder, Unity Income continues forever, so the mandatory portion of Unity Income reserved for URA funding could be used for other purposes by the recipient, most likely for additional healthcare spending once the magic 4 percent level is reached, at any age.

Once Social Security is eliminated (which will likely take one to two generations), Americans will have three sources of income beyond work—Unity Income, URAs, and personal savings and investment. How many young adults believe Social Security will be available for them, never mind check their future benefits regularly with the Social Security administration? However, a lot of investors check their investment accounts at least monthly, and many follow the stock market daily. By making investing mandatory from birth, many Americans who have been left behind will contribute to and benefit from capitalism.

Under Unity Income, Americans will receive in their URAs $100 per month to invest from birth to high school graduation and $300 per month thereafter for life. Withdrawals may begin when

4 percent of the URA balance reaches the benefit that would have been received under the old Social Security system.

To transition out of the current Social Security system, there are two key points that need to be reiterated:

1. Under the American principle of no negative rights, no current or future Social Security recipient will receive less than they do today, from the combination of Unity Income and Social Security, and many will receive much more. Unity Income is the consistent amount received by all American citizens under the American principles of fairness and equality, whereas Social Security becomes a variable, diminishing benefit over time. Each dollar contributed by the federal government to URAs reduces the future Social Security obligation. As the URA accounts grow tax-free and combine with Unity Income, the Social Security benefit is reduced and eventually reaches zero obligation over time. For current seniors on Social Security, Social Security may never be eliminated, as Social Security cost of living allowances may require it to be continued.

2. Once Social Security is eliminated as a benefit to the individual, URA holders are free to transfer URA money to another URA account holder (any American citizen, young or old) or spend it any way they wish. Unlike an IRA or 401(k), this can be done at any time without penalty, so long as the URA holder is no longer eligible for Social Security. Also, unlike other monetary gifts, the transfer is not taxable and has no government-controlled, artificial

limits or regulations. The only rule is that URA money can only be transferred to another eligible URA account or Unity Healthcare Account (UHA), and this in turn further reduces America's future obligations under the current social safety net systems.

Rather than some receiving more and some receiving less under the current Social Security program, every American citizen would receive the exact same amount into their URAs starting immediately or at birth. This amount is guaranteed regardless of their life decisions—to stay home and care for the family, to marry, how many years they worked, how much income they made, or anything else. Any additions to personal wealth and financial security would be through personal savings and investment. Just the fact that every American would be an investor would increase financial literacy and encourage lifetime investment.

However, those who do not save and invest, whether by choice or life's circumstances, will have a safety net for later in life that is better than what they get today. URAs are modeled for the average recipient, but the reality is that people who receive more in Social Security benefits today have more in their 401(k)s, IRAs, and other retirement savings, as well as home equity. They were higher earners during their working years. The poor will be the biggest beneficiaries of URAs.

My father retired at age sixty-five, and my mother retired at age sixty-one, both with very modest 401(k)s. For twenty-three years of retirement, they took only the required minimum distributions to supplement Social Security. There was more money in their 401(k) s after twenty-three years than when they first retired. Their secret? They put the money in market index funds and forgot about it. Brilliant!

The argument against privatizing Social Security due to risk and mismanagement is false. As any investor knows, dollar cost averaging over long periods of time is the key to both contributions and withdrawals. Investors get into trouble trying to time the market and withdrawing money during down markets. Time and compounding interest are your friends. My parents used dollar cost averaging to fund contributions at only 3 percent of their modest incomes for about twenty years. Then, they dollar cost averaged minimum required distributions for the next twenty-three years, through several recessions and bear markets. This strategy created a comfortable retirement and savings for healthcare needs later in life. Imagine if they had started saving at age twenty-one instead of their forties, when 401(k)s first became available, or better yet, at birth.

The guarantee of Social Security meant that my parents did not need extra money during market downturns and could capitalize on the average gains of the market over two generations. Similarly, the guarantee of Unity Income will allow every URA holder to dollar average contributions and minimum withdrawals for life. At death, account holders transfer the residual generational wealth to whomever they choose who has a URA or UHA without fear of government confiscation, gift taxes, and other arcane rules. Simple wills will eliminate much of today's estate planning, which is set up mostly to avoid unnecessary estate taxes and burdens on heirs. This reduces the risk of losing the home or farm. Also, the need for disability income insurance, which many people pay through employers or buy on the open market, will be reduced because of the Unity Income safety net. In sum, the cost of managing life and death is reduced, which frees more money to be spent, saved, invested, or gifted.

Another subtle but important point to make here is the relationship between wealth and Medicaid. Many people who have some savings but not enough to cover healthcare needs later in life will drain their savings to be eligible for Medicaid. This entire concept is eliminated because of the Unity Healthcare Accounts, as discussed in the next chapter. Seniors should never be forced by government policy to be drained of life savings and unable to pass their wealth to future generations.

Incidentally, why is the government telling us when to retire? What is magic about sixty-two, sixty-five, sixty-seven, or seventy years of age? Many lifetime investors retire early, choose to defer Social Security because they do not need the money, and wait to receive more benefits later in life. They live off savings or bridge the retirement-to-Social-Security gap via equity in their homes. With Unity Income and URAs, all Americans can retire when they financially, physically, and psychologically want, without artificial government timetables, knowing Unity Income provides a safety net forever, not just when they reach an artificial age. Also, many American seniors enjoy working to stay active or choose to work to make extra income. With the American Unity Plan, they are not penalized by the tax code for working longer and contributing their time and experience. This is freedom from government intrusion in our life decisions.

Social Security benefits are calculated based on lifetime earnings using the average of the thirty-five years when you earned the most. Someone who is now sixty-two, assuming they entered the workforce in their twenties, would still be eligible for Social Security calculated the way it is now. However, with Unity Income, the Social Security benefit when they retire would be reduced by the Unity Income payment. If they claim Social Security at sixty-two, that is fine. They could continue working and receive income-tax-free benefits until they spend it. Under the American Unity Plan, many more people would use Unity Income to retire early under Social Security and reduce the long-term obligation of the Social Security trust fund. The recipient is much better off than under just Social Security as it is today. However, this would put a strain on the workforce, which is another reason for increased sponsored immigration, as discussed in a later chapter.

Conversely, someone who is twenty-five today would begin receiving Unity Income and funding URAs immediately. When they reach sixty-two, if they have not already built enough wealth in the URAs to be ineligible for Social Security, they would claim Social Security under the same formula as today. Likely, they would build enough wealth that sometime in their sixties or maybe their early seventies, they would no longer be eligible and would be phased out of Social Security. A baby born today would likely no longer be eligible for Social Security in their fifties or early sixties at the very latest, and probably much earlier in life.

The point is that the American Unity Plan will phase out Social Security within most American's lifetimes and will preserve the retirement safety net without accounting gimmicks or government promises that will be hard to keep due to changing demographics. The year when Social Security is phased out will be based entirely on the free-market rate of return. Does anyone think the current Social Security system will survive for forty, fifty, or sixty more years without significant economic pain? The American Unity Plan is a smooth transition and is part of an overall plan to balance the federal budget.

As a side note, one question would be why not allow people to save more in URAs than the federal government contributions or gifts from other URA holders? The answer is that there is no incentive to contribute more. Why would a forty- or fifty-year-old put more money into a URA when they could simply invest on their own in any asset they choose? There are no tax ramifications whatsoever. Also, if they contribute more, they will lose a potential Social Security benefit sooner than if supplementing their URAs and Social Security with their own private accounts. To a child today, it will not matter one way or the other, but most would rather not have the government see any more of their wealth than is necessary.

The American government spends approximately $1.3 trillion annually on Social Security for retirement, survivor benefits, disability, federal employees, and civil servants. Under the American Unity Plan, it is estimated that $500 – $600 billion, or over 40 percent of the annual spend, could be replaced by Unity Income immediately, and this includes benefit increases for the poorest American seniors.

Unlike current government spending and accounting gimmicks, URA funding is very easy to budget. The annual funding for URAs, as a portion of Unity Income, is set at $1,200 for the young and $3,600 for adults. To budget, we simply need to multiply

URA contributions by the number of American citizens in each of these two demographic groups. Federal URA total spending will only grow if the American citizenry grows or if the benefit is increased. When passed, the benefit should not be linked to automatic increases like the current Social Security COLA system. Let the free market produce better rates of return and let any Unity Income increases be debated and passed annually by Congress as part of a balanced budget solution.

To put URA market performance into perspective, the average Social Security check is between $1,600 and $1,700 per month, with military and federal retirees receiving much more and lower lifetime wage earning spouses receiving less. Remember, Social Security recipients have taxes withheld and pay for their healthcare premiums and deductibles. Social Security grows, on average, about 1.3 percent per year as a Cost-of-Living Adjustment (COLA) and higher during inflationary periods such as 2022 and 2023. To understand the budget impact, we can compare the return of average Social Security recipients who get annual 1.3 percent COLAs to URAs.

With URAs, a child born today would not be eligible for Social Security until 4 percent of the URA value is greater than the calculated Social Security payments. From a worst-case perspective, if the market returned a pathetic 4 percent for URAs over a long period of time, and there was never an increase in URA funding, a child born today would still receive some Social Security until age eighty-two, though the benefit amount after reaching the Social Security retirement age would be smaller and smaller each year because of Unity Income. However, to put this in perspective, we are comparing Social Security to only 4 percent of a URA. There is 96 percent wealth remaining in the URA when Social Security is eliminated for this American recipient, or over $1.2 million in the account!

Now we'll look at a moderate return scenario. If the market returned only 6 percent for URAs, a child born today would be ineligible for Social Security at age fifty-seven. The wealth in the URA account would be over $900,000 when the eligibility for Social Security is eliminated.

Finally, if the 8 percent average market return in the United States over a long period of time is used for URAs, and assuming no increases in URA funding (which is unlikely, as demonstrated by generations of Congresses), a child born today would be ineligible for Social Security at age forty-seven. The wealth in the URA account would be over $800,000 when the eligibility for Social Security is eliminated.

By the way, if we applied the same 1.3 percent average annual COLA increase to URA funding that we do to Social Security, the 4 percent return breakeven gets reduced from age eighty-two to age sixty-seven! Also, we are only comparing Social Security against the URA portion of Unity Income. As we will discuss, there are also healthcare accounts funded by Unity Income that will act as a risk mitigator to catastrophic healthcare costs, as well as a portion for flexible uses, including investment. All of the above scenarios were worst cases. Are there any other acceptable solutions to continue Social Security for the next forty years without significant pain?

Time is our friend. The math is better for a newborn than for a recent college graduate than for someone in the middle of their life. Because of the Unity Tax, we switch the equation. In the future, the wealthiest, who buy more goods and services, pay the most federal taxes and directly fund the future retirements of the youngest. This is sustainable, predictable, cost-efficient, and much more flexible to manage than the reverse generational transfer of today. The Unity Tax rate and the URA funding amounts can be adjusted based on the demographics at the time within, hopefully, the context of a balanced budget.

Once again, companies can reduce their expenses, and thus their selling prices for goods and services, by eliminating 401(k) matches to employee contributions, as well as the cost of administering these programs. Employees can simply invest a portion of their larger, tax-free, take-home pay on their own without being constrained by the investment options employers decide to provide and having to worry about rollovers and tax implications later in life.

It is possible our politicians will put additional restrictions on URAs because they cannot help "protecting" people from themselves. We need protection from the politicians! Every investor makes mistakes, some worse than others. We recover, learn, and adapt. It is a good thing. Once we let politicians and regulators put rules on our money, they never stop. The rules for URAs are simple: no withdrawals, without exception, before Social Security is eliminated for the recipient; invest only in federally approved, regulated accounts; and then do what you want with your money after you're eligible to withdraw funds—spend it, invest it, gift it, or transfer it to another URA or UHA account holder.

The argument that Social Security cannot be replaced is garbage, however it is correct that we need a long transition period. Under the American Unity Plan, we have downside protection against sustained bear markets if the market returns are poor, but we have significant upside potential gain in both wealth and freedom to decide when to retire. Limited downside risk and significant upside potential is the dream of every investor!

There have been other proposals in the past to allow Americans to simply opt out of Social Security and allow them to be responsible for their own savings. In theory, this is a valid proposal. In reality, those who make poor investment choices should be on their own, but the compassion of the American people would not let that happen. They would be rewarded for poor choices with a new social safety net at some point. With URAs and Unity Income, the social safety net is always in place, even if someone is foolish with their URAs.

The unifying message will appeal to every American's sense of fairness and equality and specifically to younger Americans who may support the concept of Universal Basic Income.

> Unity Retirement Accounts provide every American citizen a guaranteed income for life that far surpasses their expected Social Security benefits. Every American will receive the exact same amount, with the poorest Americans receiving the greatest protection against financial insecurity to close the wealth gap. Every American will be an investor, and no American will receive less than they do today from Social Security. Unity Retirement Accounts will save the soon-to-be-bankrupt Social Security system and eventually replace it with a modern American retirement program.

So, exactly when does Social Security get eliminated from the federal budget? The beauty of the American Unity Plan is that there is no government timetable arbitrarily set by politicians based on getting reelected. It is a plan based on market performance and individual responsibility. If market performance is low and people do not invest wisely, the current octogenarian Social Security system may live for another fifty or sixty years. If market performance mirrors the past, the number of people who will not have reached their personal Social Security elimination wealth will be extremely small. At some point, with less than say 1 percent of the American citizens needing some supplemental Social Security beyond their Unity Income benefits, we will need to have a funeral. Maybe the savings from the elimination of the Social Security bureaucracy can be refunded to the American people. Maybe the American people or charities will transfer some of their wealth from their URAs to the URAs of the few who are still eligible for Social Security to put it to rest finally. Maybe, for once in our lives, we can watch a bureaucracy face the inevitable without crisis.

Can much of the same logic apply to healthcare? Yes.

12

THE HEALTHCARE SOLUTION FOR ALL

It is amazing that people who think we cannot afford to pay for doctors, hospitals, and medication somehow think that we can afford to pay for doctors, hospitals, medication and a government bureaucracy to administer it.

— Thomas Sowell, author and economist

W hen studying healthcare rankings globally, one might think the United States is a third-world country. Yet, people travel here to use our medical facilities and be treated by our best-in-class doctors and hospitals. We lead the world or are near the top in healthcare innovation and drug discovery. The disconnect is in how healthcare success is measured. We value life and do not ration care or create delays for services as a means of cutting costs. When you are sick, speed to service is vitally important. We have not yet implemented single-payer, socialized medicine, but that path is being traveled. There is no comparison to quality of care and service time between a free-market system and socialized medicine for those in need, and life span outcomes are equivalent. Nationalized healthcare has one advantage, and that is lower cost, though it's achieved through rationing care and service. If this is important to healthcare pollsters, we will never score well.

In the United States, we pay more for everything we value, and healthcare is no exception. We want high-quality, timely, and affordable care available for all in need. So, we need to define the problem we are trying to solve before we discuss solutions. The problem statement is how do we reduce healthcare costs without limiting or rationing the care, services, and breakthrough medicines we and much of the world are accustomed to receiving?

Some claim that private sector care funded by employer or individual private insurance plans have much better medical outcomes than Medicaid. In fact, some studies show people with no insurance (self-funded) have better medical outcomes than people with Medicaid. Other studies try to account for wealth, demographics, behavior, and other factors to determine quality of outcome, but almost none claim Medicaid performs better or is more cost-effective.

Clearly, having three systems of healthcare (public, private, self-pay) causes division. The current political direction focuses on moving more people to the highly government-subsidized healthcare marketplace for those without employer-provided plans, which are subsidized as a business expense and limit portability. Yet, the Democrat-led Affordable Care Act (ACA) clearly fell short of their stated goal of insuring all Americans. The Republicans ran on "repeal and replace the Affordable Care Act" but once again offered no solution of their own. The only proposal on the table is Democrat-led single-payer healthcare. To build broad unity across the political spectrum, we must address the 28 million people with no healthcare insurance. Can these people be added voluntarily to the private healthcare plans rather than socialized, single-payer plans? Can those with private healthcare move from employer plans to personal plans to increase choice, flexibility, and portability?

The Medicare trust fund is projected to go bankrupt as soon as 2027, yet it is not front and center in discussions. There is an expectation that it will be saved by either new taxes or a reduction in services. According to CMS.gov, US healthcare spending is growing at almost 10 percent annually and reached over $4 trillion in annual costs, or about $13,000 per person. As a share of the nation's gross domestic product, health spending accounts for about 20 percent. About 60 percent of the total healthcare cost is private health insurance or out-of-pocket spending, and 40 percent is government funded. The federal government spends almost $1.5 trillion per year on Medicare, Medicaid, CHIP, and other benefits. Whether private or public, the amount we spend on healthcare is approximately twice that of most industrialized countries.

Clearly, we have a cost issue. Healthcare costs are far outpacing the US inflation rate. How have other nations solved the problem? Singapore is one of the freest societies on the planet and has implemented innovative solutions, albeit on a smaller scale. In the book *The Cure That Works* by Sean Flynn, PhD, he describes how free-market incentives can radically reduce costs while maintaining or improving outcomes. Singapore spends one-third the amount the US does per person on healthcare. By many measures, Singapore is the world's healthiest country. Singapore's GDP per capita is equivalent to the US but leads almost every European nation. It would be hard to argue that Singapore has sacrificed anything to achieve good and cost-effective healthcare. In fact, one could argue that Singapore has raised its standard of living because of the lower cost healthcare, freeing its citizens to spend and invest in other places.

What did Singapore do, and could it be applied to the United States? Singapore focused on providing financial incentives to consumers to shop for services and ensured there is competition among service providers, including public hospitals. There is free-market incentive for businesses to innovate and compete for consumers while maintaining high healthcare standards. (After all, it would be hard to maintain a business if you kill or injure your customers!) Singapore provides public funding to personal healthcare accounts and has eliminated much of the third-party payer system.

One example of innovation and competition is in hospitals. Hospitals are high-capital, low-margin businesses that must cater to customers in every socio-economic class. From a business perspective, they have financial models similar to that of airlines. Unused hospital beds and airline seats are forever lost revenue, but these assets still cost the businesses money. Airlines have business, comfort, and economy class, where some passengers subsidize others on price. Safety and convenience are consistent for all, as hopefully we all arrive together in one piece. Singapore's hospitals allow patients to "upgrade" to more private settings with added comforts and features than semiprivate or community settings. There is no difference in medical care between any price range.

Compared to the other social safety net programs of Social Security and education, healthcare is by far the hardest to solve simply due to the complexity of the current system. There are many proposals to incrementally "fix" the current system, but almost every proposal tackles only parts of the problem. Why do foreign countries pay less for prescriptions than Americans? How do we insure 28 million more Americans? How do we improve healthcare for the poor, ensuring outcomes and convenience are equivalent to those with private insurance? How do we solve for insurance companies denying claims and canceling coverage? How do we focus on prevention instead of just treatment? Why are prices not published? Why do we pay different prices for the same services depending on our insurance company or whether we pay cash?

What is missing is a holistic, bold approach to change healthcare based on free-market American principles. This plan must provide a smooth transition that hurts no one in the process, as healthcare is critical to society. Incremental improvements to the current broken system are not working. We need a new, bold approach to move more Americans to not only private insurance but personal healthcare insurance owned and managed by the consumer rather than employers.

The healthcare element of the American Unity Plan is structured around several core strategies, working together, that will result in reduced costs while improving the quality of care, especially for those who are uninsured or have government subsidies. These strategies set the goal, or the long-term end state, rather than incrementally trying to patch a cost- and outcome-inefficient process. These strategies also contain proper guardrails. We must set the end state before we discuss the transition using the American principles of fairness, equality, and doing no harm to anyone in the process.

1. **Universality.** Everyone will have a Unity Healthcare Account (UHA) that will be controlled by the individual to ensure flexibility and portability. There will be no such thing as family or group coverage, simplifying policies and reducing costs; however, consumers will be able to access buying groups or procure plans together to reduce premiums. UHAs will be provided by public funding for healthcare insurance and other medical expenses for every American citizen. The 28 million American citizens without health insurance will now have almost unlimited policy options that fit their needs, without the restrictions in current insurance and one-size-fits-all government programs, such as the ACA. The UHA portion of Unity Income provides individuals from birth to high school graduation $200 per month and adults $400 per month, with adults currently without a high school diploma or GED grandfathered. A family of four will receive $1,200 per month in their collective four UHAs.

2. **Transference.** UHA recipients can spend UHA funds as they wish on insurance or direct healthcare payments. They can save and invest the cash balance of their UHAs for life and leave any account balances to the UHAs of their heirs.

Unlike Unity Retirement Accounts, UHA funds can be transferred to anyone else at any time. This promotes charitable giving and allows families and groups of individuals to pool resources. This also allows charities, businesses, and even state and local governments to add to the federal funding of specific UHA holders where there is a need. This idea has far-ranging implications to address many societal problems.

3. **Standards of Coverage.** Universal standards are needed to define a valid healthcare spend amount and ensure transparency regardless of which insurance company or policy is selected. In this case, we want healthcare to be defined as broadly as possible to be inclusive of as many unique situations as there are people. This could include mental health, preventive medicine, vision, dental, experimental treatments, gym memberships, hearing aids, medical marijuana, birth control, drug and alcohol treatment, and more. This cannot be political or based on any judgments or moral values to limit or ration care, within reason (no, a glass of excellent red wine will probably not be classified as medicinal). It is recommended that an independent agency, free from federal government politics, such as the American Medical Association, provide these healthcare standards that will be the universal standard for every private insurance policy. There are many examples of independent agencies setting standards, such as Underwriters Laboratories for product safety and the Financial Accounting Standards Board for financial reporting standards used by banks and

the federal government. These "UHA approved policies" give consumers confidence in selecting policies under which no claim can be denied for any reason.

4. **Undeniability.** UHAs must reduce fraud and lawsuits, a major healthcare cost and problem in the current health-care–insurance–legal complex. We must reduce denial of payment to those insured. Under this idea, medical claim issues will mostly be limited to claims above the maximum out-of-pocket cost where claimants request insurers to reimburse for nondefined expenses. Essentially, no licensed hospital, doctor, pharmacy, assisted living, or home care service claim can be denied.

5. **Noncancelable.** UHA approved plans are private insurance policies that cannot be canceled once underwritten and have no maximum lifetime limit. Each policy has a maximum annual out-of-pocket cost provision to reduce catastrophic financial risk for the consumer. The maximum out-of-pocket cost, insurance premiums, and annual increases are negotiated between the insured and the insurer based strictly on demographics and risk profile. Of course, older Americans will pay more than younger, and smokers will pay more than nonsmokers. However, there are no exclusions to any government approved healthcare expenditures. In other words, the coverages are the same across policies, and insurance companies will compete for consumers on price and service, balancing cost and risk. These healthcare policies must have no lifetime out-of-pocket limits and are noncancelable, mirroring many

permanent life-insurance and long-term care policies in place today. Insurance, once in place, cannot be canceled for any reason whatsoever. In addition, newborns must be covered under the same plan as the mother unless the parents choose a new policy at a lower cost. This ensures, over time, that infants born with preexisting conditions requiring more medical attention are not priced out of the insurance market. The goal is to eliminate the entire concept of preexisting conditions. However, in the short run, those with preexisting conditions will obviously pay more for the same coverage but not as much as today when the cost of healthcare itself is reduced.

6. **Direct Payments.** Only patients or their custodians, not third parties, are allowed to pay for any defined healthcare expense. This provides the consumer with an incentive to shop and drive down prices, as we do for all other products and services. It is up to the patient to seek reimbursement from the insurance company after the annual out-of-pocket limit is reached. The entire concept of a deductible will most likely disappear, since UHAs provide consistent monthly funding. Most will want no deductible and instead will simply choose an affordable out-of-pocket annual limit to reduce insurance premiums and build equity in their UHAs. Fewer insurance claims also result in lower insurance and healthcare service provider costs. Payment between service providers and patients will be arranged in the same manner that any product or service, large or small, is bought today—cash or credit at the point of sale.

UHAs allow people with no or minimal existing credit to finance healthcare purchases or obtain extended credit. There should be no difference between financing a car and a medical procedure. By ensuring all American citizens have UHAs, service providers will assume all patients have the means to pay for services. There will be no waiting or service delays based on whether someone can afford to pay or is insured.

7. **Transparency.** Along with eliminating third-party payments, transparency must be significantly increased for all healthcare services to allow consumers to shop for cost-effective services and medicines. No one would buy a car without understanding the final price and financing terms before signing. Why is healthcare any different? Consumers should be able to pull up an app and compare cost, availability, and quality of service to select the right provider for them without worrying about "in or out of network" or cash versus insurance price. When there is no time to shop, as with emergency room visits, patients have limited cost and fraud exposure due to maximum annual out-of-pocket limits. If there remains price gouging—service providers taking advantage of those "unable to be informed"—this is the purview of government. The role of the federal government in healthcare is only to eliminate fraud and ensure standards are set.

This is a lot to digest, but we all recognize that our healthcare system, despite services being provided by mostly private enterprises, is too complex, opaque, costly, and unfair to many. To simplify, the above seven strategies can be condensed to three simple goals.

1. Eliminate the risk of financial catastrophe for healthcare consumers.
2. Reduce the cost of healthcare to the consumer and to the federal government (American taxpayers).
3. Maintain or improve quality of care.

Instead of incrementalism, which is how government grows and problems never get solved, these three goals can be achieved by applying the seven strategies as one bold, integrated healthcare solution as part of American Unity Plan.

Let us start with the elimination of risk. Hopefully, we can all agree that if every American citizen had permanent, noncancelable health insurance, and if there was an annual cap or maximum on the amount of money any consumer spent on healthcare services, risk would be mitigated. An annual healthcare expense cap, whether $2,500, $5,000, or even $10,000, could be painful, but it would not be catastrophic. This would be equivalent to replacing a broken-down car, roof, or home heating system. These costs are painful and usually inconvenient to budgets, but we figure it out and move on. The middle class and wealthy have noncancelable life insurance and umbrella insurance coverages, and many have long-term care and disability insurance. These are relatively inexpensive and protect against catastrophic events but have one thing in common: the coverage is established well in advance of the probable need for insurance. Can catastrophic insurance be provided to all Americans?

If an insurance company already knows someone is spending a lot of money on healthcare or has a serious preexisting condition, then the cost of insurance is high and is therefore unaffordable. This results in government dependency for care. However, this problem can be solved by having catastrophic healthcare insurance in place well before the risk occurs to spread risk across both time and a greater population of people insured.

Over time, about 1 percent of patients incur about 25 percent of healthcare costs, and 5 percent of patients incur about 50 percent of total annual cost. It is estimated that only one hundred people per one million, or about thirty thousand American citizens, incur healthcare costs over $1 million in any one year. The problem is that, for the most part, we do not know which patients will have the need and cost at any one moment in time. Except for preexisting conditions that may be more predictable but incredibly expensive, we can use demographics like gender, age, lifestyle, and geography to our advantage to predict future risk and solve for cost catastrophes without sacrificing quality of care.

So, the ideal solution in the long term would be for every American to have healthcare insurance well before birth. How we get there in the interim is difficult, but we need to focus on the long-term objective before addressing implementation. Assuming we want to provide healthcare insurance to every American born (as opposed to healthcare services, which we all have available at varying levels of effectiveness, cost, and convenience), there are two possible solutions. Our choices are private insurance policies or single-payer government coverage.

Single-payer proposals are a perfect example of a bad government solution to a well-defined cost problem. The problem, according to many, is that even after passing the Affordable Care Act (ACA) addressing preexisting conditions, 28 million Americans still do not have healthcare coverage. The reason is that even with government subsidies, many people still cannot find or afford policies that fit their individual needs or simply prefer to take the risk and save their money. The problem is the cost of healthcare, and therefore insurance is too high. The ACA was not the long-term solution but a stepping stone to single-payer system, where the government assumes full control of our healthcare system. In single-payer systems, such as those prevalent in Europe and especially the UK, costs are controlled by rationing care, resulting in services that are unavailable or have long queues. Like our failing government-run schools, the wealthy work around this by paying for private healthcare services directly.

Prescription medicines, the same ones we can purchase in the US when they are available, do cost less overseas because other governments regulate and negotiate new prescription drugs. However, this results in far less investment in new drug research and development and experimental treatments. With socialized medicine, there is no incentive for manufacturers to create breakthrough treatments like there is in the US unless the government finances the endeavor, as we witnessed with the pandemic.

In sum, Americans mostly agree that coverage should be "universal," but Americans do not agree on the best solution. We must leverage what the US does better than any other country—free-market capitalism, innovation, and individual freedom.

To allow everyone to purchase private insurance, Unity Income provides individuals from birth to high school graduation $200 per month and adults $400 per month. A family of four will receive $1,200 per month. The question is whether this is enough money for every American to purchase catastrophic private coverage (relative to their own finances) without mandating that they spend additional funds beyond federal payments to their UHAs. It is one thing to require Americans to spend money everyone is given equally; it is another to require some to pay more than others or to buy something they might not want, need, or afford.

Unfortunately, it is difficult to compare this allocation of UHA funds to current healthcare insurance costs. In 2020, the average national cost for health insurance was less than $500 for an individual and $1,200 for a family per month for an ACA plan. These insurance costs are equivalent to UHA funding. However, these national averages do not tell the entire story because they are highly subsidized and these subsidies vary wildly from state to state. In addition, there are no standards of coverage and availability between policies at these average insurance costs.

For employer-provided plans, on average, companies pay 70–80 percent of the insurance cost for an employee. Pharmacy benefit managers provide hidden rebates for prescription drugs. Buying groups negotiate prices for some but not others. For those with no insurance or high-deductible plans, prices for the same services can be much lower with cash payments. Then, of course, we have government programs such as Medicare and Medicaid shifting much of the total cost burden to the private sector.

In effect, there are so many programs, subsidies, side deals, administrative costs, middleman companies, and bureaucracies that we really do not know the true cost of providing services at the individual level and therefore what price an insurance company would charge the consumer for standard coverage across a wide population. We have sliced and diced healthcare costs and payments so many ways, the system cannot be pieced back together.

We do know for certain that relative to cost, insurance costs come down as deductibles and out-of-pocket maximums increase. We do know the more consumers pay directly for services and medicines themselves and eliminate insurance filings, the lower the cost to provide services. We do know for certain that if people pay premiums for longer periods of time, the higher cost of later-in-life healthcare can be amortized, reducing insurance prices today. We do know that pricing transparency produces lower costs as consumers shop and save. We do know that standardization of coverage reduces fraud, claim denials, and legal battles. And, most importantly, we do know that Americans will help people in need when given the opportunity to provide direct assistance, as opposed to when being taxed more.

Therefore, the only reasonable solution is to simply start the process of a long-term transition using these seven strategies. We pass legislation to create the standards for UHAs so policies can be provided by the insurance industry. Then, without mandates, we simply provide every American with the funds in their UHAs as part and parcel of the American Unity Plan and watch what happens.

Clearly, many of the 28 million uninsured will buy insurance with this new source of funding, but some will not for their own reasons. Rather than pay premiums, they may build up equity in their UHAs and continue to pay for healthcare services in cash. Of course, they run the risk of a catastrophic event, but for now, that is their choice, and they are no worse off than today.

Many people who are uninsured use public facilities essentially as a doctor's office for nonemergency services. This usage drains state and local resources. How much would local governments contribute to their citizens UHAs to buy private insurance?

The vast majority of people on Medicare will not buy private insurance, except for potentially a low-cost supplemental policy. Medicare mostly works as a benefit for them, and they have paid over a lifetime of work for this benefit. The UHA funds can be used for their out-of-pocket expenses.

Many with Medicaid, CHIP, VA, and other government programs without significant existing conditions will purchase private insurance policies because of the better healthcare and availability of services they will receive. This will be especially true of children and young adults. Many will simply want out of the current system.

Finally, many employees with healthcare insurance through their work, or those who have selected ACA policies, will move themselves or family members to private policies because of the portability and access to a wider range of services (everyone is "in-network"). Employers will also encourage employees to buy plans directly. Suppose employer-provided insurance costs $1,000 per month with the employer picking up $750 of the tab and the employee only $250. How much would an employer pay to an employee to buy their own policy? This is not a trick question!

The transition from the current healthcare mess to a more transparent and efficient system is not as much a transition plan as it is a process using free-market economics. We simply will not be able to predict how many people will transition to private policies and when. Many will see the benefits immediately. They will want standards of coverage in the policy with no denial of claims, non-cancelable policies that are portable for life, and the elimination of catastrophic financial risk—in other words, the ability to sleep easier and not worry.

Given a UHA is "free" money, it would not be hard to imagine that the younger and healthier we are, the more we will use private insurance if the plans are more affordable. Some may wait for a few years to build up their UHA value and, when ready to buy insurance, will do so with much higher deductibles and maximum out-of-pocket limits to reduce their premiums and continue to save.

UHA approved insurance plans will have many similarities to car insurance. The rich could theoretically buy a plan with a $100,000 maximum annual out of pocket, almost eliminating the premium. The less fortunate may buy a plan with a $2,500 maximum out of pocket (set aside only $2,500 of the $4,800 annual UHA funding for catastrophic costs) and choose to use more money in their UHAs for premiums. As people age and their income and UHA values increase, they can choose to raise their annual maximum out-of-pocket limits to reduce premium costs. The risk-return relationship is controlled by the patient, not the insurance companies, employers, or the government, who often limit the flexibility of insurance companies to provide policies that meet individual needs. Once UHAs have a large enough balance, consumers may decide to purchase policies such as long-term care insurance or disability insurance during their working years or grow their accounts tax-free until needed.

Now we will discuss the impact on the federal budget. How do we end up with a balanced budget and predictable healthcare spend by eliminating the current healthcare system? We showed we can achieve the elimination of Social Security over time with Unity Retirement Accounts by simply funding accounts earlier and having a set trigger when people are ineligible for Social Security. Most of the net $2.4 trillion first-year budget increase in the American Unity Plan is associated with healthcare. This is much less than most proposals for a single-payer healthcare system. It is easy to predict that very few Americans on Medicare will change to private policies. Predicting how many people will switch from Medicaid, other government provided programs, employer-provided plans, and heavily subsidized ACA policies to reduce the federal spend is difficult. When the majority of the 28 million uninsured Americans get private coverage, there is no federal savings. The same is true for employer plans.

But what happens to healthcare cost reduction, our primary goal? As healthcare costs are reduced, federal spending on government programs will be reduced, thus reducing the budget deficit. As costs are reduced, more and more people will select private insurance, which will continue to reduce costs further. We can predict how many people die each year to reduce the federal spend, so the goal over time is not to add any more people to the current system. Each year, the federal deficit from healthcare spend will be reduced.

This benefits the Medicare budget but ironically also helps noncitizens who are not eligible for Unity Income. They can buy the same less expensive private insurance with standardized coverage with their own money, their sponsors can provide insurance, and there are charities who would step in as well. US Customs mandates that foreigners who enter the US legally show IDs. Maybe immigrants' sponsors should be required to show proof of healthcare coverage?

Even for those who have entered the US illegally, no one wants to deny them care. The American taxpayers currently subsidize those without insurance. The question is how to provide them care. If sanctuary cities want to treat everyone without question with local funds, they are free to do so. If a healthcare provider chooses to provide non-life-threatening services, they are responsible for collecting the bill or raising money. For those who believe in legal immigration, the path is simple. Sponsorship and legal immigration require healthcare to be paid or insured by the parties involved, not funded by American citizens. If you are sponsoring someone to come to school or work in your business, you are responsible for making sure they are protected financially from unforeseen events.

Many articles and studies have estimated that 30 percent to as much as 70 percent of all healthcare spending in America is waste and fraud. Eliminating this through free-market consumerism would be enough to reduce the incremental budget increase in American Unity Plan spending by half! One study cited that less than 30 percent of all healthcare dollars go to clinicians. The rest is absorbed by bureaucracy and middlemen in the supply chain that provide little to no value to consumers. This is consistent with the Singapore results. Most healthcare is delivered locally, but we pay for it by sending vast amounts of money outside the community to then be rerouted back to our local doctors and hospitals. The big insurance companies and pharmacy benefit managers are keeping 20–25 percent of that money for themselves in administrative fees, overhead, and profits. Another large percentage of healthcare spending is outright fraud. What is needed is local control and self-policing, with demand driven by the consumer, and what the consumer wants is transparency and simplicity. They want to be treated fairly—to pay a fair, transparent price for good service when they need it.

Payments must be between the patient and the provider to lower the cost of providing services. This eliminates all the back-office, non-value-added tasks service providers must perform for insurance filing and reporting. All costs must be transparent and agreed to before the service is performed. Many medical services cost less than a pair of sneakers, a set of new tires, or a trip to Costco. We do not need insurance between us and this facet of life. For bills that are large but affordable (the medical equivalent of fixing a transmission or buying a sofa), medical providers will offer credit, just like the rest of society does from car dealers to furniture stores. Buy now, pay later services are growing exponentially. There is an explosion of innovative financial services that could be applied to healthcare to reduce costs, improve credit, and increase convenience.

For large bills, credit bridges the gap between when the service is performed and when the patient is 100 percent reimbursed by insurance after the annual out-of-pocket limit is reached. The key is the maximum out-of-pocket provision in all insurance plans, which should have no ifs, ands, or buts as a federal standard. When a patient reaches the maximum limit, insurance pays the patient, and the patient pays the service provider. This is no different than paying other large bills like a mortgage or car payment. The patient is responsible and has the necessary protection to eliminate financial catastrophe. Unity Income provides a government guarantee of credit to American citizens. The IRS can confiscate a paycheck following due process for nonpayment of taxes, and the legal system provides for creditors to collect bad healthcare debts. The key is to reduce the cost of healthcare itself, so it is more affordable and there are less bad debts, credit collectors calling monthly, and hits to credit scores from healthcare service providers. Simplicity and transparency reduce costs and minimize fraud and waste. The insurance industry being between the patient and provider has totally distorted the free market, where innovation and competition drive down costs.

The goal is to bring down costs through scale by leveraging capitalism. Big cities have proven that governments cannot lower costs through scale, but big companies like Amazon, Walmart, Best Buy, and Costco can. Maybe UHA policies will be discounted with an Amazon Prime account! Or, for those who opt in, at some point Google will know not just where we are at any moment but how sick we are through a smartwatch and AI, route us to the most cost-effective and high-quality clinic as reviewed by the public (Dr. Smith has 4.9 stars), allow us to book an appointment, and bill us automatically.

As with Social Security, the plan may take a couple of generations to complete before we can say goodbye to every one of the current federal programs. In the interim, as more people sign up for UHA private policies and our seniors exit our world, the budget deficit gets less and less every year. Remember, the UHA funding part is perfectly predictable. It is the current healthcare system in America that is unpredictable, inefficient, and costly.

The twin goals are healthcare cost reduction and risk mitigation to both the consumer and the federal government in budgeting for and controlling long-term costs without sacrificing healthcare quality or availability. The federal government, or an independent agency, will certify policies that private insurance provides as "UHA approved." This means they have several key features that we already discussed—they are noncancelable, follow standards of coverage for nondeniability of claims, and allow for direct payments by consumers to service providers. How is the goal of a transition to 100 percent private coverage reached?

1. A UHA approved policy provided by a private insurer is one that meets the criteria of a UHA policy. It has the standards of coverage, with no exceptions or modifications, so the consumer knows exactly what they are buying. It is a "no surprises" policy. Once purchased, it cannot be canceled for any reason by the insurance company. Unlike car insurance, all premiums for life must be clearly stated in the policy, and the premiums can be paid directly to the insurance company from a consumer's UHA account or paid by the consumer out of pocket. A twenty-year-old would know the exact annual cost and their maximum out-of-pocket risk at age seventy. Insurance companies will clearly target the young, enticing them with low premiums and high deductibles (or no deductibles and simply a

maximum out-of-pocket annual cost). Why would insurance companies sell these policies? First, because they will get predictable premiums for decades, which improves their business value. They will get the ability to compete for 28 million uninsured consumers, many of the almost 100 million recipients of some form of government healthcare assistance, new American citizens as well as visitors living in the US, and a large part of the employer-insured group. The insurance company costs will be reduced, as they no longer deal with corporate purchasing departments and the federal government, no longer pay corporate and payroll taxes, and lower their overhead by eliminating significant amounts of claims processing (alas, claims processors will need to retrain as customer acquisition consultants). They will want to acquire these consumers to cross-sell other products such as life, auto, and property insurance. They will further innovate, as rules and regulations are eliminated when consumers and providers deal directly, and they will create new products that appeal to more consumers. (Why are vision and dental not included with medical?) In sum, this will create a bidding war between insurance companies for new customers and result in lower-cost healthcare premiums.

2. Consumers cannot cancel their policy once established and can only change to another UHA approved policy to keep insurance competition high while eliminating catastrophic risk. Once they select a UHA approved policy, they are no longer eligible for any government subsidy or program,

including Medicare, for life. They own noncancelable insurance and the monthly funding to pay for it!

3. Americans will no longer be automatically enrolled in Medicare at age sixty-five. There are plenty of Americans who have existing policies and are healthy enough to opt out of Medicare on their own, especially if they choose a UHA approved policy.

4. As part of the standards of coverage, if a biological woman of any age has a noncancelable UHA plan, the plan would automatically cover not just the cost of childbirth, but it would guarantee the same insurance coverage for the child. The child would arrive with its own UHA policy with the same premiums and maximum out-of-pocket cost as the mother's policy. The parents or custodians could then select a new, more affordable UHA approved policy for the child whenever the time is right. Under this concept, along with the immigration mandate, if every young biological female chose a UHA policy, the idea of a preexisting condition could be eliminated over the next fifty years or so. This rule could also cover adoptions. UHA policies need to be flexible to account for advances in medicine and societal changes.

5. Money can be transferred from any UHA to another, so long as both parties have approved UHA policies in place or the contributor is a state or local government, a legal business entity, or a charity. The idea of allowing only UHA holders with approved private policies to transfer funds with each other provides incentive for more people to obtain policies. The transfer process can be as easy as

Zelle and Venmo, since UHAs are owned by the individual and are regulated. This promotes charity, like the St. Jude Children's Research Hospital model, where donations supplement insurance and families pay nothing for care. This will be especially important for the 5 percent of the patients who incur 50 percent of healthcare costs and the millions of people who want to help. Charities will spring up to pool donations, just as organizations like Tunnels to Towers pool contributions to help disabled veterans. In addition, state and local governments will contribute directly to the UHAs of those in need to allow more people to buy UHA approved policies. This state and local funding, as well as charitable giving, will supplement the federal Unity Income funding. This will reduce the funding burden for public healthcare facilities. As corporations will provide direct UHA deposits to reduce and eliminate company provided policies, state and local governments will do a similar return on investment calculation for their citizens.

These policy changes will reduce the cost of healthcare by quite a bit, probably over 50 percent, benefiting not only UHA policy holders but anyone buying services, including the uninsured and governments. At some point, the cost of UHA policies will be lower than UHA funding. We can then require the remaining few people not on Medicare to buy a UHA policy. This will eliminate all government healthcare programs once the last Medicare recipient has left us. Then, when there is no government program as a backup for people with no insurance, consumers and insurance companies will simply need to provide proof of owning a UHA plan, like we do with car insurance.

Once free from government regulations and controls, the free market will work its magic. Companies like GoodRx negotiate prices with pharmacies on behalf of their customers, who pay a monthly subscription. Many doctor groups are now charging a small, flat, monthly fee allowing patients to get basic care at any time and to budget their expenses. These doctors do not accept insurance, their costs are much lower than traditional medical practices, and services are much more available to patients. We have witnessed what happens to prices for elective procedures such as LASIK that are not covered by insurance. (In case you don't know, they go down.) In addition, fee-based buying groups will work directly for consumers in many areas of healthcare, including prescription medicines, and maybe across states. Patients negotiating with service providers in a free market have driven costs down while maintaining or improving outcomes.

Models such as these incentivize lifestyle prevention to make treatment less expensive in the long run without rationing care, as is customary in most single-payer government plans. For example, custodians for the homeless can arrange to purchase UHA approved plans on their behalf. The premiums would be paid directly from their UHA accounts. Given many of the homeless are addicts or have a mental illness, the premiums would be very high but could be supplemented by local communities and charities as direct con-tributions, thereby spending much less than they do now and en-suring that undeniable treatment is available.

Let capitalism promote innovation and show the best value for consumers. Let charities and concerned Americans help our fellow citizens individually. America knows how to do this if we let it. Over time as we transition, the role of the federal government in healthcare will be to enforce the law and set guidelines for approved UHA policies. Once an individual has a UHA approved plan and, of course, has the guaranteed government funding under Unity Income, it will still be against the law to not pay an insurance premium or a service provider. Enforcing the law is a proper function of government, not providing one-size-fits-all healthcare. The best path forward is public funding and free-market delivery!

The message for the American people to build unity is compelling, even for many supporting single-payer healthcare systems.

We will transition the 28 million Americans who have no insurance to private insurance plans that are permanent and noncancelable and for which claims cannot be denied. We will provide all American citizens with equal funding for Unity Healthcare Accounts to shop for the best policy at the right cost that fits their individual needs. We will provide an opportunity for all Americans, especially the poor, to have the best private insurance plans to improve their health outcomes and prevent disease. Everyone living in America will benefit from dramatically reduced healthcare costs. We will lower the cost of healthcare as part of a balanced budget, and no one will have less coverage than they do today.

This is the progressive's dream, but without the socialized, one-size-fits-all medicine that has serious healthcare outcome flaws everywhere it has been implemented. Under the Unity Plan, we will all pay taxes fairly and equally based on our purchases of goods and services. We will all get the same Unity Income to buy healthcare and eliminate catastrophic financial risk. We will all have the same opportunity to buy preventive care based on our individual needs and life circumstances. We will all be reasonably accommodated over a long transition period to ensure no negative consequences for those who have already paid into the existing system and are used to their current standards of care and cost.

Now on to education, the most controversial social safety net program today—and the easiest to change!

13

PUBLIC SCHOOL COMPETITION

Forty years ago, tuition in some of the great American public universities and colleges was virtually free. Today, the cost is unaffordable for many working-class families. Higher education must be a right for all—not just wealthy families."

— Bernie Sanders, US senator, Vermont

t has been said that if you want to ensure a solid middle-class life, just do three things: finish high school, get married, and do not have children before marriage. Well, that is wonderful except for two things. First, only one of the three is somewhat controllable through public policy—education. Second, we need to recognize that many people were born into situations not in their control. They lack the parenting and economic means to overcome many obstacles in life, despite living in the one country where success is more possible than anywhere else. It is America, and everyone is capable of achievement, but we also need compassion.

We already agree we need a social safety net, but ensuring retirement savings and managing healthcare costs are only part of the answer. Education is the best way to make generational change. Education is still the most cost-effective and humane way to ensure a social safety net and to guarantee America survives well into the future.

Unlike healthcare, education in the US has both a quality-of-outcome problem and a cost problem. Depending on the source, the average K-12 education cost per student is roughly $13,000 in the US. As with both socialized healthcare and the Social Security system, the rich and many of the middle class choose to avoid the poor performance of government-delivered education by sending their children to private schools or faith-based schools or homes-chooling them instead. The poor and most of the middle class do not have this option.

The federal government provides a little less than 8 percent of funding for public education, but its control is greater due to mandates and regulations. State and local governments split the remaining 92 percent funding about evenly. The current funding is both a problem and an opportunity. It would have been easy not to include education in the American Unity Plan because of the small federal funding and the high cost if federal funding to individuals begins. However, education is part and parcel of the social fabric of America. The American Unity Plan is a long-term strategy, and one that promotes self-reliance and reduction of government dependency over time. There is no greater way to reduce dependency than education.

Education is mostly funded by the states and local jurisdictions, but only a federal program can provide the flexibility and consistency to promote economic mobility and freedom, along with ensuring fairness in education opportunity availability to all. We need education to promote economic growth and financial literacy and to be the foundation to accommodate many more American citizens without abandoning federalism. The federal government could provide the true safety net, with minimum management and regulation, and ensure private citizens have more control over the government-run schools they are mostly forced to use. In fact, the federal government could fund education without the department of education!

The only recent Republican initiative to change education was the No Child Left Behind Act of 2001. It was clearly not a solution founded in American principles and had minimal success. It did provide more flexibility for local school districts to use federal funds, which does at least align somewhat with federalism. However, it mandated testing, which increased federal control and bureaucracy. Over time, teachers and schools do what Americans do. They innovated and simply began to "teach to the test" as they were highly incentivized to do. Grades improved, but unfortunately learning and outcomes did not, especially for the poor. Costs continue to rise.

Then the focus changed to Common Core curriculum, which goes against the American value of freedom for each child to develop their own unique skills instead of what the government deems important for the masses. Now that the Republicans have dropped any semblance of federal education reform, progressives have clearly seized control of the education agenda in many states and school districts with teachings such as critical race theory (CRT).

No Child Left Behind and Common Core were the typical incrementalism favored by so many Republicans rather than bold, holistic solutions. Conservatives and libertarians had mostly abandoned education because they believed it should be a private issue between parents, students, and schools. Many are now rallying around education because of infringements on parents' rights and freedoms. Some are calling for more school choice, vouchers, charter schools, and homeschooling. The time is right for a bold solution for not just K-12 education but all education, including new proposals to eliminate college student debt.

There are three ways to approach the education problem: public funding and public delivery, private funding and private delivery, or public funding and private delivery. In this case, private funding means direct consumer payment for services, as opposed to payment of taxes or vouchers from government. Currently, private delivery of education ranges from a fraction of the cost of public education to quite expensive, as do all services delivered by the private sector. Yes, a BMW costs more than Honda, but both get you from point A to point B. Can we create reliable, high-quality, and less expensive education for all Americans by utilizing the private sector for delivery much more than we do now? Absolutely!

The idea of American Unity Education is to publicly fund parents and custodians directly with real cash, instead of vouchers, tax credits, and other bureaucratic schemes. We give parents and custodians the freedom to do as they believe is necessary for their children's education and related expenses. With this funding, parents will create the need for a supply of free-market, private education competing with public schools for their business. Private school in a competitive environment would cost much less than publicly delivered education, and we have many examples to prove it. The goal is very simple. If education was publicly funded directly to parents and custodians but privately delivered, and every child had the funding to attend the schools of their choice, and there was true competition for students, we would not have an education crisis in this country! If consumers were free to select schools based on their own needs, with the freedom to move their money and their child to more cost-effective and better-quality schools as they see fit, outcomes for all American children would dramatically improve.

Would school vouchers achieve the same goal? No, because vouchers come with government strings attached. Governments may add regulations that force vouchers to be used with teachers who are members of unions or have certain government approved accreditation or limit the ability of family members to homeschool, seek vocational training, attend religious affiliated schools or schools that use new and innovative methods. The distribution of vouchers would be means tested, denying choice for many middle-income families. Regulations, whether federal, state, or local, run deep in education. It becomes difficult to run even charter schools, therefore private schools become the only option. The focus should be on parents and custodians being responsible for their children's education and giving them the maximum freedom to meet the needs of their families.

American Unity Education provides the ability for every parent or custodian of American citizens who have not graduated high school to open Unity Education Accounts (UEAs). The federal government will fund $500 per month or $6,000 per year into UEAs. The total federal spending for UEAs is approximately $400 billion. This is compared to the approximately $750 billion spent annually for K-12 public education for over sixty million young people. Since the federal government funds less than $60 billion in education today, there will be a short-term federal deficit. However, as you will see, state and local funding for publicly delivered education will be dramatically reduced as the total cost of education is reduced. Total taxes (federal, state, and local) paid by Americans will drop accordingly. Here is how American Unity Education works.

As with healthcare, the definition of education needs to be exceptionally broad to allow parents, custodians, and teachers to help children develop the skills they need for college or employment. This could include everything from daycare to pre-K to college. Special needs, technical and specialized training, and student loan payments are all included. As with retirement and healthcare, UEA accounts can be invested and grow tax-free for life. Parents who choose not to use the funds for early childhood would have more funds available for their children's higher education or other training later in life.

Education accounts allow any American with an account, a nonprofit, a charity, or state and local governments to contribute funds to UEA holders. Local governments are free to supplement federal money. Red and blue states and counties will experiment with different education funding models over time as many parents migrate to private schools and the cost of education delivery is reduced. Some may choose to piggyback on the federal model and contribute local tax dollars to UEAs while maintaining some funding for public schools until the transition is complete. As private schools will cost less, local and state taxes could be reduced. Some may choose to keep public schools in place, competing with private schools, and simply reduce local taxes by the amount of the federal funding. Many will wait and see where parents choose to educate their children.

The argument here is not against funding of public education; it is against the almost exclusive government monopoly of education delivery. By having the funding directed to the student and not the local government, as we do with college funding, parents can make the best choice, both financially and academically, for their child.

Relative to the American principle of fairness and equality of opportunity under the law, American citizens with no children have always had issues paying to educate others. Local taxes are paid with the hope that the educated will stay and build communities, but many leave. This is an argument for more federal funding, as education helps America in total more than just local communities. What would not change under the American Unity Plan is paying federal taxes to educate others' children, so these parents would be no worse off than they are today.

What is even more unfair is how parents pay for both others' children and their own to go to private schools due to the poor delivery of government education. We accept the public benefit of education for all. Once again, we need to create a better solution that is fair, accommodates all Americans, treats all Americans equally, and does no harm to one group while benefiting another. Paying taxes, whether locally or federally, to finance poorly delivered and costly government education while personally financing private schools is hard for many to accept.

We need to rapidly expand the number of private schools and transition away from the almost-monopoly on government-delivered education. This is not to say that all public schools are performing poorly. Some, primarily in affluent suburbs, are excellent but simply cost too much. However, many of America's poorest students are trapped in failing schools, which also cost a fortune to operate.

With public funding going directly to the student through UEAs, private schools would expand at an incredible rate. There will be an education gold rush. Currently, the government delivery of education provides mainly a one-size-fits-all educational experience in K-12, whereas two- and four-year colleges and technical and trade schools produce specialized education. The concept of public funding and private delivery of K-12 education opens an entire world of possibilities for innovative education to make America competitive again and give the poorest Americans an equal opportunity to succeed. Education is effectively being run by the local bureaucracies and has become entirely too political. Parents and students have little say and little choice compared to the power of local school boards, politicians, and teachers unions.

With private delivery, schools would cater to the specific needs of the students as guided by parents and custodians. Ironically, the entire concept of a college-level, "liberal arts" education is to explore and find yourself. I would say that by the time kids enter high school, they have some idea of their strengths and interests—math

and science, computers and technology, literature and history, economics and finance, medicine and healthcare, political science and
law, social and public work, fine arts and music, sports and fitness,
the military, or marketing and sales. Do they envision having a
stable job or starting a business? By the time they have taken the
SAT and are applying for college (or not), they have a better idea
of their ambitions. There are charter schools, magnet schools, and
electives within traditional schools, but students still follow a set
course curriculum. Using the county where I live as an example,
here are the current requirements to pass high school: English
(four units), math (four units), science (three units), US history
(one unit), economics (half a unit), government (half a unit), other
social studies (one unit), physical education or ROTC (one unit),
computer science (one unit), foreign language (one unit), and electives (seven units).

I can tell you the curriculum looks the same in 2022 as it did
when I graduated high school in 1978, other than the computer
science class that replaced typing. Can you imagine any other organization remaining stagnant for that long? Of the twenty-four
units needed to graduate, seventeen are dictated by the school and
only seven are chosen by the student based on interest. This is
one-hundred-fifty-year-old rote learning not applicable to probably
80–90 percent of today's students. The electives are even limited in
their approach to a few courses.

There are two basic goals of K-12 education—prepare a student
to be accepted into higher education or give them the skills to get
a job. A job may even include starting your own business or working as an independent contractor. The customers of these future

graduates, either the job market or colleges, will decide when and if they are ready.

The pace of the real world is moving much faster than the education bureaucracy can change. A mostly private education system would offer courses that approach the real-world needs of students, similar in many ways to how technical colleges adjust to meet the needs of employers and local communities. The government-delivered education of today must, by definition, be broad enough to service everyone, and therefore it lacks the necessary flexibility to keep up with the times and provide the specializations to keep most students interested.

Here is a real-world example. By the ninth grade, I knew I was interested in both engineering and business. I loved math but also dreamed about being an entrepreneur and having my own business. Every math class I took, I excelled in. However, of all my high school science classes, I only liked physics, and that was an elective at the time. I absolutely knew I would have no use for chemistry or biology. And frankly, my weak high school chemistry class was of little use when I took three mandatory chemistry classes for college engineering. However, I bet there were people who knew they were going into healthcare and medicine who wanted more biology and chemistry and loathed physics. And for those of you who scored twice as much on your verbal SATs than your math, you may be thinking, "Why take any of it?"

Now if someone with engineering and business administration degrees thinks most of his high school science was a waste, imagine what someone who is now a journalist, a human resources manager, or a digital marketer thinks? On the other hand, someone in these professions probably liked their English literature classes much more than me. Now, after forty years in the professional world, I know that writing classes would have been beneficial to me. Writing never interested me until I had to write my first business proposal for a potential customer.

When has a top-down government initiative ever personalized and tailored anything to the individual (customer) based on their needs? The high school syllabus, like any product or service, needs to be tailored to the specific needs of the consumer, in this case the individual intellectual and emotional needs of the students, as guided by their parents and custodians. The goal is to build individual strengths, not train an army of clones. It is great to experience and explore new interests, and many do not "find themselves" until college and beyond, but I submit the government school system does not excel here either.

If education were provided solely by the private sector, using public funding, schools would absolutely be personalized, because parents and students would choose where to spend their money. For students, twenty-four units of work in exchange for direct payment for four years from their UEAs is fair. Here might be a curriculum that an average, college-bound, future engineer might want:

- Math (six units) – Geometry, algebra, trigonometry, calculus, applied business math, probability and statistics (for gaming, of course, and a field trip to the World Series of Poker).
- Science and engineering (three units) – physics, introduction to engineering and problem-solving, data science and analytics.

- Business and finance (six units) – entrepreneurship, economics, introduction to accounting and business finance, personal financial literacy and investing (your kid probably has a Robinhood account already), applied writing and communications, introduction to supply chain, sales, and marketing.
- Technology and computer science (three units) – fundamentals of computer science, business applications (Microsoft, not Google!), programming basics.
- Other (three units) – health science and exercise, government and law, American history.
- Electives (three units) – Preferably at a junior college, junior achievement program, or an internship.

Of course, there would be similar schools created that focus on arts and the humanities, or human sciences (biology, chemistry, sociology, psychology, medicine, etc.), or sports and fitness, and they would be much more specific to the needs of the student consumer. It is not hard to imagine classes common across these diverse schools that could be taught remotely. Courses such as entrepreneurship, financial literacy and investing, applied writing, communications, business applications, and more would be just as appealing to a future English teacher as a scientist.

With competition, each school will show different results and adjust much faster to the needs of students than government-run schools. Schools will collaborate to create virtual classrooms and mixed teaching models that span geographies. Why are public schools so limited by geography? If businesses can collaborate virtually across the globe, can senior high school students across the US be taught by an entrepreneur in Silicon Valley or a rocket scientist at SpaceX?

Another interesting twist will be the business models of privately delivered education competing for your education dollars. Some schools will likely be for-profit and some not-for-profit. Some schools will teach critical race theory and some traditional American values. Some will incorporate religion into the school week, and some will be agnostic. Some will have incredible sports facilities, and others will provide a pass to the local Y. Some will have cafeterias, and others will have food trucks. Some will have pristine campuses in the woods, and some will be on commuter lines. Some will have local cultures and traditions incorporated into school life. Some will be year-round, and others will follow the typical school year. Some will even stagger school to align with the workweek needs of the community (medical communities, factories and warehouses shift work, etc.).

The style of teaching might even change. Might a school emerge around the Socratic method? How about in-person schooling mixed with virtual learning as a strategy as opposed to a response to the pandemic?

Will some parents send children to schools that teach CRT? If there is demand for CRT teaching in schools, the market will provide it. Would private schools arise that serve the needs of everyone, from children with special medical needs, to the LGBTQ community, athletes, and more?

Our freedoms and American principles mandate that we hold people accountable for their actions and their outcomes, not the process or thinking that leads to their actions and outcomes. If we believe in freedom and the rights of parents to decide what is best for their children, then we live with the legal outcome of the parents' decisions whether we agree with that outcome or not. Therefore, we need to free our children from the bondage of government-delivered, one-size-fits-all education. Government education reduces the rights of parents and limits choice. Unfortunately, anytime the private sector competes with the government, the government wins. Education is the great equalizer in society, with the biggest beneficiaries of delivery privatization being the poor.

One special group is older adults who do not have a high school education and therefore have reduced opportunities in life. These adults can range from early twenties to much older. This group includes many who have been or are currently incarcerated. The public education system has failed them. American Unity Education allows for these adults to use the younger Americans' portion of Unity Income funds for the sole purpose of completing their GEDs. It is not hard to envision establishing private schools that cater to older Americans in any circumstance who want not only degrees but maybe additional life skills they may be lacking. However, this provision is only for those who are grandfathered in when UEAs are established. We need to provide incentives for more teenagers to finish high school on time, which impacts many aspects of life.

After high school graduation, Unity Education would continue funding adults through the completion of their education by using their "other" adult Unity Income as well as eighteen years of savings in their UEAs. A young adult may use this funding for tuition, living expenses, or anything they see fit. This other funding is permanent and can be used to pay down student debt later in life. Students who currently have student debt could use Unity Income for that purpose. Since everyone receives the same amount of Unity Income, Americans who worked through college or have already paid down their student debt do not get penalized and incur negative rights because others used the same funds to pay their student debt.

With Unity Income, we can also get the government out of financing higher education and reinvigorate the private lending market due to the credit Unity Income provides. Traditional college funding through the myriad rules, regulations, forms, and applications may go away. With the federal government less involved except for funding UEAs, any additional funding beyond the savings of the students and parents for expensive secondary education could be provided by scholarships or financed by the colleges themselves, banks, and nonfinancial institutions. Loans, especially for the poor, will be easier to obtain because Unity Income can be used as collateral as a guaranteed income source for life.

UEAs would significantly reduce the need for student loans in the first place, whether that be for a two-year technical or trade school or for a four-year university. The intent is not for UEAs to provide a free ride to Harvard. The point is for them to provide the opportunity for everyone to get an education beyond high school if they so wish or any training needed to gain employment. Secondary education loans will still be needed by many but will not be as severe. In addition, parents and students will learn to assess the quality and value of education against their spend at an earlier age, and chances are less people will take out quarter-million-dollar loans to get a near minimum-wage job. Ideally, the loans would be provided by the educational institution, not government backing.

Would K-12 private schools start providing loans as well to supplement UEAs? Imagine the marketplace potential, where an elite sports high school would provide loans to the most promising athletes that would be paid back only from a professional sports contract? Would elite sports universities provide funds to high schools to run feeder programs like the baseball minor leagues? Would schools provide scholarships to promising biologists or mathematicians to build their reputations for excellence? When the public system no longer provides the services and the choices are up to the individual, American innovation will flourish!

The transition to private schools will be long, and to be clear, it is probable that some public schools will remain. Many public schools, especially those in affluent suburbs, are satisfactory to parents. Those parents may choose to keep their children in government-provided education and invest their education accounts for college. The point is that many parents and children do not currently have this choice.

On the other hand, UEAs are funded only for American citizens. Non-Americans also need to educate their children, and states and local communities share this burden. Would conservative-leaning local communities simply eliminate public schools and force immigrants, legal or illegal, to fund their own educations? Many immigrants will also pay for private education as the cost is reduced and many will continue with government schools, if available. However, we cannot underestimate the power and compassion of the American people to fund underprivileged children, American citizen or not, to attend better-performing private schools.

The funding of UEAs will be immediate, and this will create demand for education delivery choices. But it takes time to finance and build schools, even in the private sector. Although there would be immediate demand, there simply is too little supply. Private schools are scarce and available mostly for the wealthy, American citizen or not. Charter and magnet schools are often blocked or influenced by local school boards, and therefore are still small compared to the traditional government-run schools. Local boards are becoming increasingly political and often block parental choice. Currently, we have incredible demand for school choice but too little supply. In fact, many private schools are now teaching ideas contrary to parents' wishes and expelling students whose parents complain. There are so few private schools that their only option may be homeschooling.

We need to create the environment of the technology industry that started in the 1990s and continues to this day. We need massive education capital chasing great, innovative delivery ideas. With American Unity Education, money would go directly to the parents to pay directly for services. In addition, states, local counties, and school districts could redirect money currently supplied by state income taxes and local property taxes away from the public schools and simply add to the private accounts of the children. As the market demands alternative schools, more taxes will be directed toward parents and away from government-delivered education. Entrepreneurs working with private equity, venture capital, and charities would provide the capital necessary to acquire the assets and talent to meet the market demands.

We do not need to defund the current public schools. They would simply downsize when forced to truly compete with private education, unless they improve cost and outcome. Taxes for schools would not be eliminated, but they would be significantly reduced. Counties would sell assets to fund private education. At some point, any public schools that remain uncompetitive with the private market will go away, along with their school boards and bureaucracies.

This transition from public to private delivery of education will be difficult, and the federal government must maintain neutrality. The American principles of fairness, reasonable accommodation, and equality must be maintained. Under the Unity Tax, all products and services are taxed equally to ensure the government does not pick winners and losers. It would be easy to not tax education. However, we define the term "education" as broadly as possible to meet the needs of parents and children. Is daycare education or not? How about fitness training for a future athlete? Once again, if it is a service that benefits from the elimination of taxes on labor, capital, and profits, the Unity Tax must be applied. New schools that are built or acquired will benefit from reduced costs like any other business. This would prevent future politicians from deciding whether to tax schools based on their government accreditation, unionization, for-profit status, curriculum, or anything else.

Conversely, any government delivery of services that competes with the private sector will be taxed in a similar manner. Government schools will benefit from reduced costs such as payroll taxes, insurance, supplies, maintenance, transportation, and more. Since their cost per student is a public record, they will pay the federal Unity Tax as well. All things being equal, public schools will have no federal tax advantage over their private school, religious, and homeschool counterparts. This will either expedite the transition to the private sector or will force them to use public money more efficiently. Either outcome is acceptable. The federal government already allocates education funding only to the school districts that follow their guidelines. The federal government clearly has the power to regulate local schools and therefore the ability to tax as well.

Once the environment with demand for private education is in place, American innovation would take over. Is it so hard to imagine competing national chains of privately run schools at scale, as we have in other industries including healthcare, groceries, fitness, and more? They would only be successful by providing a superior education at a much lower cost due to size and scale, as evidenced by their outcomes and the demand from parents. Would education clusters pop up to share resources and drive demand? Many cities have motor miles, malls with competing and complimentary stores, and business clusters where all the law and insurance firms operate. Would private schools utilize abandoned assets in shopping malls or neglected neighborhoods? Could underutilized government schools simply be purchased by the private sector?

Could private schools form education clusters and collaborate as they see fit? This would allow for bus routes, car pools, sports facilities, food services, security, healthcare, and even specialized education (art, music, language, etc.) to have scale across multiple private enterprises, improving the convenience for parents and students and further lowering the cost of delivering education, which drives demand for all.

Schools that specialize in one area could have reciprocal education agreements with schools in another specialty. This is no different than corporations that create strategic partnerships to leverage customer base, geography, or expertise. In addition, outside partnerships would be much easier to establish with private instead of public procurement.

Like healthcare, the goal is to reduce the cost of education itself through private enterprise innovation and competition. With federal funding and without bureaucratic strings attached, more private schools will emerge to change the paradigm of education. Recently, a private school announced opening in my hometown. Tuition cost is between $4800 and $6200 per year, less than 50 percent of the cost of public education. At the school, there is one administrator, one assistant administrator, and everyone else is a teacher. Parents and volunteers provide whatever additional support is needed, from counseling to coaching. UEAs provide $6,000 per year, before any additional contributions from states and local governments. This is very doable!

Currently, 90 percent of teachers belong to a union. A large percentage of teachers, however, are not enamored with the politics of their unions and their support for certain teachings in the classroom, but they have almost no choice where to work. Teachers are one of the most well-respected professions but now are being maligned because of what a few are teaching in the classroom, as well as their unions' open politics. Public education delivery is literally dividing the country.

With privatization of schools, more and more teachers will shift to private schools and not vote to be part of a union. Many current teachers in private schools choose to work for less wages than their public-school counterparts to avoid politics and have more freedom to serve their students. These schools outperform most of the public schools. However, private schools will compete for the best teachers, and as in any industry, the best will be paid more because of performance, not artificial wage scales and tenure.

The message of Unity Education is appealing across the political spectrum.

> We will provide funding to Unity Education Accounts to all Americans who have not graduated high school and assist those adults who have not yet obtained their high school degrees. This will allow parents, custodians, and students to choose the school that best fits their needs and will create an innovation revolution in the delivery of quality education, especially helping those trapped in failing public schools. The cost of education will be reduced dramatically to minimize property taxes and not penalize any parent who chooses what is best for their children.

Parents, custodians, and children in a free market for private education delivery will decide what is best for them, not a school board with a one-size-fits-all approach. American values ensure competition provides the best approach and trusts parents and custodians to make the best decisions for their children by voting with their publicly funded American Unity Income. The only role of government is to ensure that the law is not broken. We tried No Child Left Behind, but children were left behind. We tried

Common Core and standardized testing, and now we have high school graduates who can pass a test but are ill-prepared for college and the real world. We tried all this while spending more per student than almost any country. We need to combine public funding and free-market competition to deliver the best education results.

Unity Education does shift more of the financing burden to the federal government, so a discussion of federalism is important to define the role of the federal government in many aspects of our lives and our finances.

14

REINVENTING GOVERNMENT, AGAIN

> *No government ever voluntarily reduces itself in size.*
> *Government programs, once launched, never disappear.*
> *Actually, a government bureau is the nearest thing to*
> *eternal life we'll ever see on this earth!*
>
> — Ronald Reagan, former US president

U nification requires us to decide if a policy should be enacted at the federal or state level. Enactment could entail funding, delivery, or coordination. For example, coordination of environmental policy clearly concerns the federal government, as problems in one state or country may impact another, especially regarding air and water quality, as well as land use. The American Unity Plan promotes retirement, healthcare, and education as social safety net issues funded but not delivered at the federal level. National defense and border security fall into the category of federal delivery of service.

Where possible, policy should be enacted by the states because different states have different values and priorities on issues ranging from taxes to homelessness. Accommodation is far easier with federalism. As we witnessed during the pandemic and continue to witness to this day, our ability to migrate between states where personal values are aligned is much easier than ever. Within states, there is also a migration from urban to suburban and rural areas. This is making our divide wider as Americans move into their corners of the country. Issues that cross state lines (border security, environmental policy) cause the biggest divides. The right federal policies and solutions can unite us more than state policies.

There are two ideas that must be central to any unifying policy platform. What is the constitutional role of the federal government, and how do we balance the budget?

Democrats almost always support government growth through increased taxes and regulations. Republicans used to talk about reducing the size of the government rather than limiting the rate of growth. The size of the government can only be reduced with a return to federalism and a fundamental rethinking of the structure of government. Except for the military and law enforcement, the entire concept of "public service" has changed. When the counties surrounding Washington DC are some of the richest in the US, the power has clearly shifted beyond the Constitution's mandate for government. There is little altruism in working for the federal government when they pay higher wages than the private sector for comparable skills and education and have more job security and greater benefits.

In the 1990s we tried "reinventing government." This was another bold "moderate" proposal destined for failure because of misalignment of goals. The goals of both parties are now to grow government, which results in reducing our freedoms. Their definition of reinvention worked. Government does more and is in more control of our lives every day, but there has been some improvement in service levels at places like the Social Security Administration and the IRS. Service improvements are needed to justify growth without revolt, but what about reducing actual spending?

One of the key lessons from the Contract with America for anyone wanting to scale back the size of government is that it is best to eliminate a program completely, as that engenders just as much opposition as reducing funding for a program. Only when a program is eliminated is the battle over that program won. In contrast, incremental growth reduction, as opposed to actual spending cuts, simply means revisiting the issue every year.

Many Republicans have campaigned on reducing the size of government and eliminating federal departments, most notably the Department of Education, but has a department or program ever been eliminated? One bold solution is to not only eliminate programs or departments from the existing bureaucracy but to completely reorganize the federal government around its constitutional mandate.

When a new CEO comes into a position in the private sector, usually there is a complete reorganization aligned to the vision of the executive and the board of directors he or she serves. How many Republican presidents have served since Republicans campaigned on reducing the size of government? How many bold government restructurings have occurred? The Republicans failed once again to promote a plan aligned to the constitutional role of the federal government and reorganize the shape and even the location of federal departments to better serve the stakeholders of this country.

Here is the current executive branch organization by cabinet level department and its stated mission:

- State Department – Advises the president on foreign policy and negotiates treaties.
- Defense – Provides military forces to deter or wage war and protect the nation's security.
- Veteran Affairs – Administers benefits, pensions, and medical programs for veterans.
- Homeland Security – Provides border and transportation security and emergency preparedness and response.
- Justice – Prosecutes those accused of violating federal law, represents the US in court, provides legal advice to the president.
- Treasury – Produces coins and bills, collects taxes; enforces alcohol, tobacco, and firearm laws; manages the Secret Service and IRS.
- Commerce – Conducts census, grants patents, and registers trademarks.
- Transportation – Administers programs to promote and regulate highways, mass transit, railroads, and air travel.

- Energy – Promotes production of renewable energy, fossil fuels, and nuclear energy.
- Agriculture – Manages national forests, inspects food, administers food stamps and school lunch program.
- Interior – Manages public lands, wildlife refuges, and national parks; helps Native Americans.
- Labor – Enforces federal law on minimum wages, maximum hours, and safe working conditions.
- Education – Administers federal aid to schools, conducts education research.
- Health and Human Services – Enforces pure food and drug act, manages Medicare and Medicaid, oversees the Social Security Administration as an independent agency.
- Housing and Urban Development – Operates home financing and public housing programs, enforces fair housing laws.

Is there anything to prevent the government from adding even more bureaucracies to assume more control of our lives? The department of culture and speech? The department of technology regulation and cybersecurity? If energy and agriculture are important, why not have the department of semiconductors and electric vehicles?

Why are the Republicans focused on incremental changes to costs and regulations instead of starting anew? Why have the Democrats abandoned reinventing the government to reduce waste and fraud so more tax receipts could be applied to other programs and help people needing assistance rather than funding high-wage earners in the Washington suburbs? If the structure of the bureau-cracies of the federal government was changed, more money that impacts the country as a whole could be applied to other priorities, such as the social safety net, including education. For each current area of the bureaucracy, we need to decide if the role is coordination, funding, or delivery.

The American Unity Plan proposes fundamental changes to the way the government raises taxes and funds around 75 percent of fed-eral spending in social safety net programs. In typical government fashion, without a complete restructuring of the government itself, any savings and progress toward a balanced budget and fighting inflation would be wasted. To ensure an actual cost reduction, we need to reorganize the government around its constitutional man-date and implement these changes as the American Unity Plan is fully transitioned in. It is now time to implement a balanced budget around a new organizational structure to fight inflation and climate change to ensure an adequate social safety net aligned to American principles. Here is a concept of what a constitutionally mandated federal government organization might look like:

President and Chief Executive Staff:

- Budget, Benefits, and Taxation (Treasury)
- Justice and Law Enforcement
- National Defense, Intelligence and State (Foreign and Domestic)
- Federalism

One of the complaints we constantly hear from government bureaucracy is lack of interdepartmental coordination. There are currently fifteen executive branch departments and massive organizations within each one to provide some level of coordination. Well, how about we consolidate and rightsize the number of departments themselves to reduce coordination and streamline operations?

- Budget, Benefits, and Taxes – If all taxes are paid through retailers and end service providers collecting sales tax on behalf of the government, it seems like the role of the Treasury and IRS gets relegated to that of banker and auditor. Manage the money supply, deposit the tax checks from retailers, budget federal government operations, pay bills, and make sure each American gets a Unity Income check each month. The IRS becomes an auditor to make sure each entity collecting taxes pays the right amount and suspected fraud is turned over to justice. Over time, Social Security Administration, Health and Human Services, Veterans Affairs, and the rest can be consolidated and streamlined into this department to manage the few remaining federal services. Also, this department should not have any security, policing, or law enforcement role as it does now.
- Justice – Simply enforce federal laws including benefits fraud, enforce the payment of taxes, and focus heavily on protecting our liberties and human rights under the doctrine of equal justice under the law.
- National Defense – Why is the State Department separated from intelligence and military services? It seems like they

go hand in hand, as each treaty is part and parcel of national security. We must stop bureaucrats from negotiating complex trade deals that lead to unintended consequences that reduce our national security. Under the American Unity Plan, trade policy is simple reciprocation.

- Department of Federalism – This is my favorite. The three departments above are mandated by the Constitution, but anything not mandated is in the purview of the states. The other departments deliver services directly to the American people. The Department of Federalism is focused on funding and coordination between the states so services can be delivered by the states or the private sector. We should think of this department more like the surgeon general's office than the departments of interior, labor, commerce, transportation, and energy. The budget of this department should never be increased and should probably be reduced until a minimal level is reached.

All functions and jobs not listed that currently operate in the federal realm should be returned to the states. Will a massive government downsizing hurt the economy? No. The federal workforce is 2.1 million strong, excluding the post office (over 500,000 employees) and the department of defense. The federal government is on pace for 100,000 federal employees to retire annually. The annual retirement number is increasing because the federal workforce is aging. If we simply stopped hiring once the American Unity Plan became effective and allowed the federal workforce to reduce with retirements as programs and departments sunset, this would go a long way toward balancing the budget and reducing the scope and influence of the federal government.

The annual workforce reduction could be much greater if entire departments are eliminated immediately (energy, transportation, etc.) and control returned to the states and independent organizations to set policy, with the federal government having coordination oversight only. The states might have to increase budgets, but they have the infrastructure to do so now. The states manage parks, build roads, regulate utilities, provide healthcare and education services, and much more. They perform these functions more compassionately than the federal government, as they are closer to the citizens and are more cost-effective because almost all states require a balanced budget.

A fiscal deficit occurs when tax receipts are insufficient to support spending. This has not concerned Washington DC for many years, but the states are different. Almost all states require some form of a balanced budget requirement. In general, state balanced budget requirements typically require the governor to propose a balanced budget and the state legislature to pass a balanced budget, and any deficits cannot be carried over into the next fiscal year. State and local governments do not have the economic ability to run fiscal deficits to "stimulate" their economies like the federal government nor can they create money out of thin air. Under federalism, the states will gladly take more control, using the fiscal discipline they already have.

The federal bureaucracy must be reduced. Some states have used the approach to write new, modern, streamlined regulations from scratch. Besides a federal department reorganization, could a bold, new president use the same approach and eliminate the idea of executive orders and executive branch regulations altogether and replace them with actual laws, except for true military emergencies, as voted on by Congress? A president of any party who cares about the long-term success of the country instead of their personal legacy would offer Congress a gift by ceding power back to Congress where it belongs. Anything that requires the regulatory compliance of the electorate and punishes by controls, fines, or imprisonment is a law and must be applied equally to all. Laws must be passed by Congress, instead of Congress providing "guidance." When regulations are written by the executive bureaucracy or ordered by the executive like an autocrat, we lose freedom, no matter the party in charge. Rather than a fourth branch of government, "regulators" should effectively be consultants or advisors to Congress and in fact do not always need to work for the government. Any regulations should be voted as law. If that is inconvenient for Congress, so be it.

We have consultants embedded in Washington DC now. They are called lobbyists. However, with the Unity Tax, there would be no reason to lobby for tax breaks or special industry incentives. Rather, lobbyists would argue for fewer regulations to reduce the cost of products to stimulate demand or increase profits for their clients. The point is that without the tax incentives, industry experts would provide guidance to Congress and the final regulatory environment we all live with would be voted on by members of Congress who would be held accountable. Bureaucrats and regulators have political bias but no accountability.

No policy solution is complete without a long-term vision to reduce the size and scope of government to balance the budget. This is a key reason many libertarians, independents, and moderates do not vote Republican. For example, Health and Human Services (HHS) will take a generation or two to eliminate, but as URAs and UHAs are funded, under, say, the Department of Budget, Benefits, and Taxes, HHS can be reduced in size each year and eventually eliminated. This long-term vision implemented over decades must be policy that carries from administration to administration.

There is over $6 trillion currently proposed in new federal spending as of this writing, in addition to the trillions of spending already committed from the pandemic. This new spending does not include the Green New Deal, student debt forgiveness, or Medicare for All. It does not include security for Ukraine or our southern border. Do deficits matter to Republicans or anyone in Washington anymore? Or is it just lip service? This is a living experiment over how much deficit spending can be realized without massive inflation due strictly to fiscal policy rather than pandemic-related spending and supply chain issues.

Without a balanced budget, progressives will typically want to raise Unity Income payments without increasing the Unity Tax or reducing other spending. Republicans will want to reduce the Unity Tax without reducing other spending. Both parties align on not reducing spending. Unfortunately, this is not where we want to build unity. Deficits will grow to potentially crisis levels. The American Unity Plan aligns everyone, though for different reasons, to keep the Unity Tax as low as possible. But without a focus on spending, Unity Income will add to the deficit if there are no other offsets. We simply cannot rely solely on GDP growth. We need specific, bold spending reduction proposals. Here are some examples.

The government does not do anything exceptionally well except fight wars and enforce laws when we have the will. There is not a single other function of government where it is best in class in cost, quality, and service, as government has no incentive to be that. Does anyone believe Amazon could not deliver the mail cheaper and better than USPS? What cannot be outsourced should be incentivized. Every private organization pays based on performance one way or the other. The goal is to increase the pay of government employees who are performing constitutionally mandated roles to attract the best while reducing the overall budget.

There will always be a gray area as to what is the proper role of the federal government. For example, we should all agree that food and drug safety is required, but does it need a federal department and does the service need to be delivered by the government itself? Do we need government employees doing testing and research? Instead, could the role be strictly advisory?

Maybe for nonconstitutionally mandated functions, the federal government should operate more like Berkshire Hathaway and less like the Soviet Union. Many organizations operate in a decentralized manner with limited operational management but provide oversight and guidance to ensure the strategic vision is achieved, benefiting stakeholders.

Going further, could the FDA, CDC, and the NIH be independent bodies, whether appointed or not, and have no legal authority? We witnessed the lack of unity when government employees appear to be political in decision-making, defaulting to the opinion of the chief executive in either party. The idea that federal government employees are apolitical and neutral is a relic of the past. Can these organizations be more like the Federal Reserve and give the appearance of political neutrality, at least after their appointment? Or could industry associations like the American Medical Association, the American Institute of Certified Public Accountants, and others replace much of the work done by government bureaucrats and regulators?

In many cases, federal regulators can be replaced with industry associations that can provide governing rules and practices. We do this in a wide range of fields now, from accounting to real estate to medicine. Industry peer review, guidance, and testing is more effective and produces better results. The last thing any association would want is to have a bad actor take down the entire industry.

The goal is to remove politics where possible to balance the needs of industry members, customers (society), and stakeholders. The longer bureaucrats remain in government, even if they are disguised as professionals such as doctors, they naturally become political to remain in power. Society would be much better served if industry experts recommended Congress to pass laws, rather than regulations. The cost of industry associations is borne by the private sector, not the US taxpayer.

One concern about implementing Unity Income is that regulators will insist on volumes of regulations, increasing cost and complexity. Usually, their intentions are to reduce risk, but they only add to compliance costs. Regardless, the rules that accompany Unity Income need to be passed by Congress, not written by regulators. For example, would regulators limit what investments could be made in Unity Retirement Accounts? Would crypto held in a US regulated brokerage account be off-limits because it may compete with the US dollar? The idea of Unity Income is that, over time, mistakes will average out, and the ongoing Unity Income provides for a social safety net. Could the rules simply be that accounts cannot go negative (no margin) and all investments must be in SEC regulated accounts (Coinbase, not FTX)? Could a law be written in fewer words than the US Constitution? That would be refreshing.

Regulation is different from transparency. There is nothing wrong with reporting that the money received from taxpayers has been contributed to the appropriate education, healthcare, and retirement accounts. It is important to have transparency to monitor account growth to plan for future spending and to advise whether contribution adjustments are needed. We need full transparency but minimum regulation.

Perhaps the greatest opportunity to unify the country across party lines and align the government to constitutionally mandated roles is around federal lands. Opportunity zones were passed as one of the greatest yet largely unrecognized achievements of the modern Republican Party. Opportunity zones are designated "economically disadvantaged" areas throughout the country that offer tax incentives to real estate investors. Opportunity zones are an example of good incremental legislation but within a bad long-term strategic framework, and it certainly is not a bold solution people can rally around.

Opportunity zone legislation is needed because of the current tax code. When corporate and personal income taxes are eliminated and replaced with the American Unity Tax, there will be less incentive to invest in opportunity zones. What can replace good legislation that will no longer be needed? First, states and local governments provide most of the incentives now when companies are deciding where to locate operations. State incentives include state income tax reductions, property and inventory tax holidays, job training, state and local tax credits for hiring, and more. Consistent with federalism, states and specific opportunity zones would compete for business investment.

More importantly, the federal government is the largest landowner in the United States, and land provides an incredible opportunity under federalism. If we believe in capitalism and private property rights, as much property as possible should be returned to the American people by the federal government. As a bold solution, we can sell or donate every bit of federal land that is not mandated in the Constitution to individuals and corporations, where it is used for commercial purposes, and the remainder can be given to the states for management to reduce the size and control of the federal bureaucracy. Land sales could be used to fund new spending, such as for Unity Education Accounts or climate defenses.

Why are private citizens leasing land from the federal government to run their businesses and putting up with excessive regulations? For example, when in power, could the Republicans have sold the federal land for the Keystone Pipeline to the owners and operators so this project could never be blocked? If we sell federal lands that have no strategic purpose, we could use the proceeds to finance environmental infrastructure, as discussed in the next chapter, or reduce the debt.

There is a movement to privatize land ownership for conservation. Besides several well-known landowners who happen to be some of the richest people in the US, there are many groups raising capital to privately finance land purchases. In addition to providing protection from development, it provides a sustainable operating budget for land management. This in turn provides property taxes for local governments and relieves local government of making the difficult choice between land conservation and development.

There must be guidelines entities must follow to acquire US assets. National security is clearly a primary concern. Should lands with oil and mineral reserves or farmland be sold to a Chinese or Russian company? Anyone who acquires land must be bound by US regulations and full transparency requirements.

What land and assets should the federal government own? This is an interesting question that should be answered only in the context of the Constitution. It was historically necessary to acquire the current American landmass to protect the American continent from European imperialism and the inevitable wars that would follow. North America has a unique advantage over every other continent, except Australia, of having experienced no wars with its neighbors for over one hundred years. There have been skirmishes but nothing on par with the European continent. Despite the treatment of the American Indians, this accomplishment was a huge success, saving countless millions of lives if Europe had gotten a foothold on the American continent. But like all federal programs, the bureaucracy that was built to unify the continent never went away or restructured to support a modern America.

The federal government owns around 640 million acres of land, or about 28 percent of the 2.27 billion acres of land in the United States. Four federal agencies—the US National Park Service

(NPS), US Fish and Wildlife Service (FWS) and US Bureau of Land Management (BLM) within the US Department of the Interior, and the US Forest Service (USFS) in the US Department of Agriculture—oversee roughly 95 percent of federal land.

We can argue whether national parks could just as easily be managed by the states at less cost (as they manage state parks). Very few parks cross state lines. Military bases clearly should be federal property, as well as special purpose assets, like federal prisons and courts, that have constitutional and strategic purpose. But farm and grazing lands? Oil fields? These have no strategic interest and are better managed by the private sector or the states to lower the cost of providing these products and services to the consumer.

When private sector leases are subservient to the government as a landlord, one of two possible scenarios occurs: the cost is artificially low to the true value, therefore effectively becoming a government subsidy; or the cost and regulation is too high, thereby becoming a tax. In addition, as a landlord, the government gives itself the right to impose new regulations and to shut down economic activity for some businesses in some industries but not others, violating equality under the law. In either case, the government is competing with the private sector or regulating private industry beyond its constitutional right.

All nonconstitutionally mandated land and assets should be sold to the private sector at fair market value or donated, and 100 percent of the proceeds should be used to pay down the national debt or finance environmental infrastructure as an insurance prepayment against future federal relief for environmental catastrophe.

It is estimated that this value is almost $20 trillion. Selling even a small fraction of these assets each year would go a long way toward both paying down the debt, reducing compliance costs, and growing GDP without impacting national security.

The federal government manages livestock grazing on 158 million acres. Why? More than one-third of US land is used for pasture, and nearly 25 percent of that land is administered by the federal government and open to grazing for a fee.

In their article "Here's How America Uses Its Land" published by Bloomberg on July 31, 2018, authors Dave Merrill and Lauren Leatherby provide a very interesting chart detailing how land is used in the US. The aggregate amount of land used for national defense is depicted as a small swatch in South Texas. Yet the federal government owns 28 percent of the land in the US. Why is the federal government a landlord when the Constitution mandates and protects private property?

About a quarter of US oil and an eighth of the nation's natural gas are produced on federal lands. About 11 percent of all hydraulic fracturing occurs on federal land. The remainder occurs on private and state-owned land. Ironically, energy independence, and thereby national security, would improve if the federal government did not own these lands. American manifest destiny was needed as defense against European imperialists. We can now return the land to the American people.

Another interesting byproduct of the America Unity Tax is that profits generated overseas can be repatriated at any time without tax consequences. Capital will flow globally to locations, with opportunity for profit. How do we invest in foreign nations to promote freedom and benefit the US taxpayer? Rather than exclusively using our military to secure our freedom or providing aid, could we also use our intellectual capital and financial acumen, leveraging the American Unity Tax?

Our economic freedom is critical to provide the funds to protect our political freedom. Using Cuba as an example, could we export our intellectual capital and freedoms to countries that would benefit more from dealing with the US than our enemies? We lead the world in investment bankers and management consultants. The wars of the twenty-first century will mostly be economic and political (Communism / socialism vs. capitalism / freedom) rather than militaristic, with just a few remaining exceptions. The measure of success with our alliance partners will be how many countries move up the Freedom Index (the US has dropped to twenty-fifth).

Think about all the money spent defending against the threat from Cuba (Russia) and allowing Communism to have a foothold ninety miles from our shores. We have the best finance, mergers, and acquisitions people in the entire world. Did anyone ever think of a leveraged buy-out instead of using the military? The GDP of Cuba is about $100 billion, with almost no prospects for growth. Heck, Apple could buy the entire island with cash! We just spent trillions paying people not to work. Here is an idea that is both economical and humane: Why not offer the entire Cuban leadership, political and military, however many billions they need to leave the country, with complete asylum to the country of their choice, as well as anyone else who does not want to be an American? Or we can simply wait for the Cuban people to revolt and do it the hard way.

As a reminder, we bought Puerto Rico from Spain in 1898 following the Spanish-American War.

Return the land, 100 percent of it, to the people of Cuba and allow Cuba to voluntarily become a territory of the United States, like the US Virgin Islands and Puerto Rico, with full voting rights after democratic elections are in place. Between tourism, the return of industry, trade with the US and surrounding nations, and the freeing of incredible talent, Cuba will grow its GDP enormously and the US can reduce all associated military spending. With Cuba as a US territory, the American Unity Tax would go into effect and produce an incredible net income stream toward deficit reduction. With all taxes eliminated except the Unity Tax, businesses would flock to Cuba because of the opportunity.

For that matter, our biggest immigration problem seems to stem from people making the dangerous trek from the northern triangle countries of El Salvador, Honduras, and Guatemala through Mexico to the United States. The total GDP of these three—and we can throw in Nicaragua for good measure—is about $140 billion. A significant portion of their income is from expats sending money back to their homelands from the US. Remittance fees are very high. Suppose we injected into each country as private equity three times their GDP, or around $400 billion. In return, after a positive vote on the proposal in each nation, they would agree to adopt the US Constitution as their own, use our currency (actually El Salvador should just go with Bitcoin), implement the US federal code as the rule of law to come under the protection of the US military, and upon successful transition, would become territories of the US. If accepted, immigration from these countries would come to a halt.

In addition, China's advances in our hemisphere would be reduced. We spend much more annually on border security, courts, social welfare, foreign aid, and more, besides the human toll as a magnate for human trafficking and drug cartels. Sounds like a great acquisition strategy for the US to solve several large-scale problems. These countries would be magnets for investment and tourism, as Costa Rica and Belize are now.

This type of idea is anti-imperialist. It supports freedom without bloodshed and returns the land to the people of their home countries, operating under US property rights law, as more land should be returned from the federal government to the people in these fifty states. More importantly, they would be protected by the US military, freeing up domestic revenue for nonmilitary spending.

These are ideas to reduce the size of government and fund a transition to more freedom and away from government regulation and control. If the budget is not balanced, maybe Congress should not be paid! Yes, this is symbolic, but it is a thought. Without a balanced budget, politicians in both parties will continue with rampant spending, draining the funds needed to fight inflation, address climate change, and provide national security. The message is easy to unify voters.

We believe in private property rights and returning nonstrategically important lands controlled by the federal government to the American people. This is a critical step in balancing the budget. The proceeds for all land sales will be used to reduce the federal debt, reduce the size of government, eliminate unnecessary and harmful regulations, fund education, and protect the environment. This ensures that American citizens doing business on federal lands have equal rights and protection under the laws.

Federalism builds unity by returning control to the states, red and blue alike, and to the American people. Federalism is freedom for states and private businesses to decide for themselves. However, there is one area of government control that is impacting every part of our lives. It is political and emotional, almost religious in nature. We will now focus on environmentalism.

15

CLIMATE SOLUTIONS

We are running the most dangerous experiment in history right now, which is to see how much carbon dioxide the atmosphere can handle before there is an environmental catastrophe.

— Elon Musk, CEO of Tesla & SpaceX

There was a famous French philosopher, theologian, mathematician, and physicist in the seventeenth century named Blaise Pascal. It was generally believed Pascal was an atheist, but he regularly attended church. When asked why, he stated it was a good bet, and this simple analysis became Pascal's wager.

	God Exists	God Does Not Exist
Wager God Exists (Attend Church)	Salvation	Wasted Time, Donations
Wager God Does Not Exist (Do Not Attend Church)	Potential Misery	No Impact

Pascal's wager allows us to think in terms of probabilities of outcomes, as well as risk and return. If you believe God exists and are wrong, you will have wasted a few days every week or year in church. However, if one does not believe God exists and is wrong, the potential impact is, well, maybe forever.

The reason for discussing Pascal's wager is because, for many, the environment is a religion. Most people are "environmentalists," including the most ardent capitalists. All Americans across the political spectrum rightly believe that we should have clean air and water, preserve our natural resources, and generally be a conscious citizen of the world.

So why has climate become divisive? Many believe that climate change is the one and only issue facing us today and solutions can only be achieved through federal government control and mandates ignoring other potential catastrophes. The looming national debt crisis, Social Security and Medicare insolvency, and warfare with rogue nations are as important to many who support the climate movement but believe issues like these cannot be seemingly ignored to focus only on climate. If China seized Taiwan, would that rise to the level of climate change? A US–China embargo like other embargos of Iran and Russia would make the 1970s seems quaint. Supply chain shortages would cause immediate inflation and, with

China holding so much US debt, could lead to a worldwide recession and long-lasting stagflation.

Nor do some believe that a more lethal, engineered pandemic than Covid or the Earth getting hit by an object from space are as much of an existential threat as climate change, thereby needing immediate solutions. Some of these events have happened in the past albeit on smaller scales. There are many doomsday scenarios that rise to the level of the impending climate crisis that garner scant attention in comparison.

The issue with the debate is not that climate change is real. It is. However, many believe the threat has been greatly exaggerated or at least not balanced against other pressing needs. The problem is one of resources. If all resources are poured into the proposed environmental solutions, it may lead to unintended consequences in inflation, debt, recession and unemployment and potentially a weaker military.

The point of this chapter is not to debate environmental science. At this point, given the lack of absolutes, as will be discussed, most people have already taken a position and are arguing their point. However, many Americans rightly think the Republicans lack a comprehensive and bold environmental policy position, and many believe the Democrats have co-opted the environmental movement for political and financial gain. The divide is getting wider and more dangerous every year.

For many potential voters, environmentalism is important but is not a make-or-break issue. They attend the environmental church on a somewhat regular basis and contribute to the cause, but it does not consume their daily lives. They do what they can to be a good environmental steward within the reasonable confines of living a normal life. They do not attend conferences or march for environmental justice. Discussions of balancing the federal budget, saving Social Security and Medicare, and managing inflation are just as important to these citizens. Any comprehensive plan must be able to articulate an environmental position that is forward-looking and reasonable and does not disillusion the many voters who are not swayed by the "change or die now" existential threat mantra but are nonetheless genuinely concerned citizens.

Ardent environmental believers do not agree that balancing the vast needs of society to have affordable energy, housing, transportation, and food, as well as to create a better standard of living and ensure national security, equates to saving the planet. The overwhelming majority of people who simply care about the environment believe in balance, and we can decide with them what policies achieve this balance. Most people rightly believe that we cannot fix one problem by causing misery elsewhere. The current default federal policy is to eliminate all fossil fuels as quickly as possible to save the planet from imminent destruction. As we have seen in the past few years, this policy potentially addresses one critical issue while creating other serious threats that are wide-ranging, from inflation to national security. Since energy is a critical part of any economy and energy shortages cause inflation, it would be difficult to present the American Unity Plan without discussing climate policy, as the biggest risk to the plan is the potential for inflation from increased demand due to more money in American pockets from the repatriation of jobs and elimination of payroll taxes and withholdings. Increased demand and energy shortages do not play well together. The question is can we solve more than one problem at once?

So, we begin with what we can agree on, and then specific solutions will be discussed. First, what is it with human beings that we cannot simply say "I don't know"? There are very few definitive conclusions when it comes to the environment. There are things we can measure such as temperature, CO_2 levels, air and water quality, and more. Many environmental science theories have certain probabilities of occurrence. They are mathematical models that have proven over time to be much more wrong than right. It is acceptable to question models. However, many take a hard stance on the environment and preach "the science is settled," when nothing could be further from the truth. Every potential event has a probability of occurrence and a magnitude of risk when that event happens. Airplanes are much safer than automobiles, but when an incident happens, the damage to humans is much greater in the air than on the ground. Airplanes have low-probability risk occurrence and high-magnitude event outcomes, and automobiles are the opposite. The proper questions can lead to the right balance between risk and reward in potential solutions. Here is how we can begin with some simple questions that will eventually lead to Pascal's wager being applied to environmental policy.

Question 1: Is Earth's temperature (climate) changing? Since we can measure temperature going back thousands or even millions of years with some confidence, we can all agree it is. Anyone denying temperature change has not done one bit of homework. We can discuss the rate of change and root causes. We can all agree that Earth has gone through heating and cooling periods from the beginning of time, and these changes can have an impact on the planet and its inhabitants. Sea levels rise and fall (our ancestors once walked from Asia to America across what is now the Bering Sea), food and water sources move, ice melts and freezes. Is the climate changing? Yes, as it has for four billion years. Is the rate of change accelerating? Maybe.

Question 2: Are humans contributing to climate change? It is unquestionable that human beings emit CO_2 and that CO_2 levels are increasing. CO_2 and temperature have a strong correlation. Since CO_2 and temperature are both measurable, and both CO_2 and temperature were around before human beings, and certainly before the industrial revolution, there is some level of doubt around cause and effect. CO_2 levels and temperature have been closely correlated for four hundred thousand years, with CO_2 increases mostly lagging temperature increases. Since we cleaned up our collective polluting act immeasurably from the smokestack and dump-in-the-river era of the industrial revolution, is it possible we have already corrected enough to reverse human contribution? Our air and water are certainly cleaner than in the 1970s thanks to the environmental movement, and we did this without hurting our economy. However, some think CO_2 levels have risen beyond what we have historically experienced. No matter the contribution of humans, mankind has clearly survived higher CO_2 in the past, regardless of the relationship between CO_2 and temperature. We may simply be at a moment in Earth's history when CO_2 happens to be naturally high. The point may be moot.

Question 3: Let us assume the theory, which has some probability of being true, that CO_2 causes temperature increases, not vice versa, which is now the consensus. Do modern humans, post industrial revolution, increase CO_2 at a rate beyond what naturally occurs? Again, the answer may be yes, but what probability do we assign to it to know what environmental policies to put into place and at what cost and return? The believers are 100 percent certain that CO_2 is 100 percent caused by human lifestyles and rising quickly. Most people assume humans probably contribute some but have no idea how much compared to nature.

Much of the talk of an existential threat is based on models and theories. There is no 100 percent certainty, just models with probabilities. The point is not to deny or to be righteous in the belief it will or will not happen. We need to create realistic policies. For example, if you were 100 percent certain that North Korea or Iran, who are testing intercontinental ballistic missiles capable of carrying a nuclear warhead, will within ten years launch missiles into a major US or European population area, what would you do now? Remember, you are 100 percent certain it will happen in less than ten years. Would you negotiate (the Neville Chamberlain approach to the Nazis), or would you preemptively strike to eliminate their capabilities now (the Iraq War approach)? Or would you incrementally build a massive army on their borders over many years, watch, and adjust as politics, technology, diplomacy, and economics play out (the mutually assured destruction approach with the Soviet Union)? The point is, when each of these monumental decisions were made, no one was certain if the approach was correct. Caution, concern, challenging assumptions, and most importantly, gathering new information is vital to success.

Question 4: Is climate change, regardless of how much humans contribute to it, a problem? This is an interesting question that only time will reveal the answer to. Since Earth has changed from the beginning of time, and humans have certainly adapted and migrated historically as temperature and weather affected food and water supplies, should we be overly concerned? Modern technology affords us more ability to adapt to environmental changes quicker than ever before. No one can be 100 percent sure that climate change would be catastrophic to the human species. However, it is far more likely that human beings will adapt to changing environmental conditions, as we have for millennia, but no one can be certain.

Environmental existentialists claim we cannot take that chance and we must act now. We may already be past the point of no return. Can we take the chance that North Korea, Iran, or Russia will not start a nuclear war? Can we take the chance that Social Security and Medicare will be saved from the brink of bankruptcy, or that our national debt will not cause US insolvency? Can we be certain China will not release a stronger biological weapon or launch their own trade war on our debt? One hundred percent certainty of an uncertain event occurring is not only foolish but dangerous.

If the environmental doomsday camp is wrong about the magnitude and the timing of the problem, a worst case might be to starve the world of fossil fuels too soon, creating supply chain shortages, poverty, and global stagflation, and we might still have climate change as a mostly natural occurrence. But at that point, we will not have the economic wealth to solve any major problem. However, the rich and elites will still fly their private jets to climate and economic summits in Switzerland. Affordable and abundant energy has been critical to the improvement of the human condition and, as we have seen in 2022, energy security is national security. To ban all fossil fuels when renewables are not yet an affordable and abundant replacement would mean that one would have to believe that human contribution to CO_2 levels beyond natural conditions is catastrophic and will occur very soon.

Question 5: What policies should we put in place? For guidance, let us return to both Pascal's wager and American principles. Pascal starts with a proposition, or policy statement. Unlike belief in the Almighty, there is not just one environmental question that needs to be answered, as demonstrated by the questions above. We cannot simply ask only "Do you believe the world will be destroyed by climate change in the next ten years?" Every question asked or problem statement has a probability of occurrence (risk analysis) and a potential solution that carries both costs and rewards. Probabilities change with time.

Let us assume we all believe climate change is an existential threat but we are uncertain of the timing. Here are two courses of action:

The world will be destroyed by climate change in <u>ten years</u> if we do not act:

- Probability: Very low, no evidence of immediate destruction
- Solution: Eliminate all fossil fuels and transition to 100 percent renewables now
- Probability of success: Extremely low
- Evidence:
    - Inability to scale renewables and countries decommissioning and divesting their nuclear energy plants

- o Lack global consensus, as China and India are major polluters
  - o No evidence of our ability to reverse weather and CO_2 trends
- Cost of acting: Extremely high
  - o Rising energy prices cause inflation
  - o Oil and rare earth minerals controlled by unfriendly nations
  - o National security concerns and threat of war
  - o Loss of freedom with intense government control and regulation

The world will be destroyed by climate change in <u>fifty years</u> if we do not act:

- Probability: Low to moderate
- Solution:
  - o Transition to 100 percent renewables without harming economies
  - o Build support with China, India, and developing countries
  - o Build infrastructure to mitigate risks from climate change
  - o Colonize another planet as a backup plan to save humanity
- Probability of success: Moderate
- Evidence:
  - o Renewable energy sources scaling each year

- ○ Technology is advancing in construction and space exploration
- ○ Environment is cleaner than the last fifty years while supporting economic growth
- Cost of acting: Low
  - ○ Free-market is investing in renewable energy
  - ○ Developing countries can accelerate progress
  - ○ Infrastructure has proven to save lives and minimize property loss

From the environmentalist imminent (ten years or less) existential threat perspective, the only rational alternative is to save the human species by rationing energy, potentially leading to widespread poverty and increasing national security threats. Remember, they are 100 percent certain that the world will be destroyed by climate change if we do not act now, despite the odds of this happening being extremely low, albeit not exactly zero. The problem is that the solution requires most of the world to suffer greatly, with central governments controlling energy policy, extremely high regulations, and massive government spending on prevention. This is the optimistic view that they are wrong about a catastrophic event! There is no scenario that improves the human condition if you believe environmental disaster is imminent. Unlike Pascal, where the cost of being wrong was minor (church attendance), the cost of extreme environmentalist policy being wrong may be losing millions of lives, impoverishing much of the planet, and compromising our freedoms to Communist regimes.

If you are one of the few billionaires who can finance space endeavors or experiment on changing weather patterns, then colonizing another world over the next fifty years (not ten years) is as rational as Pascal attending church. Your lifestyle will not change if your endeavors fail. However, for the rest of the world reliant on freedom and capitalism to create abundant energy for food, clothing, transportation, and shelter, as well as to expand the social safety net, environmental fatalism is not a good bet.

In a recent Investor Day presentation, Elon Musk, who one can argue is doing more to solve the actual problem than anyone attending environmental conferences, said he believes a 100 percent sustainable economy is 100 percent doable in fifty years. "Earth can and will move to a sustainable energy economy in our lifetime."

The solution needs to be clean, cheap, and abundant energy, whatever the source, that *also* reduces the probability of environmental disaster. We probably do not need to solve this overnight and certainly do not need to create a potentially worse economic disaster while trying. The current climate solutions of pushing clean, expensive, and limited energy before the technology is ready, rather than cleaner, cheap, and abundant energy, will exacerbate the debt and inflation problems. We have no idea which will come first and have a worse impact—climate catastrophe or inflation, debt, and widespread poverty. It is estimated that during the pandemic lockdowns, emissions fell by less than 10 percent globally but CO_2 still grew. It is rational to ask whether the solution is worth the cost.

If the climate issue is not exaggerated, then we must also understand the timing. In fact, we must assume we need to transition to 100 percent sustainability. However, we do not have the resources, technical and financial, to solve all problems at once. We know for certain that every prediction of the timing of the climate catastrophe has been wrong until now. That is not to say they will be wrong in the future. However, moving resources toward resilience and preparedness while sustainable technology improves, instead of pursuing accelerated climate change prevention, is more practical and will build unity to solve many problems, including climate change, debt, and national security. Climate change cannot be addressed in isolation.

We need to weigh the costs of potential solutions in terms of risk and reward. In your personal life, you do this calculation all the time. Some want high premiums and low deductibles on their healthcare plans, and some want only catastrophic insurance or no coverage at all and will pay as they go. This is a personal choice based on family needs.

At the societal level, the argument many make is that government must decide for us issues such as environmental catastrophe protection, as individual decisions impact us all. However, the federal government has a miserable history of making incorrect decisions because they typically exert too much centralized power and control. The pandemic is the latest example of the government not applying a balanced risk and return approach. Prior to proceeding, did anyone ask whether the cost of lockdowns (loss of businesses and jobs, mental health impact, education impact, financial stress, etc.) outweighed the benefits for society as a whole? Or did certain people (elderly, high risk of infection) benefit more and others (the young, healthy) benefit less, violating a key American principle of no negative rights? Fortunately, in the US, lockdowns were ordered at the state and local level based on federal guidance, and society can now weigh the benefits and costs. What would have happened if lockdowns had been ordered on a national level in the US, as some countries like China did? To be fair, when these decisions were made, information was scarce and fear was high. Would our leaders make the same decisions today? With environmental science, it is fair to assess solution cost and societal benefit, even if that means waiting until more data is available on both the problem and the potential solution.

Going back to the statement "the world will be destroyed by climate change," notice that when the statement changed from a ten-year to a fifty-year horizon, not only did the odds of the event happening increase, but the chance of success also increased, and the cost of applying solutions decreased. As with retirement planning, time is our friend. If we are facing an environmental disaster, we have no idea when that will happen or how severe it will be. The total elimination of fossil fuels in ten years is a different policy approach than a transition over fifty years.

The environmental movement is focused on the total elimination of man-made carbon, which if implemented too soon would cause other extreme conditions. Where there is no compromise, there is no unity. Just like in life, where extreme measures are not realistic for most people (e.g., training for triathlons as opposed to jogging a few times a week to improve your fitness), neither is the complete and rapid elimination of carbon, as the cost is poor quality of life, resulting in lack of resources, inflation, and debt. There is demand in the marketplace for a balanced approach for sustainable products, yet these products still need to be well-made, affordable, and available in large quantities. It takes time to innovate and produce. We have abundant natural gas, which is 50 percent cleaner than other fossil fuels but not 100 percent clean. Nuclear energy is 100 percent clean and scalable, yet many oppose it because of other risks.

Government policies rarely provide balance because the solutions are political, generic, and extreme. Most people want to do their part to protect the environment yet balance the cost and benefit to society as we evaluate the ongoing risks. To state with 100 percent certainty that we do not have time and that there is only one approach is not a mainstream position.

The Democratic Party has taken a strong stand on this topic. The Republican Party has pushed the issue to the back burner and has produced nothing beyond "all of the above." The country requires practical solutions and policies that can unite the overwhelming number of people that are concerned for the environment but also realize the potential harm from extreme, heavy-handed solutions. They need something specific.

Historically, many environmental and safety policy solutions provided this balance. They cost little and were only slightly inconvenient (like attending church) but had potentially huge returns. Seat belts are an easy example. We did not ban automobiles even though 100 percent of deaths were caused by humans (a manufacturer or a driver). Seat belts raise the cost of a car only marginally, are slightly inconvenient to use every time you get in a car, and affect all manufacturers equally but have an incredibly high safety return. In the environmental arena, we slowed CFCs release, which has had very little impact on our daily lives (changes to aerosols) but had huge returns in decreasing ultraviolet radiation. This change occurred over about a decade, had very little resistance from the public or businesses, and, this is key, was implemented equally and fairly around the globe.

Would eliminating all man-made carbon in ten to twenty years by switching to 100 percent renewables "save the planet"? The answer is we do not know if the planet *needs* saving. Will humans simply adapt as they have historically? Unlike reducing CFCs, what if only Western democracies adopted the Green New Deal but China and India (two of the five largest economies) did not? A Western democracy approach might have an incremental beneficial impact on first-world public health, but what is the global cost? The question comes to what approach achieves the most benefit to the environment and society for the least investment and risk? Depriving emerging nations of cheap reliable energy or making them reliant on nondemocratic nations such as China has a huge impact on global freedom, wealth, and health. There is an argument that wealth transfer from rich to developing nations will make up for the "right to pollute," as first-world countries did to create the wealth. This is an admission that cheap energy leads to prosperity. In the US, increasing the cost of energy or making the energy supply more susceptible to disruption impacts everyone around the globe.

The current environmental solutions are a bad use of economic resources that will exacerbate energy shortages and inflation and eventually lead to stagflation. Tax credits for renewable energy have been slow and painful. If you want government to accelerate the fight, eliminate taxes on both production and investment as proposed in the American Unity Plan. New investment will allow us to continue to "clean" the fossil fuel industry in the US, not make it 100 percent clean but cleaner compared to overseas production, as well as accelerate private investment in 100 percent sustainable solutions. Taxation elimination does not mean total regulatory abandonment. The key is to regulate fairly across all players to allow the best technologies to succeed quicker. There is an underinvestment in renewables because capital still requires a return!

There is certainly market demand to solve potential future environmental challenges, but the demand needs to come from the private sector. Electric vehicles (EVs) have been around for some time, but when the market offers EVs that are cost-effective (without government incentives), fun to drive, convenient to charge, and reliable, consumers will choose these products over gasoline-powered cars, all other things being equal. The environmental benefits are an incremental benefit to consumers that costs almost nothing, just like seat belts.

We do not need government policies and mandates driven by politically motivated timetables. The free market will wean us off fossil fuels because consumers are demanding it. Sustainability is done right when it is driven by consumer demand, with businesses owning the problem and creating better solutions than their competitors. This is more effective than when government action causes greater harm than good (for example, shutting down pipelines, not building refineries, or increasing the cost of drilling leases). There is nothing better than having products that are sustainable, as well as energy- and cost-efficient so people can afford them. Socialist governments ban plastic straws. Free societies wait for some entrepreneurs working in a lab, such as Loliware, to develop a biodegradable straw that feels like plastic and costs about the same. That way, when people toss their straws, the problem is solved without government controls or mandates. The free market works on its own timeline rather than under some artificial government mandate.

We cannot solve a global problem in isolation. Businesses got behind the CFC reduction because it impacted all global competitors equally. When countries like China can ignore your solution, you lose support. We know nuclear energy is the only scalable, carbon-free energy source. One would think governments would work with the nuclear energy industry to improve the cost and safety. The current course of action—phasing out nuclear power plants—is like abandoning automobiles rather than introducing seat belts. China, as a Communist country, can mandate anything it wishes. China is massively scaling nuclear power and renewables to eventually decarbonize but also building coal-fired plants to support their economic growth in the near term. A large-scale nuclear disaster in China would certainly impact the United States. The question is which country will reach carbon neutrality first and whose economy will be best supported in the process? The US and many Western democracies are decommissioning aging nuclear plants and shifting to natural gas because solar and wind are still not scalable. China is standardizing the design of their nuclear plants using modern technology that is reportedly safe (learning from the lessons of the past) and building many plants at scale, which lowers the cost. At scale, safety continues to improve. Could we build safe and small nuclear plants, with revised and smarter government regulations, at scale and at a lower cost as we now build rockets in the private sector to both save our species from environmental disaster and lower the cost of space travel?

No matter the solution, the goal should not be to save the environment or humankind from annihilation but to incrementally improve the environment as we have done for decades while promoting wealth and prosperity for all. We need to balance free-market capitalism with pragmatic environmental policy. In short, the Republicans need a solution and a message, and the Democrats need to compromise and admit climate change is not the only consideration to the American people.

We need to focus on preparedness for climate-related events while we move to 100 percent sustainability led by the private sector. This is the proper role of the federal government. This will save lives and prevent massive property damage whether we agree or disagree on why these things happen and when they will get worse. We can all agree climate-related events will happen in the future. Solutions like infrastructure spending focused on what we absolutely know cause harm to people and property will be much more beneficial to society than a blanket approach impacting prosperity, inflation, and debt. Basically, we can agree to mitigate the damage from rising seas more easily than we can agree to try to prevent the seas from rising! To Pascal's point, there is little downside, since we fix disasters after they occur anyway, and potentially a very high economic return by mitigating the impact of future disasters.

The reality is this is not a this-or-that proposition. Whether you believe in climate fatalism or natural occurrence, climate-related death and disaster has and will occur. Even if climate events may have increased, the cost measured in lives over the last century is less. Why? Because we have hardened our infrastructure by utilizing modern building technology and early warnings. However, we can do more, and this would be critical for building support for the

American Unity Plan to ensure low inflation and to reduce spending resulting from environmental events.

In most of nature, prevention is better than treatment. The cost of prevention techniques such as weight loss and exercise to prevent heart disease later in life has a great return on investment in terms of quality of life and cost reduction. In the case of climate change, the type of prevention is what we are really arguing about.

The policy needs to be focused on environmental insurance and preparedness. As with health insurance, we buy policies we can afford. People buy the appropriate amount of coverage to balance the policy costs and deductibles based on their life circumstances—economics, family history, current health, age, and more. We naturally balance perceived risk and return. If a health event does not occur, we are not upset if we do not get hospitalized or die. The return on investment on our health, life, and automobile insurance against the premiums paid is financial catastrophe risk mitigation. Peace of mind has a benefit—knowing that just in case something bad happens, we are prepared. If we built sea walls around US cities susceptible to flooding and the floods never came, no one would second-guess the decision. But if the cost of energy doubled or was unavailable in the winter to heat homes, we would certainly question the wisdom of bad environmental policy. When you are cold and hungry, saving the plant is not a priority!

Our energy and emissions policies have historically followed a similar balanced approach. When we saw pollutants spewing from smokestacks and mufflers, we all agreed the incremental cost of not polluting would have a good return. We do not want air that looks like Los Angeles in the 1970s or major Chinese cities today.

What is the best solution? Whether the seas rise or not, infrastructure (true infrastructure—tangible things) helps the health, safety, and prosperity of us all. Using federalism as a concept, why not allow states to borrow federal funds to use for environmental impact projects? Or use the proceeds from federal land sales within a state to fund environmental impact projects within that state? Or simply allocate a percentage of the Unity Tax to environmental infrastructure so we all contribute equally, as some have proposed for military spending, to ensure long-term strategic projects are funded over time and administrations? Infrastructure for 100 percent prevention is not affordable either. It needs to be directed where there is true vulnerability. In other words, it too must be budgeted and incremental to avoid spiking inflation and the deficit.

There is nothing wrong with planning to determine the best way to prepare. We need the equivalent of war games for environmental impact. Just like nuclear weapons, we hope to never "pull the trigger," but we can prepare. We need to put in place sensible prevention (dams, sewers, seawalls, building codes, zoning, etc.) where there is a higher probability of damage to address some of the known environmental threats.

We also need to prepare for the worst. If the imminent existentialists are correct, then Earth will undergo massive change. The question is whether this will be a big event as typically depicted by Hollywood, where the floods and earthquakes happen within a few days, or if rising seas will be gradual over decades or centuries? The far more likely scenario is a gradual change, giving us more time to react and respond. As we hit new heat records in the last decade, we have not experienced significant climate shocks. We have always had climate-related catastrophes, which are now more economic than life-threatening. Potential problems are drought and floods in some areas, but new opportunities become available elsewhere.

Just as capital moves globally to where it is most useful, so will humans, as we have done for millennia and continue to do to this day. People move because of war, poverty, oppression, and shortages, and maybe environmental conditions will join this list in the future. It is relatively inexpensive to absorb new immigrants if our processes for legal migration and taxation are corrected. Migration planning should be a major focus of environmental policy as the most humane and cost-effective solution available to address the climate crisis. This will allow the emerging world to develop naturally and to preserve the wealth of the developed world to fight the climate war. This is much more rational than spending trillions on preventing temperature increases with unscalable technologies in their current offerings.

Through good messaging, America can build unity around environmental infrastructure and preparedness.

We believe in environmental infrastructure insurance to prevent damage from potentially harmful environmental changes. While the free-market transitions over time to 100 percent renewable energy sources that can be produced as affordably and abundantly as fossil fuels to preserve our growing economy and keep inflation in check, we can build infrastructure to minimize the loss of lives and damage to property from climate-related events. This includes hardening our energy grids from weather-related events, securing our coastal cities from floods and wind, and helping our heartland to survive tornados and droughts. Infrastructure spending on prevention will reduce the need to budget for environmental remediation in the future and will save lives. Where infrastructure is not affordable or practical, we must increase our preparedness to respond quickly to climate-related events and human migration.

Environmentalism has become a religion to many and cannot be ignored if we are to unify the country and implement rational policy. As emotional as environmentalism has become, there is an even more hotly contested issue out there. Now we will discuss immigration.

16

COMPETITION FOR GLOBAL TALENT

*Every aspect of the American economy has profited from
the contributions of immigrants.*

— John F. Kennedy, Massachusetts senator,
A Nation of Immigrants, 1958

There is perhaps no issue more divisive in the United States than
immigration. Immigration is foundational to the American
Unity Plan. We want and need more legal immigration for
many reasons. Primarily, the American Unity Plan provides the
mechanism for immigrants to subsidize American citizens to reduce
our tax burden. Unlike our population predictions of the past, we
can absorb many more people than we have now in the US as we
have abundant energy, shelter, food, and even jobs. What we are
lacking is not just people to fill jobs but the global talent needed

to build the America of tomorrow. Talent is not just a matter of economics but also of national security.

In the American Unity Plan, immigrants receive no Unity Income benefits from the federal government until they become American citizens. However, immigrants and visitors pay taxes on every product and service bought via the American Unity Tax. In effect, immigrants and visitors pay proportionately more in taxes than American citizens, who receive income to offset potentially higher product and service prices.

In the context of the American Unity Plan, the more people who become American citizens, the worse the economics due to Unity Income, unless the naturalized citizen has a positive return on investment by paying more in federal taxes through their purchases than they receive in Unity Income. Employment and US spending can be integrated into the requirements for American citizenship. Putting moral issues aside for asylum seekers and others who dream of a better life, legal and sponsored immigration leading to naturalization simply will have a better economic result for America than unsponsored, illegal immigration. Sponsored immigration requires a purpose beneficial to America—education leading to employment in the US, founding a business leading to wealth and job creation, companies filling needed skill sets, and charitable organizations providing guidance and a head start in a new country.

Despite the politics on immigration on both sides, what America does better than any country is assimilate those new to our shores into our American customs and laws without losing their sense of birth culture and history. When assimilation fails in the United States, it is due to lack of sponsorship by Americans, and mostly this is caused by illegal immigration. There is already a global population shift from emerging economies to the US and Europe, whether due to political oppression, climate change, or simply the desire for better opportunity in life. This population shift to the US will exacerbate our debt issues by providing services that are unfunded either at the federal or state level. Under the American Unity Plan, we simply need more people in the US to solve our debt insolvency crises.

Sponsors provide a free-market solution to immigration. Other than charitable organizations, sponsors will match supply to market demand for goods and services. The supply of opportunity is literally endless for those seeking a better life in America. Sponsors provide a real-time regulation of imminent need matching new talent and skills to market demand. Sponsors will do a much better job than federal bureaucrats allocating immigration visas. Sponsors are in a better position than any government organization to evaluate the current needs of the employment market to the available supply of talent. They are in a better position to assess whether retraining of specific people is possible or new immigrants with the required skills are needed in the US. In Europe, companies can be responsible for lifetime employment and are mandated to have much higher benefits. European companies are loath to hire and have implemented automation in many industries to spend on capital rather than labor because of their social commitments. Europe generally has a much higher unemployment level than America.

Many argue that increasing immigration takes jobs from American workers. In addition, previous studies have shown that sponsored immigration, under our current system, has not been any more or less beneficial economically to the immigrant. Other studies have shown that immigration has a net benefit because immigrants have a higher rate of business and job creation. Whatever your position, under the current system, we have reached full employment for many years and need to try a different approach to both fill needed jobs and grow GDP and the tax base.

We have seen automation replace many jobs, from low-skilled workers to higher-wage earners such as programmers. Yet, the unemployment rate remains low. First, the unemployment rate does not matter compared to the talent deficit. If there are almost ten million jobs available and there are millions of people unwilling or unable to fill them, whether due to geography or skills limitations, we must look to global talent. The result of not doing so is inflationary at home, and continuing to outsource jobs overseas takes capital investment and tax base with it. From an employment point of view, it is not about wages but productivity. The right talent, matching skills with the required work, improves productivity.

In America, we compete much more with intellectual capital than other nations. We create and innovate, and immigrants are a key component to our leadership. However, this benefits highly skilled and white-collar professionals much more than semiskilled, blue-collar, and entry-level work. By eliminating corporate and payroll taxes, the American Unity Plan lowers the base cost of labor for business to keep more jobs at home in a less inflationary environment. If countries lower their wages to continue to be competitive with the US and keep the jobs outsourced to them at home, this is at least disinflationary to the US consumer. Either way, America benefits.

Under the American Unity Plan, there is no downside for increased immigration. We are only limited by the number of qualified and willing sponsors. Sponsors can absorb the market risk of failure—status reporting, social costs such as healthcare and potentially housing, and other expenses currently funded by the American people at both the federal and state level. Sponsorship is a commitment to both the immigrant and the country. If more people pay the Unity Tax and fewer people receive federal benefits, it is disinflationary, as Congress will be positioned to maintain the lowest possible Unity Tax rate necessary for a balanced or surplus budget to reduce the national debt.

In fact, America should seek out the best talent in the world. Would it be a good or bad thing if tens of millions of top Chinese and Russian talent immigrated to the United States under their own free will, with no restrictions on length of stay, business ownership, and capital investment so long as they followed our laws (including, of course, laws pertaining to national security and intellectual theft)? These individuals are different from, say, a business owned by the Chinese Communist Party acquiring US land or business interests. Companies recruit top talent from their competitors all the time. Why not let sponsors identify the best global talent? What is better for humanity—to have one billion people living under Communist Chinese rule and three hundred million people living in America, or many more people living under American-style democracy, increasing our ability to compete globally?

Before the pandemic, there were over one million foreign students attending American universities, with those from China and India accounting for more than half. They send their best and brightest to be educated in America. They are encouraged by US colleges and universities because foreign students pay more in tuition than US citizens as well as stimulate local economies. So long as a student is not a security risk and has something to add to America, why would we not want them to stay and build businesses, raise families, work, and invest here? From an economics perspective, this is equivalent to business travelers on expense accounts subsidizing the plane fare of coach passengers on vacation. It is a free benefit to the US, so long as our laws are followed and a sponsor can attest for the individual.

We must create immigration policies that encourage the best and brightest to immigrate and stay regardless of country of origin. Current immigration policy is convoluted. Between six hundred thousand and one million people become US citizens every year. Is this enough given our declining birth rate and low unemployment rate leading to inflation? By limiting beneficial American citizenship resulting from constraining immigrant populations, we are both incentivizing illegal immigration and losing potential talent important to our success. There are so many bureaucratic and arcane rules, it is disincentivizing legal immigration. Future entrepreneurs, scientists, doctors, and engineers must deal with the B-1, E-2, H-1B, L-1, O-1, and OPT visa alphabet soup. In addition, we give temporary worker status for certain industries. We need to open the talent and self-sufficiency floodgates by first addressing legal immigration and then citizenship.

To apply for an immigrant visa, a foreign citizen now must be sponsored, usually by an American citizen or employer, but there are quotas. Quotas and price controls are contrary to free-market capitalism and American principles, as they give advantage to one group or person over another. We grant fewer than 1 million permanent immigrant visas per year across the various categories, but without limits to the immediate families of American citizens. US immigration law is based on the following hierarchy: the reunification of families, admitting immigrants with skills that are valuable to the US economy, protecting refugees, and promoting diversity. Do we want the federal government dictating what skills American industry needs? If sponsors are willing, why do we need quotas?

The old argument that immigrants compete for American jobs is false under the right policy. If you believe in economic growth as the way to create wealth and jobs, then you want the top talent to start businesses, innovate, invest, build, hire, and grow the economy. Hopefully, they become American citizens one day following a streamlined legal process. In the meantime, they are living and working in the US, paying taxes, and by law receiving nothing in return but our thanks.

Are there limits to the number of people America can accept? Maybe, but those limits for legal immigration need to be set by the free market, not politicians. The politicians should focus only on American citizenship restrictions as part of the budgeting process and ensure laws are followed for border protection and sponsorship. The necessities of life are food, clothing, transportation, shelter, and energy. The world has an abundance of all, and America leads the way. The problem is logistics. We need more people living in freedom under the rule of law, where the abundant necessities are produced safely with environmental and workplace standards, and less people living under Communist and authoritarian regimes, with artificial limits controlled by government policy and rationing. Any discussions in the past of "resource limits" are wrong and have often ended in genocide (for example, China's one child rule and their famine from centralized food planning).

If we apply free-market economics to legal immigration, might too many immigrants take jobs from American citizens? Potentially, as occurs now, especially with illegal immigration impacting the poor more than middle-income workers. The people that are most hurt are those who have the least skills, but we can review this from both a supply and demand point of view.

Lower-skilled American citizens will be supplemented by Unity Income, giving them a competitive advantage over their legal immigrant competitors if they want to take advantage of this American citizen benefit. Many of these entry-level jobs are required to build skills for advancement or supplement their income while in school. Unity Income provides the safety net to give economic advantage to US citizens competing against immigrant workers. Where employers fail to attract US talent, they will sponsor legal immigrants. Yes, they could, and some would, pay less to sponsored immigrants than American citizens, but sponsorship also has costs and responsibilities.

The supply of lower-wage workers who will come to the US will decrease unless employers increase wages. Without wage increases, the cost of living in the US will be higher for lower-wage immigrants than American citizens. Higher-wage immigrants can more readily absorb the slightly higher cost of products and services with the Unity Tax. However, under the American Unity Plan, the elimination of the corporate income tax will incentivize many more companies to return business to our shores. As we have seen with the great resignation after the pandemic, the increase in the number of jobs available increases wages. This makes it more attractive for people to work here, whether American citizen or immigrant.

Over time, the market will define the equilibrium of optimal immigration and Congress can decide whether to increase American citizenship levels. America wins when immigration is legal, voluntary, unconstrained by bureaucracy, and focused on attracting the best global talent. We must unite under a rational immigration strategy. If immigrants came here voluntarily because there were jobs the market needed filled, what would be the downside of opening the spigot? More immigrants would pay the Unity Tax as legal residents of America buying retail goods and services. They would be ineligible to receive a single dollar of federal support unless they become citizens and would have sponsors to ensure assimilation and additional safeguards for compliance with our laws. This is a totally voluntary system with only the free market setting the upper limit of how many people enter and when. We have no shortage of land, energy, food, medicine, clothing, housing, transportation, or people willing to help when the free market meets the demand without government interference.

Why would we not want the best from China, Africa, Iraq, Afghanistan, Venezuela, Russia, Cuba, and many more places where talent exists but is stifled by repressive governments with no opportunity for freedom and success? Strip these repressive countries of their most precious resource—talented people! Even if this talent eventually returned home, they would have contributed to our economy without putting negative rights on American citizens, and more importantly, they would have tasted freedom, maybe importing it to their homeland. With a free-market immigration policy, the vast majority would stay and start businesses, develop the next breakthrough innovations, and hire American talent.

Innovation is America's biggest competitive advantage. Green card rules as applied to entrepreneurs are archaic. For founders, it takes years to build a company. Incentivize them to stay, become citizens, and hire Americans. America is disproportionately represented by foreign founders as business owners and patent holders. As a group, they are self-sufficient instead of government reliant. The reality is that the American welfare state has turned many more of our citizens than necessary into government dependents, whereas most non-European immigrants grow up needing to be self-sufficient.

Centralized immigration planning of human resources for the free market is a failure, as centralized planning and control of food, energy, medicines, transportation, and every other valuable resource is destined for failure. Why do we care *why* someone is coming to America so long as they are a net benefit bringing ideas, talent, and desire to our country legally?

It takes years under the current system to get a green card and even longer to become an American citizen. Why do we allocate instead of letting the free market decide who is needed here and when? Put the onus on the sponsor and the immigrant working together. Why would we limit the number of medical professionals and staff who choose to come here, so long as they are sponsored by a hospital, medical practice, or local community? Why would we limit private equity firms and venture capitalists from sponsoring global entrepreneurs? Why do we limit the number of engineers that technology, defense, and manufacturing firms employ? Why do we restrict locals who helped us fight wars overseas when we have veterans groups willing to help? Talent does not mean only degreed professionals. What government planner could have predicted a shortage of truck drivers, dock workers, daycare and restaurant workers? These skills exist globally, and many willing workers could be sponsored by companies right now to solve critical US labor shortage problems. Does our government really think so poorly of Americans' ability to compete that we need job protections?

The concept of sponsorship is embedded in immigration law. The role of the federal government should be to make sure everyone enters the country legally and poses no threat to American society. The immigrant must register, just as an American citizen is "registered" at birth with a Social Security card. This allows the federal government to perform background checks and ensure the sponsor is responsible for the immigrant. We can eliminate all types of visas, quotas, limits, programs, and bureaucracy. The rules for entry should be simply "known, safe, and sponsored." Stay, abide by our laws, and do your best!

We want people wishing to immigrate to this country, whether temporarily or permanently, to be sponsored, as this is more compassionate and accountable than centralized government monitoring. CFOs need to attest to the accuracy of their financial statements. What if sponsors had to attest to the status of the immigrants they sponsored? Sponsors can attest immigrants are working, enrolled, and progressing in America. Sponsors could ensure immigrants have healthcare insurance to mitigate the risk to our healthcare systems. Both are particularly important for asylum seekers, family members, and others here for humanitarian reasons. In other words, sponsors are people who know and care about the immigrant and provide guidance to follow our laws, learn our culture and customs, and assimilate into society without causing undue burden to American taxpayers.

The last thing this country needs is to emulate Europe and create enclaves of refugee communities subsidized by taxpayers. We need diversity of talent, with many customs and cultures assimilating into the US culture as we have had historically. Wherever possible, we need to avoid segregating first-generation immigrant communities. Sponsorship and motive to assimilate are essential to continued American progress. We expect those arriving here to be self-sufficient over time, and sponsorship provides the bridge. Eventual American citizenship and its benefits are the prize at the end of a journey.

Both federal and state governments could set the rules for "qualified sponsorship." If a family wishes to bring relatives into the US, it is not unreasonable to ask the family to provide for the immigrant with no government assistance. If we can mandate vaccines and masks, would it be unreasonable to mandate a sponsor provide healthcare and education? There is no shortage of charities that would sponsor, and local charities give immigrants the best chance of success. No American would have a problem with increased legal immigration if we knew that no immigrant put negative rights on the American taxpayer and there was a path to compassionate assimilation.

The concept of qualified sponsorship also provides an advantage for American citizens in the workforce. With Unity Income, it is likely that employers will reduce healthcare and retirement benefits for workers by simply paying them more and eliminating the cost and burden of managing these benefits. However, since immigrants are not eligible for Unity Income, employer sponsors may have to provide this benefit to immigrants, increasing their total cost of employment compared to American citizens. In addition, regardless of how they are paid, many immigrants remit their earnings to their home countries. Maybe these wealth transfers should be taxed at the Unity Tax rate since the money was earned in the US and not spent, saved, or invested here.

Our politicians do need to address the millions who have entered this country illegally, but to build unity, this could be part of a bold, comprehensive plan to increase legal immigration to achieve other goals, such as funding the social safety net, reducing inflation, and avoiding stagflation. The idea of blanket immunity is a failed concept. Using American principles, we can neither accommodate nor give preferential treatment to those who broke the law, regardless of the humanitarian reason, over those who followed the law. The idea of providing a benefit above and beyond the requirements for legal entry confers negative rights on all legal immigrants and American citizens alike.

The American principles of fairness, equality under the law, and reasonable accommodation must apply to past immigration mistakes. Every American who has contributed to the infrastructure and defense of our country understands that immigrants must contribute before receiving the benefits and opportunities of living in America. Current illegal immigrants living in the United States must be registered and sponsored. We are compassionate and can decide as a nation if illegal immigrants who register and have broken no other laws (other than entering the country illegally) can be eligible for continuing to reside in the US and maybe eventually gaining US citizenship. But in the interim, registration and sponsorship afford better assimilation than living under the radar. In fact, support to stop illegal immigration will grow if we integrate free-market legal immigration as part and parcel of the American Unity Plan.

Democrats and Republicans can unite on legal immigration as an issue, and hopefully stop illegal immigration in our lifetimes. The message will be resounding across the political spectrum.

We will bring the world's best talent to America to start businesses, perform critical jobs, and contribute to our economy by paying the American Unity Tax. No immigrants will be eligible for federal benefits until they become American citizens. We will drastically expand legal immigration using free-market American principles without preference to country of origin, religion, skill sets, family status, or other artificial quotas. We will improve our ability to humanely support those freeing repressive governments and seeking the opportunities America has to offer. Every immigrant will be supported by a sponsor to ensure they thrive and assimilate into American culture, working toward self-sufficiency. Anyone who has previously entered or will enter our country will be registered to ensure they are safe and sponsored.

Legal, sponsored immigration is needed at drastically higher levels to fight inflation, save our social safety net promises from bankruptcy, balance the budget, and pay down the national debt as part of the American Unity Plan. We cannot build unity to fight these problems on the path we are currently heading in with immigration. Increased levels of legal immigration can be a unifying argument, as both Republicans and Democrats will want the increased tax base and sponsorship process.

The focus and resolution of the current immigration debates are not prerequisites to the bigger economic and social issues that increased legal immigration can solve. We must make it easier for legal, global migration to attract the best talent to America. More legal immigration will help to end illegal immigration, as the incentive to break the law will be diminished. The constraints should be only on citizenship, not legal entry to reside in the US. Under the American Unity Plan, using free-market principles, self-sufficiency will be the driving force of American immigration, with legal immigrants and sponsors working together to assimilate using their natural talents.

Finally, we will put everything we've discussed together. How do we build a coalition to achieve unity?

CONCLUSION
ACHIEVING UNITY

History, faith and reason show the way, the way of unity. We can see each other, not as adversaries, but as neighbors. We can treat each other with dignity and respect. We can join forces, stop the shouting and lower the temperature. For without unity, there is no peace, only bitterness and fury. No progress, only exhausting outrage. No nation, only a state of chaos. This is our historic moment of crisis and challenge and unity is the path forward. And we must meet this moment as the United States of America. If we do that, I guarantee you we will not fail. We have never, ever, ever failed in America when we've acted together."

— President Joe Biden, Inaugural Address,
January 20, 2021

P olicy changes around the edges are dangerous. We all want to compromise, hoping that agreement equals societal improvement. However, we have separated into political and social factions with very little compromise.

Progressives are bold. They tell you exactly what they are going to do and implement plans incrementally and consistently over generations. Republicans compromise on their conservative principles when not in power and try to hold steady when in control, as they have no bold solutions or plans of their own.

The American Unity Plan is about uniting the American people around a bold solution that crosses party lines by including stated objectives from both major parties. For Republicans, it is about constraining the power and size of the federal government that negatively impacts our lives and freedoms. For Democrats, it is about expanding the social safety net with a new and fair version of Universal Basic Income while eliminating crony capitalism and closing the wealth gap for the poorest Americans. More importantly, it requires the federal government to refocus on American principles and on the few things it is mandated to do to restore our freedoms.

Imagine you had to start over with nothing but the Constitution in hand. How would you design a modern system to tax fairly and inexpensively, while creating a better social safety net? Can healthcare outcomes be improved while giving all Americans an opportunity for medical security? Can education be reformed to give all Americans a greater chance at economic success at a much lower cost per student? Would we require a balanced budget except under the most severe national security emergencies? How would we use immigration to our advantage, as we have historically, to build prosperity and improve national security? How do we solve climate change without causing undue hardship and rampant inflation?

Certainly, the current systems would not be the starting point. We seem to endure despite ourselves, yet as factions widen and politicians are fearful of losing power, we have evidence of impending peril. Inflation is rising, and the national debt is out of control. Social Security and Medicare are going bankrupt. We need bold change built on America's strengths—freedom, liberty, equality under the law, risk-taking, and innovation. The American Unity Plan:

- Eliminates the current tax code and replaces it with a federal tax on all goods and services only at the retail point of purchase, without exception. Unlike a flat tax, it reduces federal control of our lives by making taxes voluntary, transparent, and anonymous while eliminating crony capitalism. It eliminates the imbedded tax and compliance cost of goods and services and provides a mechanism to balance government tax receipts against spending. It abides by the American principles of fairness and equality under the law, ensuring all Americans and immigrants contribute proportionately to their spending ability.

- Eliminates all federal subsidies and benefits in favor of Unity Income. The goal is to build generational wealth for Americans and eliminate government dependency. It improves healthcare outcomes while reducing costs. It frees our children from government-run education to give greater opportunities in life to more Americans. It provides a modern social safety net, applied equally to all Americans, and transitions over generations to ensure no one is harmed during implementation.

- Brings jobs and capital back to the United States, allowing us to significantly increase legal immigration, improve national security, and fight climate change while keeping inflation and government spending under control to balance the budget.

- Reorganizes the federal government to reduce its size, cost, and bureaucratic control over our lives while returning control to the states, where care is more compassionate. It provides real-world solutions to economic growth while ensuring reasonable accommodation and no negative rights during implementation.

In short, the American Unity Plan is about freedom under uniquely American principles. It is a new direction. It is designed to unify America to drive change and compromise by combining bold policy with compassionate messaging. It requires the courage to propose bold solutions and follow through over decades. As with anything new, there will be short-term disruptions, potentially to prices, supply chains, immigration, climate policy, and more. We deal with recessions, debt limits, and underfunded social systems every few years and manage to move forward. Now, we have a looming debt crisis with no long-term path to a balanced budget or saving Social Security and Medicare. The Federal Reserve may not be able to stimulate our way out of a recession in the future, so the sooner we act, the better.

When the American Unity Plan is implemented, Congress will have to set both the Unity Income benefit to Americans and the Unity Tax rate on all retail spending. We know they will get this exactly wrong. We know once they set the tax rate, it will be much easier to lower than raise. They will avoid a "read my lips, no new taxes" moment. If the Unity Tax rate is set high enough, and the Unity Income level is relatively modest, the federal budget could be in balance in short order. This will reduce the cost of borrowing and give the means for future Congresses to agree on tax cuts that help the poor more and fight inflation, when all goods and services are taxed equally.

We can no longer take an incremental approach to solve problems at this scale. The law of unintended consequences creates other issues that may or may not be worse than our current dilemma. We cannot solve climate change without addressing the cost, energy supply, and national security. We cannot increase immigration without addressing the tax base, unemployment, and social unrest. We cannot close the wealth gap by creating generational government dependency, but rather the poorest among us need a chance for a better life through education and investment. The American Unity Plan is a holistic approach addressing many major needs simultaneously.

It appears the art of political compromise has been permanently severed. Each party wants to "win," while America loses and becomes more divided. We have seen how Republican tax cuts without spending offsets increase the national debt. We have witnessed how Democrat federal healthcare plans and mandates limit consumer choice and increase healthcare costs while still millions go without coverage. We cannot compromise to add Unity Income on top of the current social programs disguised as Universal Basic Income. This will explode the budget and do nothing to solve the insolvency of Social Security and Medicare or the failed government education system. We cannot compromise to increase legal immigration without changing the tax code to ensure jobs and capital repatriate to the US and tax receipts are increased to fund the social safety net. We cannot propose new spending on environmental infrastructure without insisting on a balanced budget and reducing the risk of stagflation.

The American Unity Plan is a holistic solution. Both parties need to compromise to solve the problem. Moderates, libertarians, and independents will see benefits that are supported by both parties. Here is how each major political party will win:

Social Safety Net:

- Democrats and progressives: Implement a form of Universal Basic Income called Unity Income.
- Republicans and conservatives: Medicare and Social Security solvency without raising taxes and equal payments only to American citizens.

Wealth Gap:

- Democrats and progressives: Poorest Americans increase savings, invest in their financial futures, and improve access to credit.

- Republicans and conservatives: Eliminate all taxes on savings, income, and investment.

Education:

- Democrats and progressives: Increased federal funding with a primary focus on increasing opportunities for the disadvantaged.
- Republicans and conservatives: Public school privatization and choice directed by parents and sponsors.

Healthcare:

- Democrats and progressives: All Americans able to secure healthcare based on their needs; improved healthcare outcomes for the disadvantaged.
- Republicans and conservatives: Reduced healthcare costs with increased transparency and patient control.

Climate Change:

- Democrats and progressives: Spending on infrastructure and improved responses to future climate catastrophes.
- Republicans and conservatives: Time to transition to clean energy without destroying the budget and the US energy sector.

Immigration:

- Democrats and progressives: Dramatically increased immigration levels and increased humanitarian support through sponsorship.
- Republicans and conservatives: Immigrants paying proportionately more to fund the federal government than American citizens.

National Security:

- Democrats and progressives: In the short-term, defense as a smaller percentage of federal spending by increasing social safety net spending.
- Republicans and conservatives: Refocus on the national security role of the federal government, and repatriation of critical industries to the US.

Federalism:

- Democrats and progressives: New $2 trillion in social spending, benefiting the poorest Americans more while not favoring Republican over Democrat states in the tax code.
- Republicans and conservatives: Reduced intrusion and control of our lives; ability for states to experiment and provide services locally without federal mandates; return to the constitutional role of the federal government.

Federal Spending:

- Democrats and progressives: Increased federal tax receipts supporting increased government spending on social safety net programs.
- Republicans and conservatives: Path to a balanced budget regardless of federal government spending by annual legislation on Unity Tax and Unity Income rates.

Taxes:

- Democrats and progressives: Maintain highly progressive tax system by eliminating tax incentives, crony capitalism, tax cheats, and fraud; increased number of people paying taxes.
- Republicans and conservatives: Freedom from the IRS and excessive reporting and regulation.

Inflation:

- Democrats and progressives: Protection of the poor with Unity Income.
- Republicans and conservatives: Elimination of government waste, fraud, and tax compliance costs to reduce the embedded cost of products and services.

Freedom:

- Democrats and progressives: Equal protection under the law.
- Republicans and conservatives: Payment of taxes fairly, anonymously, and voluntarily.

Ideally, our leaders would compromise their ideologies and work together to solve these monumental problems. If there can be consensus to transition to a plan this bold, the ideal solution would also include a balanced budget amendment; a repeal of the Sixteenth Amendment, eliminating the current tax system; and codifying the Unity Income and Unity Tax, with the rate to be set annually by Congress. Are there modern leaders with the courage and conviction, the generational stamina, and the vision to propose and articulate a new direction?

SOURCES

Where possible, unbiased government or politically neutral sources were used for baseline facts. Progressive and conservative sources and perspectives were researched to formulate policies and solutions, as well as to develop messaging seeking to build unity. These sources are relevant to the topics in the American Unity Plan but are not necessarily recommended reading.

Introduction: The Need for Unity

Vital Statistics on Congress. (2022, November 29). *Brookings.* https://www.brookings.edu/multi-chapter-report/vital-statistics-on-congress/

Dimock, M., & Wike, R. (2021). America Is Exceptional in Its Political Divide. *The Pew Charitable Trusts.* https://www.pewtrusts.org/en/trust/archive/winter-2021/america-is-exceptional-in-its-political-divide#:~:text=This%2047%2Dpercentage%2Dpoint%20gap,the%2013%20other%20nations%20surveyed

Burnett, J. (2022, February 18). Americans are fleeing to places where political views match their own. *NPR.* https://www.npr.

org/2022/02/18/1081295373/the-big-sort-americans-move-to-areas-political-alignment

Smith, D. (2022, January 10). Is the US really heading for a second civil war? *The Guardian.* https://www.theguardian.com/us-news/2022/jan/09/is-the-us-really-heading-for-a-second-civil-war

CBS News. (2022, February 20). How free speech is under attack in the U.S. *CBS News.* https://www.cbsnews.com/news/how-free-speech-is-under-attack-in-the-u-s/

Report, C. P., Report, C. P., & Report, C. P. (2022). What Do Voters Want: Confrontation or Compassion? | Cook Political Report. *Cook Political Report.* https://www.cookpolitical.com/analysis/national/national-politics/what-do-voters-want-confrontation-or-compassion

Thrush, G. (2021, September 9). Why Biden Can Undo Much of Trump's Legacy Via Executive Orders. *The New York Times.* https://www.nytimes.com/2021/01/22/us/politics/biden-executive-orders-trump.html

1. American Principles – Uniter or Divider?

Oxford Languages and Google - English | Oxford Languages. (2022, August 12). https://languages.oup.com/google-dictionary-en/

Charities Aid Foundation. (n.d.). *World Giving Index 2022 | CAF.* https://www.cafonline.org/about-us/publications/2022-publications/caf-world-giving-index-2022#:~:text=The%20most%20generous%20country%20in,ever%20donated%20money%20in%202021

Pandey, E. (2022, March 12). America the generous: U.S. leads globe in giving. *Axios.* https://www.axios.com/2022/03/09/america-charitable-giving-stats-ukraine

2. It Is Fair to Accommodate Fairness

Crews, C. W., Jr. (2020, February 18). We're Not Biased, We're Liberals: How Cultural Leftism Will Slant Social Media Regulation. *Forbes.* https://www.forbes.com/sites/waynecrews/2020/02/17/were-not-biased-were-liberals-how-cultural-leftism-will-slant-social-media-regulation/?sh=86b44d0503c2

The Liberal Media:Every Poll Shows Journalists Are More Liberal than the American Public — And the Public Knows It. (n.d.). Media Research Center. https://www.mrc.org/liberal-mediaevery-poll-shows-journalists-are-more-liberal-american-public-and-public-knows-it

Record Breaking Turnout in Georgia's Runoff Election | Georgia Secretary of State. (n.d.). https://www.sos.ga.gov/news/record-breaking-turnout-georgias-runoff-election

Alexander, A. (2022, December 10). Effect of Georgia's voting law unclear, despite high turnout. *AP NEWS.* https://apnews.com/article/2022-midterm-elections-georgia-state-government-89b374bfafdba5b673a46b240a5e3e1f

Potter Stewart. (n.d.). The First Amendment Encyclopedia. https://www.mtsu.edu/first-amendment/article/1359/potter-stewart

What is Communism? Definition of Communism, Communism Meaning - The Economic Times. (n.d.). The Economic Times. https://economictimes.indiatimes.com/definition/communism

Stewart, M. (2021). The pros and cons of universal basic income. *College of Arts and Sciences.* https://college.unc.edu/2021/03/universal-basic-income/

Positive and Negative Liberty (Stanford Encyclopedia of Philosophy). (2021, November 19). https://plato.stanford.edu/entries/liberty-positive-negative/

How to Destroy America in Three Easy Steps: Shapiro, Ben: 9780063001879: Amazon.com: Books. (n.d.). https://www.amazon.com/Destroy-America-Three-Easy-Steps/dp/006300187X

Judge rules against Kentucky clerk who denied same-sex marriage licenses. (2022, March 21). NBC News. https://www.nbcnews.com/nbc-out/out-news/judge-rules-kentucky-clerk-denied-sex-marriage-licenses-rcna20858

Supreme Court gives victory to baker who refused to make cake for same-sex wedding. (2018, June 4). [Video]. NBC News. https://www.nbcnews.com/politics/supreme-court/narrow-ruling-supreme-court-gives-victory-baker-who-refused-make-n872946

Americans with Disabilities Act. (n.d.). DOL. https://www.dol.gov/general/topic/disability/ada

Interpretation: The Equal Protection Clause | Constitution Center. (n.d.). National Constitution Center – constitutioncenter.org. https://constitutioncenter.org/the-constitution/amendments/amendment-xiv/clauses/702

FindLaw. (2022, July 27). *The Tenth Amendment - Reserving Power for the States.* Findlaw. https://constitution.findlaw.com/amendment10.html

14ᵗʰ Amendment. (n.d.). LII / Legal Information Institute. https://www.law.cornell.edu/constitution/amendmentxiv

Understanding the 14 Amendment's Equal Protection Clause. (n.d.). http://constitutionallawreporter.com/amendment-14-01/equal-protection-clause/

Krishan, N. (2022, February 10). Washington Examiner. *Washington Examiner*. https://www.washingtonexaminer.com/policy/cancel-culture-pressure-ramps-up-on-tech-platforms-spotify-airbnb-and-gofundme

What you should know about Section 230, the rule that shaped today's internet. (2023, February 21). PBS NewsHour. https://www.pbs.org/newshour/politics/what-you-should-know-about-section-230-the-rule-that-shaped-todays-internet#:~:text=That's%20thanks%20to%20Section%20230,by%20another%20information%20content%20provider.%E2%80%9D

FindLaw. (2022a, July 18). *Defamation and False Statements Under the First Amendment*. Findlaw. https://constitution.findlaw.com/amendment1/defamation-and-false-statements-under-the-first-amendment.html

Castro, A. J. D. (2021, February 22). *Overview of Section 230: What It Is, Why It Was Created, and What It Has Achieved*. ITIF. https://itif.org/publications/2021/02/22/overview-section-230-what-it-why-it-was-created-and-what-it-has-achieved/

Spacey, J. (n.d.). *13 Examples of Crony Capitalism*. Simplicable. https://simplicable.com/en/crony-capitalism

3. The Great Political Compromise – Policy and Principle

7 Core Principles of Conservatism | *U.S. Congressman Mike Johnson.* (2023, April 25). https://mikejohnson.house.gov/7-core-principles-of-conservatism/

Times, P. (2018, March 25). Principles of a Modern Progressive Movement - The Progressive Times - Medium. *Medium.* https://medium.com/tptimes/principles-of-a-modern-progressive-movement-a2c3f9e5d25a

https://www.axios.com/2023/04/17/poll-americans-independent-republican-democrat

Overview | *Progressive Era to New Era, 1900-1929* | *U.S. History Primary Source Timeline* | *Classroom Materials at the Library of Congress* | *Library of Congress.* (n.d.). The Library of Congress. https://www.loc.gov/classroom-materials/united-states-history-primary-source-timeline/progressive-era-to-new-era-1900-1929/overview/

Grunwald, M. (2016, December 4). *The Victory of 'No.'* POLITICO Magazine. https://www.politico.com/magazine/story/2016/12/republican-party-obstructionism-victory-trump-214498/

Younge, G. (2020, February 26). How being "the party of no" is working for the GOP. *The Guardian.* https://www.theguardian.com/commentisfree/cifamerica/2012/may/14/how-being-party-of-no-working-for-gop

4. Bold Solutions Revisited

What Was the New Deal? | *Living New Deal.* (2019, August 28). Living New Deal. https://livingnewdeal.org/what-was-the-new-deal/

The Great Society - Bill of Rights Institute. (n.d.). Bill of Rights Institute. https://billofrightsinstitute.org/essays/the-great-society

Summary of the Affordable Care Act. (2018, December 17). KFF. https://www.kff.org/health-reform/fact-sheet/summary-of-the-affordable-care-act/

What is "Medicare for All" and how would it work? (2019, June 20). NBC News. https://www.nbcnews.com/politics/elections/what-medicare-all-how-would-it-work-n1014256

https://judiciary.house.gov/media/press-releases/us-house-judiciary-republicans-doj-labeled-dozens-of-parents-as-terrorist

What Is a Green New Deal? (n.d.). Sierra Club. https://www.sierraclub.org/trade/what-green-new-deal

How economists see Biden's $15 wage proposal. (2021, February 17). PBS NewsHour. https://www.pbs.org/newshour/health/how-economists-see-bidens-15-wage-proposal

House, W. (2022). FACT SHEET: President Biden Announces Student Loan Relief for Borrowers Who Need It Most. *The White House.* https://www.whitehouse.gov/briefing-room/statements-releases/2022/08/24/fact-sheet-president-biden-announces-student-loan-relief-for-borrowers-who-need-it-most/

Gayner, J. (n.d.). *The Contract with America: Implementing New Ideas in the U.S. | The Heritage Foundation.* The Heritage Foundation. https://www.heritage.org/political-process/report/the-contract-america-implementing-new-ideas-the-us

StructureCMS. (2021, April 8). How FAIRtax Works. *FAIRtax.* https://fairtax.org/about/how-fairtax-works

Peters, J. W. (2019, August 30). The Tea Party Didn't Get What It Wanted, but It Did Unleash the Politics of Anger. *The New*

York Times. https://www.nytimes.com/2019/08/28/us/politics/tea-party-trump.html

TPC: The Number Of Those Who Don't Pay Federal Income Tax Drops To. (2022, October 27). Tax Policy Center. https://www.taxpolicycenter.org/taxvox/tpc-number-those-who-dont-pay-federal-income-tax-drops-pre-pandemic-levels

Statista. (2022, November 2). *U.S. households that paid no income tax 2022, by income level.* https://statista.com/statistics/242138/percentages-of-us-households-that-pay-no-income-tax-by-income-level/

What Happened to Health Care Reform? (n.d.). https://www.princeton.edu/~starr/20starr.html

Harvard Health. (2016, June 27). *Single payer healthcare: Pluses, minuses, and what it means for you.* https://www.health.harvard.edu/blog/single-payer-healthcare-pluses-minuses-means-201606279835

Engels, K. M. a. F. (n.d.). *Manifesto of the Communist Party.* https://www.marxists.org/archive/marx/works/1848/communist-manifesto/

Bandow, D. (2017, April 6). A Century Ago Woodrow Wilson Took America Into WWI: Blame Him For Communism, Fascism And Nazism. *Forbes.* https://www.forbes.com/sites/dougbandow/2017/04/06/a-century-ago-woodrow-wilson-took-america-into-wwi-blame-him-for-communism-fascism-and-nazism/?sh=22b7097868e2

Engels, K. M. a. F. (n.d.-a). *Communist Manifesto (Chapter 2).* https://www.marxists.org/archive/marx/works/1848/communist-manifesto/ch02.htm

Today, S. S. U. (2019, October 29). Here's how much land the government owns in your state. *WLST.* https://www.usatoday.com/

story/money/2019/10/29/how-much-land-government-owns-in-every-state/40453833/

Summary of the Latest Federal Income Tax Data. (2023, March 31). Tax Foundation. https://taxfoundation.org/publications/latest-federal-income-tax-data/#:~:text=The%20top%201%20percent%20of%20taxpayers%20(AGI%20of%20%24548%2C336%20and,the%20bottom%20half%20of%20taxpayers.

The Founding of the Fed - FEDERAL RESERVE BANK of NEW YORK. (n.d.). https://www.newyorkfed.org/aboutthefed/history_article.html#:~:text=Owen%20incorporated%20modifications%20by%20Woodrow,law%20on%20December%2023%2C%201913.

Regulatory Information By Business Sector | US EPA. (2022, September 12). US EPA. https://www.epa.gov/regulatory-information-sector

https://www.dhs.gov/news/2022/08/24/following-hsac-recommendation-dhs-terminates-disinformation-governance-board

House, W. (2021). Executive Order on Worker Organizing and Empowerment. *The White House.* https://www.whitehouse.gov/briefing-room/presidential-actions/2021/04/26/executive-order-on-worker-organizing-and-empowerment/

Union membership dropped to record low in 2022. (2023, January 19). POLITICO. https://www.politico.com/news/2023/01/19/union-membership-drops-to-record-low-in-2022-00078525

Brey, J. (2022). The $1.6B Federal Plan to Spur Local Zoning Reforms. *Route Fifty.* https://www.route-fifty.com/infrastructure/2021/12/16b-federal-plan-spur-local-zoning-reforms/359974/

https://www.whitehouse.gov/briefing-room/statements-re-leases/2022/05/16/president-biden-announces-new-actions-to-ease-the-burden-of-housing-costs/

National Center for Education Statistics. (n.d.). *Fast Facts: Public and private school comparison (55).* https://nces.ed.gov/fastfacts/display.asp?id=55

To Renew America: Gingrich, Newt: 9780061095399: Amazon.com: Books. (n.d.). https://www.amazon.com/Renew-America-Newt-Gingrich/dp/0061095397

5. The American Unity Plan

Barnes, M., Bauer, L., Edelberg, W., Estep, S., Greenstein, R., & Macklin, M. (2022, March 9). The social insurance system in the US: Policies to protect workers and families. *Brookings.* https://www.brookings.edu/research/the-social-insurance-system-in-the-u-s-policies-to-protect-workers-and-families/

The Budget and Economic Outlook: 2020 to 2030. (2020, January 1). Congressional Budget Office. https://www.cbo.gov/publication/56073

USAFacts. (2023, March 20). *2023 Current State of the Union: US Federal Budget.* https://usafacts.org/state-of-the-union/budget/

The White House. (2023, March 13). *Historical Tables | OMB | The White House.* https://www.whitehouse.gov/omb/budget/historical-tables/

U.S. GDP 1960-2023. (n.d.). MacroTrends. https://www.macrotrends.net/countries/USA/united-states/gdp-gross-domestic-product

Fiscal Data Explains Federal Spending. (n.d.). https://fiscaldata.treasury.gov/americas-finance-guide/federal-spending/#:~:text=Since%20

2015%2C%20the%20Spending%20to,from%2020%25%20
to%2025%25.

Nearly 30 Million Americans Have No Health Insurance. (n.d.). pgpf.
org. https://www.pgpf.org/blog/2022/11/nearly-30-million-
americans-have-no-health-insurance

Amadeo, K. (2022, March 7). U.S. Real GDP Growth Rate by Year
Compared to Inflation and Unemployment. *The Balance.* https://
www.thebalancemoney.com/u-s-gdp-growth-3306008

Paulson, M. (2022). Measuring Fertility in the United States —
Penn Wharton Budget Model. *Penn Wharton Budget Model.*
https://budgetmodel.wharton.upenn.edu/issues/2022/7/8/
measuring-fertility-in-the-united-states

China Population Growth Rate 1950-2023. (n.d.). MacroTrends.
https://www.macrotrends.net/countries/CHN/china/population-
growth-rate

6. Paying Your Fair Share

The Constitution of the United States: A Transcription. (2023, February
3). National Archives. https://www.archives.gov/founding-docs/
constitution-transcript

*Research Guides: 16th Amendment: Topics in Chronicling America:
Introduction.* (n.d.). https://guides.loc.gov/chronicling-america-
16th-amendment

16th Amendment to the U.S. Constitution: Federal Income Tax (1913).
(2022, September 13). National Archives. https://www.archives.
gov/milestone-documents/16th-amendment

The Sixteenth Amendment. (n.d.). https://constitutionallawreporter.com/amendment-16/

What is Double Taxation? (n.d.). Tax Foundation. https://taxfoundation.org/tax-basics/double-taxation/

https://taxfoundation.org/tax-basics/salt-deduction/

What states impose sales/use tax? | Sales Tax Institute. (2019, January 23). Sales Tax Institute. https://www.salestaxinstitute.com/sales_tax_faqs/what_states_impose_sales_use_tax

The Fair Tax Book: Saying Goodbye to the Income Tax and the IRS: Neal Boortz: 9780060875497: Amazon.com: Books. (n.d.). https://www.amazon.com/Fair-Tax-Book-Saying-Goodbye/dp/0060875496

Personal Saving Rate | U.S. Bureau of Economic Analysis (BEA). (n.d.). https://www.bea.gov/data/income-saving/personal-saving-rate

What is the difference between a tax-exclusive and tax-inclusive. (n.d.). Tax Policy Center. https://www.taxpolicycenter.org/briefing-book/what-difference-between-tax-exclusive-and-tax-inclusive-sales-tax-rate

The Compliance Costs of IRS Regulations. (2023, February 28). Tax Foundation. https://taxfoundation.org/tax-compliance-costs-irs-regulations/

What is VAT? (n.d.). Taxation and Customs Union. https://taxation-customs.ec.europa.eu/what-vat_en

Value-added tax (VAT) rates. (n.d.). https://taxsummaries.pwc.com/quick-charts/value-added-tax-vat-rates

Reuters. (2020, December 31). U.S. slaps tariffs on French and German wines, aircraft parts amid EU dispute. *Reuters.* https://www.reuters.com/world/europe/us-slaps-tariffs-french-german-wines-aircraft-parts-amid-eu-dispute-2020-12-30/

Import customs procedures in France - Santandertrade.com. (n.d.). https://
santandertrade.com/en/portal/international-shipments/france/
customs-procedures#:~:text=Customs%20Duties%20and%20
Taxes%20on%20Imports&text=Duties%20range%20from%20
0%2D17,the%20general%20tariff%20averaging%204.2%25.

7. There Is No Unity Like Inflation

Fiscal Data Explains the National Debt. (n.d.). https://fiscaldata.trea-
sury.gov/americas-finance-guide/national-debt/

How Much Is the National Debt? What are the Different Measures Used?
(n.d.). pgpf.org. https://www.pgpf.org/blog/2023/03/how-much-
is-the-national-debt-what-are-the-different-measures-used#:~:-
text=In%20dollar%20terms%2C%20debt%20held,bills%20
to%2030%2Dyear%20bonds.

Lockert, M. (2022). What is Modern Monetary Theory?
Understanding the alternative economic theory that's becoming
more mainstream. *Business Insider.* https://www.businessinsider.
com/personal-finance/modern-monetary-theory

The Very Model of Modern Monetary Policy. (2023, March 1). IMF.
https://www.imf.org/en/Publications/fandd/issues/2023/03/
modern-monetary-policy-kaplan-moll-violante

What is inflation? (2022, August 17). McKinsey & Company. https://
www.mckinsey.com/featured-insights/mckinsey-explainers/
what-is-inflation

Your Guide to America's Finances. (n.d.). https://fiscaldata.treasury.
gov/americas-finance-guide/#:~:text=In%20fiscal%20year%20

2023%2C%20the,income%20taxes%2C%20and%20excise%20
taxes.

Policy Basics: Federal Payroll Taxes. (2022). *Center on Budget and Policy Priorities.* https://www.cbpp.org/research/federal-tax/federal-payroll-taxes

Corporate income taxes paid - USAFacts. (n.d.). USAFacts. https://usafacts.org/data/topics/economy/taxes/corporate-taxes/corporate-income-taxes-paid/?utm_source=google&utm_medium=cpc&utm_campaign=ND-StatsData&gclid=CjwKCAjwuqiiBhBtEiwATgvixDqgxqPAUPQL3cbuX5jN9p3zZ80gn-5VCrTFjayUaOF0Jr_FMm-QH-hoCB_8QAvD_BwE

Sources of Government Revenue in the United States. (2023, April 19). Tax Foundation. https://taxfoundation.org/publications/sources-government-revenue-united-states/#:~:text=Corporate%20income%20taxes%20accounted,U.S.%20tax%20revenue%20in%202021.&text=Source%3A%20OECD%-2C%20%E2%80%9CRevenue%20Statistics,OECD%20Countries%3A%20Comparative%20Tables.%E2%80%9D

US Inflation Calculator. (2023, April 12). *Historical Inflation Rates: 1914-2023.* US Inflation Calculator | Easily Calculate How the Buying Power of the U.S. Dollar Has Changed From 1913 to 2023. Get Inflation Rates and U.S. Inflation News. https://www.usinflationcalculator.com/inflation/historical-inflation-rates/

Inflation Rate for Medical care between 1935-2023. (n.d.). https://www.in2013dollars.com/Medical-care/price-inflation

Hanson, M. (2022, August 10). *College Tuition Inflation {2023}: Rate Increase Statistics.* Education Data Initiative. https://education-data.org/college-tuition-inflation-rate

When Taxpayers Ignore Less Visible Taxes. (n.d.). NBER. https://www.
nber.org/digest/jan08/when-taxpayers-ignore-less-visible-taxes

Sommer, J. (2023, March 25). The Fed Has Targeted 2% Inflation.
Should It Aim Higher? *The New York Times.* https://www.ny-
times.com/2023/03/24/business/inflation-federal-reserve-inter-
est-rates.html#:~:text=%E2%80%9CWe%20will%20get%20
inflation%20down,Fed%20doctrine%20settled%20years%20ago.

*Why does the Federal Reserve aim for inflation of 2 percent over the longer
run?* (n.d.). Board of Governors of the Federal Reserve System.
https://www.federalreserve.gov/faqs/economy_14400.htm

BEA Interactive Data Application. (n.d.). https://apps.bea.gov/
iTable/?reqid=19&step=2&isuri=1&categories=survey#eyJh-
cHBpZCI6MTksInN0ZXBzIjpbMSwyLDNdLCJkYXRhI-
jpbWyJjYXRlZ29yaWVzIiwiU3VydmV5Il0sWyJOSVBBX-
1RhYmxlX0xpc3QiLCI1Il1dfQ==

*Shares of gross domestic product: Personal consumption expendi-
tures.* (2023, April 27). https://fred.stlouisfed.org/series/
DPCERE1Q156NBEA

Meyer, D. (2022, September 14). Europe's antitrust enforcer talks
about the coming reckoning for Big Tech and corporate tax
dodgers. *Fortune.* https://fortune.com/longform/margrethe-ve-
stager-eu-interview-big-tech-corporate-taxes-europe/

*Economic Issues No. 30 -- Hiding in the Shadows : The Growth of the
Underground Economy.* (2002, April 20). https://www.imf.org/
external/pubs/ft/issues/issues30/

Echavarria, P. R. (2021, December 9). Measuring Underground
Economy Can Be Done, but It Is Difficult. *https://www.
stlouisfed.org/publications/regional-economist/january-2015/*

underground-economy. https://www.stlouisfed.org/publications/
regional-economist/january-2015/underground-economy

8. American Unity Income – UBI without Going Broke

Federal UBI - Universal Basic Income for all Americans. (n.d.). MoveOn.
https://sign.moveon.org/petitions/federal-ubi-universal

Gilberstadt, H. (2021, January 6). More Americans oppose than
favor the government providing a universal basic income for all
adult citizens. *Pew Research Center.* https://www.pewresearch.org/
short-reads/2020/08/19/more-americans-oppose-than-favor-the-
government-providing-a-universal-basic-income-for-all-adult-
citizens/

Countries with Universal Basic Income 2023. (n.d.). https://worldpop-
ulationreview.com/country-rankings/countries-with-universal-
basic-income

English, M. (2022, January 10). Universal Basic Income Payments
2022: Which cities and states offer these payments up to
$12,000? *MARCA.* https://www.marca.com/en/lifestyle/
us-news/2022/01/11/61dcc637e2704e66478b456c.html

TRADING ECONOMICS. (n.d.). *United States Gross Federal Debt
to GDP - 2022 Data - 2023 Forecast.* https://tradingeconomics.
com/united-states/government-debt-to-gdp

*Turn CERB into Universal Basic Income - Sign the Petition for Recovery
UBI.* (n.d.). https://www.ubiworks.ca/cerb-to-basicincome

Petition: Introduce a progressive Universal Basic Income (UBI). (n.d.).
Petitions - UK Government and Parliament. https://petition.
parliament.uk/petitions/634213

When Did Social Security Become the Third Rail of American Politics? (n.d.). History News Network. https://historynewsnetwork.org/article/10522

US Census Bureau. (2023, April 3). *Growth in U.S. Population Shows Early Indication of Recovery Amid COVID-19 Pandemic.* Census.gov. https://www.census.gov/newsroom/press-releases/2022/2022-population-estimates.html#:~:text=DEC.,components%20of%20change%20released%20today.

Kamarck, E., & Stenglein, C. (2020, October 27). How many undocumented immigrants are in the United States and who are they? *Brookings.* https://www.brookings.edu/policy2020/voter-vital/how-many-undocumented-immigrants-are-in-the-united-states-and-who-are-they/

Budiman, A. (2022, December 1). Key findings about U.S. immigrants. *Pew Research Center.* https://www.pewresearch.org/short-reads/2020/08/20/key-findings-about-u-s-immigrants/#:~:text=-Most%20immigrants%20(77%25)%20are,census%20data%20adjusted%20for%20undercount.

Total population by child and adult populations | KIDS COUNT Data Center. (n.d.). https://datacenter.aecf.org/data/tables/99-total-population-by-child-and-adult-populations#detailed/1/any/false/2048,574,1729,37,871,870,573,869,36,868/39,40,41/416,417

The Accuracy of CBO's Budget Projections for Fiscal Year 2022. (2023, January 1). Congressional Budget Office. https://www.cbo.gov/publication/58893#:~:text=Although%20CBO%20has%20often%20overestimated,2021%20period%20was%209%20percent.

House, W. (2023). Update on the Administration's Economic Assumptions. *The White House.* https://www.whitehouse.gov/omb/briefing-room/2023/03/09/update-on-the-administrations-economic-assumptions/

2021 Poverty Guidelines. (n.d.). ASPE. https://aspe.hhs.gov/2021-poverty-guidelines

Poverty Guidelines. (n.d.). ASPE. https://aspe.hhs.gov/topics/poverty-economic-mobility/poverty-guidelines

9. What's in It for Me?

Millsap, A. A. (2021, April 28). Higher Corporate Taxes Affect Everyone. *Forbes.* https://www.forbes.com/sites/adammillsap/2021/04/28/higher-corporate-taxes-affect-everyone/?sh=4877f00a6808

The 35 Percent Corporate Tax Myth. (n.d.). ITEP. https://itep.org/the-35-percent-corporate-tax-myth/

US Census Bureau. (2022, September 13). *Income in the United States: 2021.* Census.gov. https://www.census.gov/library/publications/2022/demo/p60-276.html

Caporal, J. (2023). Are You Well-Paid? Compare Your Salary to the Average U.S. Income. *The Motley Fool.* https://www.fool.com/the-ascent/research/average-us-income/#:~:text=National%20average%20income%3A%20The%20national,income%20in%202021%20was%20%2469%2C717.

Summary of the Latest Federal Income Tax Data. (2023, March 31). Tax Foundation. https://taxfoundation.org/publications/latest-federal-income-tax-data/

Lopez, J. (2023). Self-Employed? Everything You Need to Know About Taxes. *Business News Daily.* https://www.businessnews-daily.com/9315-self-employed-tax-guide.html

Self-Employment Tax (Social Security and Medicare Taxes) | Internal Revenue Service. (n.d.). https://www.irs.gov/businesses/small-busi-nesses-self-employed/self-employment-tax-social-security-and-medicare-taxes

Cohen, P. (2023). Small Business or Big Business: Which Really Creates the Most Jobs? *Factor Finders.* https://www.factorfinders.com/blog/small-business-job-creation-vs-big/

Taxation of foreign nationals by the United States—2022. (n.d.). Deloitte United States. https://www2.deloitte.com/us/en/pages/tax/arti-cles/taxation-of-foreign-nationals-by-the-us.html

Expert, N. G. F. L. (2022). Are You Rich? U.S. Wealth Percentiles Might Provide Answers. *Kiplinger.com.* https://www.kiplinger.com/personal-finance/605075/are-you-rich#:~:text=How%20much%20money%20do%20you,your%20assets%20minus%20your%20liabilities.)

How Much Does Assisted Living Cost? Prices by State & Ways to Pay - Caring.com. (2022, April 28). Caring.com. https://www.caring.com/senior-living/assisted-living/how-to-pay/

10. Social Safety without Dependency

Government benefits | USAGov. (n.d.). https://www.usa.gov/benefits

Division, D. C. (2022). Social Services. *HHS.gov.* https://www.hhs.gov/programs/social-services/index.html

Probasco, J. (2023). Government Assistance Programs: What's Available, Where to Apply. *Investopedia*. https://www.investopedia.com/government-assistance-programs-4845368

List of 80+ Federal Welfare Programs. (2023, February 11). https://singlemotherguide.com/federal-welfare-programs/

Social Services Block Grant Program (SSBG). (2023, February 14). The Administration for Children and Families. https://www.acf.hhs.gov/ocs/programs/ssbg

Work Requirements and Work Supports for Recipients of Means-Tested Benefits. (2022, June 1). Congressional Budget Office. https://www.cbo.gov/publication/58199

Walsh, C. (2022, November 3). *What is federalism?* State Policy Network. https://spn.org/articles/what-is-federalism/

Paycom. (2023, January 24). Your 2023 Guide to Every State's Minimum Wage. *Paycom.com*. https://www.paycom.com/resources/blog/minimum-wage-rate-by-state/

Blakemore, E. (2021, May 4). What was the Neolithic Revolution? *Culture*. https://www.nationalgeographic.com/culture/article/neolithic-agricultural-revolution#:~:text=The%20Neolithic%20Revolution%E2%80%94also%20referred,current%20geological%20epoch%2C%20the%20Holocene.

Gordon, D. (n.d.). *The States That Are Most Reliant on Federal Aid*. MoneyGeek.com. https://www.moneygeek.com/living/states-most-reliant-federal-government/

Lapera, G. (2023). U.S. states with the most and least debt. *Credit Karma*. https://www.creditkarma.com/insights/i/states-with-most-debt#states-with-the-highest-and-lowest-debt-to-income-ratios

Income Inequality by State 2023. (n.d.). https://worldpopulationreview. com/state-rankings/income-inequality-by-state

Credit Markets for the Poor. (n.d.). RSF. https://www.russellsage.org/ publications/credit-markets-poor

Lack of Access to Financial Services Impedes Economic Mobility. (2018, October 16). https://www.atlantafed.org/economy-mat- ters/community-and-economic-development/2018/10/16/ lack-of-access-to-financial-services-impedes-economic-mobility

Houlder, V. (2018, February 16). Wealthy give to charity to feel good, not avoid tax. *Financial Times*. https://www.ft.com/ content/0797b95c-083b-11e8-9650-9c0ad2d7c5b5

Cfp, K. D. (2022, September 22). Nearly 6 in 10 donors may give more to charity despite economic fears, study finds. *CNBC*. https://www.cnbc.com/2022/09/22/despite-fears-of-a-recession- many-may-give-more-to-charity.html

How to Integrate Back Into Society After Serving Time. (2020, February 17). Jared Justice. https://www.jaredjustice.com/blog/ how-to-integrate-back-into-society-after-serving-time/

How Money Traps Victims of Domestic Violence. (n.d.). theatlan- tic.com. https://www.theatlantic.com/sponsored/allstate/ how-money-traps-victims-of-domestic-violence/750/

Gaille, B. (2017, May 25). *25 Important Deadbeat Dads Statistics - BrandonGaille.com*. BrandonGaille.com. https://brandongaille. com/23-deadbeat-dads-statistics/

Baetjer, H., Jr. (1984, April 1). Does Welfare Diminish Poverty? *Foundation for Economic Education*. https://fee.org/articles/ does-welfare-diminish-poverty/

11. Generational Wealth for the Rest

Daly, L. (2023). How Many Americans Own Stock? About 150 Million -- But the Wealthiest 1% Own More Than Half. *The Motley Fool.* https://www.fool.com/research/how-many-americans-own-stock/

Fast Facts & Figures About Social Security, 2021. (n.d.). Social Security Administration Research, Statistics, and Policy Analysis. https://www.ssa.gov/policy/docs/chartbooks/fast_facts/2021/fast_facts21.html

Quick Facts on Social Security. (n.d.). https://www.uvm.edu/~dguber/POLS21/articles/quick_facts_on_social_security.htm#:~:text=In%201940%2C%20there%20were%2042,at%20current%20payroll%20tax%20levels.

Hager, T. (2023, February 5). Is Social Security Going To Go Bankrupt? *Forbes.* https://www.forbes.com/sites/tomhager/2023/02/05/is-social-security-going-to-go-bankrupt/

FastStats. (n.d.). Births and Natality. https://www.cdc.gov/nchs/fastats/births.htm

U.S. Population Growth Rate 1950-2023. (n.d.). MacroTrends. https://www.macrotrends.net/countries/USA/united-states/population-growth-rate

Americans Are Living Longer Than Ever. (n.d.). PRB. https://www.prb.org/resources/americans-are-living-longer-than-ever/

Elkins, K. (2018, November 2). Here's the age at which you'll earn the most in your career. *CNBC.* https://www.cnbc.com/2018/11/02/the-age-at-which-youll-earn-the-most-money-in-your-career.html

Individual Retirement Account (IRA) Resource Center. (n.d.). Investment Company Institute. https://www.ici.org/ira

Berger, R. (2023, February 19). What Is The 4% Rule For Retirement Withdrawals? *Forbes Advisor.* https://www.forbes.com/advisor/retirement/four-percent-rule-retirement/

Reduce Social Security Benefits for High Earners | Congressional Budget Office. (2022, December 7). https://www.cbo.gov/budget-options/58628

Berry-Johnson, J. (2023). Estate planning is an important strategy for arranging financial affairs and protecting heirs — here are 5 reasons why everyone needs an estate plan. *Business Insider.* https://www.businessinsider.com/personal-finance/why-is-estate-planning-important

Rodeck, D. (2021). You Can Keep Some Assets While Qualifying for Medicaid. Here's How. *Kiplinger.com.* https://www.kiplinger.com/personal-finance/insurance/health-insurance/602819/you-can-keep-some-assets-while-qualifying-for-medicaid

Benefits Planner: Retirement | Retirement Age and Benefit Reduction | SSA. (n.d.). https://www.ssa.gov/benefits/retirement/planner/agereduction.html

Social Security Benefit Amounts. (n.d.). https://www.ssa.gov/oact/cola/Benefits.html

Chantrill, C. (2020, December 6). *US Social Security Spending for FY2022 was $1,219 billion according to US Treasury.* https://www.usgovernmentspending.com/social_security_spending_by_year

USAspending.gov. (n.d.). https://www.usaspending.gov/

Monthly Statistical Snapshot, March 2023. (n.d.). https://www.ssa.gov/policy/docs/quickfacts/stat_snapshot/

Waggoner, J. (n.d.). *History of Social Security COLA Increases by Year*. AARP. https://www.aarp.org/retirement/social-security/info-2020/colas-history.html

12. The Healthcare Solution for All

Best Healthcare in the World 2023. (n.d.). https://worldpopulationreview.com/country-rankings/best-healthcare-in-the-world

Statista. (2023, April 12). *Health ranking of countries worldwide in 2023, by health index score*. https://www.statista.com/statistics/1290168/health-index-of-countries-worldwide-by-health-index-score/

Ireland, S. (2021). Revealed: Countries With The Best Health Care Systems, 2021. *CEOWORLD Magazine*. https://ceoworld.biz/2021/04/27/revealed-countries-with-the-best-health-care-systems-2021/

Pharma IQ. (2022, October 5). *Top five countries running the most clinical trials*. https://www.pharma-iq.com/pre-clinical-discovery-and-development/articles/top-five-countries-running-the-most-clinical-trials

World Index of Healthcare Innovation – FREOPP.org. (2001, March 16). FREOPP.org. https://freopp.org/wihi/home

Allen, H., Gordon, S., Lee, D., Bhanja, A., & Sommers, B. D. (2021). Comparison of Utilization, Costs, and Quality of Medicaid vs Subsidized Private Health Insurance for Low-Income Adults. *JAMA Network Open*, 4(1), e2032669. https://doi.org/10.1001/jamanetworkopen.2020.32669

Van De Water, P. N. (2023). Medicare Is Not "Bankrupt." *Center on Budget and Policy Priorities.* https://www.cbpp.org/research/health/medicare-is-not-bankrupt

Historical | CMS. (n.d.). https://www.cms.gov/research-statistics-data-and-systems/statistics-trends-and-reports/nationalhealthexpenddata/nationalhealthaccountshistorical

How Does Government Healthcare Spending Differ From Private Insurance? (n.d.). pgpf.org. https://www.pgpf.org/blog/2023/02/how-does-government-healthcare-spending-differ-from-private-insurance#:~:text=Government%20insurance%20programs%2C%20such%20as,percent%2C%20or%20about%20%241.2%20trillion.

How much does the federal government spend on health care? (n.d.). Tax Policy Center. https://www.taxpolicycenter.org/briefing-book/how-much-does-federal-government-spend-health-care

U.S. Health Care from a Global Perspective, 2022: Accelerating Spending, Worsening Outcomes. (2023). *www.commonwealthfund.org.* https://doi.org/10.26099/8ejy-yc74

Rao, P. (2023, March 29). *Ranked: The World's 25 Richest Countries by GDP per Capita.* Visual Capitalist. https://www.visualcapitalist.com/worlds-richest-countries-2023-gdp-per-capita/

How does health spending in the U.S. compare to other countries? - Peterson-KFF Health System Tracker. (2023, February 15). Peterson-KFF Health System Tracker. https://www.healthsystemtracker.org/chart-collection/health-spending-u-s-compare-countries/#Health%20consumption%20expenditures%20per%20capita,%20U.S.%20dollars,%20PPP%20adjusted,%202021%20or%20nearest%20year

Aldridge, M. D., & Kelley, A. S. (2015). The Myth Regarding the High Cost of End-of-Life Care. *American Journal of Public Health*, *105*(12), 2411–2415. https://doi.org/10.2105/ajph.2015.302889

Agboola, S., Simons, M., Golas, S., Buijs, J. O. D., Felsted, J., Fischer, N., Schertzer, L., Orenstein, A., Jethwani, K., & Kvedar, J. C. (2018). Health Care Cost Analyses for Exploring Cost Savings Opportunities in Older Patients: Longitudinal Retrospective Study. *JMIR Aging*, *1*(2), e10254. https://doi.org/10.2196/10254

NHE Fact Sheet | CMS. (n.d.). https://www.cms.gov/research-statistics-data-and-systems/statistics-trends-and-reports/nationalhealthexpenddata/nhe-fact-sheet

Hartman, M., Martin, A., Washington, B., Catlin, A., & Team, N. H. E. A. (2022). National Health Care Spending In 2020: Growth Driven By Federal Spending In Response To The COVID-19 Pandemic. *Health Affairs*, *41*(1), 13–25. https://doi.org/10.1377/hlthaff.2021.01763

Almost 25% of Healthcare Spending is Considered Wasteful. Here's Why. (n.d.). pgpf.org. https://www.pgpf.org/blog/2023/04/almost-25-percent-of-healthcare-spending-is-considered-wasteful-heres-why

Key Facts about the Uninsured Population. (2023, February 7). KFF. https://www.kff.org/uninsured/issue-brief/key-facts-about-the-uninsured-population/#:~:text=In%202021%2C%2027.5%20million%20nonelderly,and%20people%20in%20working%20families.

eHealth Insurance. (2022). How Much Does Individual Health Insurance Cost? | eHealth. *www.ehealthinsurance.com*. https://

www.ehealthinsurance.com/resources/individual-and-family/
how-much-does-individual-health-insurance-cost

Gordon, D. (n.d.). *The Average Cost of Health Insurance in 2023 |
MoneyGeek.com*. MoneyGeek.com. https://www.moneygeek.com/
insurance/health/average-cost-of-health-insurance/

Freedman, M. (2023). Health Insurance: Employer and Employee
Costs in 2023. *business.com*. https://www.business.com/articles/
health-insurance-costs-this-year/

Topic: Medicaid. (2023, February 21). Statista. https://www.statista.
com/topics/1091/medicaid/

Impact the lives of St. Jude kids. (n.d.). St. Jude Children's Research Hospital.
https://www.stjude.org/promotion/impact-giving-pm.html-
l?sc_dcm=58700008005633801&sc_cid=kwp&sc_cat=b&ds_
rl=1291300&ds_rl=1285465&ds_rl=1290690&gclid=Cj0KC-
Qjw6cKiBhD5ARIsAKXUdyYG31btHYvshIMG0lK7Imqw-
3pZv32FrEV-FHGJFHf0cnin6379U2QsaAh5xEALw_wcB&g-
clsrc=aw.ds

Tunnel to Towers Foundation. (2023, March 10). *Tunnel to Towers
Foundation*. https://t2t.org/

GoodRx - Error. (n.d.-b). https://www.goodrx.com/how-go-
odrx-works?utm_campaign=127243741&utm_con-
tent=121594327405&utm_source=google&utm_medium=cp-
c&utm_term=kwd-353253197642&gclid=Cj0KCQjw6cKiBh-
D5ARIsAKXUdyZ7h6O2UPhFzRW7GWnj5vk3YBlGhWm-
Cimhs-WWu6bkYV7IoGwZxR1caAtLMEALw_wcB&gcl-
src=aw.ds

13. Public School Competition

Hanson, M. (2022b, August 24). *U.S. Public Education Spending Statistics {2023}: per Pupil + Total*. Education Data Initiative. https://educationdata.org/public-education-spending-statistics#:~:text=Public%20education%20spending%20in%20the,or%20%2413%2C185%20per%20pupil%20annually.

Lieberman, M. (2022, May 11). What America Spends on K-12: The Latest Federal Snapshot. *Education Week*. https://www.edweek.org/policy-politics/what-america-spends-on-k-12-the-latest-federal-snapshot/2022/05

US Department of Education (ED). (n.d.). *Federal Role in Education*. https://www2.ed.gov/about/overview/fed/role.html

Hanson, M. (2022c, August 24). *U.S. Public Education Spending Statistics {2023}: per Pupil + Total*. Education Data Initiative. https://educationdata.org/public-education-spending-statistics#:~:text=States%20contribute%20a%20total%20of,total%20or%20%246%2C868%20per%20student.

US Department of Education (ED). (n.d.-a). *Archived: Executive Summary of the No Child Left Behind Act of 2001*. https://www2.ed.gov/nclb/overview/intro/execsumm.html

Barrington, K. (2023). An In-Depth Look at Common Core – What's Working and What Isn't? *Public School Review*. https://www.publicschoolreview.com/blog/an-in-depth-look-at-common-core-whats-working-and-what-isnt

Alfonseca, K. (2023, February 6). Critical race theory in the classroom: Understanding the debate. *ABC News*. https://abcnews.go.com/

US/critical-race-theory-classroom-understanding-debate/story?id=77627465

Greene, P. (2022, June 20). GOP Proposes Federal School Voucher Program. *Forbes.* https://www.forbes.com/sites/peter-greene/2022/06/20/gop-proposes-federal-school-voucher-program/?sh=5d07e9d56c53

National Center for Education Statistics. (n.d.-a). *Fast Facts: Back-to-school statistics (372).* https://nces.ed.gov/fastfacts/display.asp?id=372#:~:text=Preliminary%20data%20for%20fall%202021,students%20(source%2C%20source).

Academics/Curriculum. (n.d.). https://www.greenville.k12.sc.us/Parents/main.asp?titleid=academics

COE - Education Expenditures by Country. (n.d.). https://nces.ed.gov/programs/coe/indicator/cmd/education-expenditures-by-country

14. Reinventing Government, Again

Walsh, C. (2022, November 3). *What is federalism?* State Policy Network. https://spn.org/articles/what-is-federalism/

US Census Bureau. (2023, March 30). *Domestic Outmigration From Some Urban Counties Slowed, Smaller Gains in Rural Counties.* Census.gov. https://www.census.gov/library/stories/2023/03/domestic-migration-trends-shifted.html

Schmidt, A. (2019, December 19). The 20 wealthiest counties in the U.S., including these Washington, DC, suburbs: Report. *Fox Business.* https://www.foxbusiness.com/money/washington-dc-suburbs-richest-counties

Agresti, J. D. (2018, September 5). A Look at Pay for Federal Employees Compared to Their Private-Sector Counterparts. *Foundation for Economic Education.* https://fee.org/articles/a-look-at-pay-for-federal-employees-compared-to-their-private-sector-counterparts/

Hamilton, J. (2021, March 23). *Why Would Anyone Want a Federal Government Job? Top 10 Reasons - ClearanceJobs.* ClearanceJobs. https://news.clearancejobs.com/2021/03/10/why-would-anyone-want-a-federal-government-job-top-10-reasons/#:~:text=But%20there%20is%20a%20lot,their%20job%20stability%20is%20high.

Kamarck, E. (2016, July 28). Lessons for the Future of Government Reform. *Brookings.* https://www.brookings.edu/testimonies/lessons-for-the-future-of-government-reform/

Singer, E. (2023, April 25). *GOP presidential candidates want to abolish the Department of Education.* The American Independent. https://americanindependent.com/department-education-tim-scott-donald-trump-nikki-haley-2024-presidential-election/

The Cabinet. (2017, January 5). whitehouse.gov. https://obamawhitehouse.archives.gov/administration/cabinet#:~:text=The%20Cabinet%20includes%20the%20Vice,Affairs%2C%20as%20well%20as%20the

Light, P. C. (2023, February 15). The true size of government is nearing a record high. *Brookings.* https://www.brookings.edu/blog/fixgov/2020/10/07/the-true-size-of-government-is-nearing-a-record-high/

Retirement Statistics. (n.d.). U.S. Office of Personnel Management. https://www.opm.gov/retirement-center/retirement-statistics/

What are state balanced budget requirements and how do they work? (n.d.). Tax Policy Center. https://www.taxpolicycenter.org/briefing-book/what-are-state-balanced-budget-requirements-and-how-do-they-work

What Is an Executive Order? (n.d.). https://www.americanbar.org/groups/public_education/publications/teaching-legal-docs/what-is-an-executive-order-/

Tankersley, J. (2023, March 10). Biden's $6.8 Trillion Budget Proposes New Social Programs and Higher Taxes. *The New York Times.* https://www.nytimes.com/2023/03/09/us/politics/biden-budget.html#:~:text=President%20Biden%20proposed%20a%20%246.8,one%20of%20his%20centerpiece%20promises.

McBride, J. (2017, May 1). Greece's Debt Crisis Timeline. *Council on Foreign Relations.* https://www.cfr.org/timeline/greeces-debt-crisis-timeline

Knispel, S. (2020, October 23). *The politicization of the CDC was under way before Trump.* News Center. https://www.rochester.edu/newscenter/cdc-politicization-health-risk-assessment-459152/

Opportunity Zones | Internal Revenue Service. (n.d.). https://www.irs.gov/credits-deductions/businesses/opportunity-zones

State Business Incentives Database. (n.d.). https://www.stateincentives.org/

Federal land ownership by state - Ballotpedia. (n.d.). Ballotpedia. https://ballotpedia.org/Federal_land_ownership_by_state

Keystone XL Pipeline Lawsuits. (2021, November 1). https://www.nrdc.org/court-battles/keystone-xl-pipeline

What is a Conservation Easement? – National Conservation Easement Database | NCED. (n.d.). https://www.conservationeasement.us/what-is-a-conservation-easement/

O'Keefe, E. (2023). 2022 Land Report: Who owns the most land in the United States? *Successful Farming*. https://www.agriculture. com/farm-management/farm-land/2022-land-report-who-owns-the-most-land-in-the-united-states

New Estimates of Value of Land of the United States | U.S. Bureau of Economic Analysis (BEA). (2015, April 1). https://www.bea.gov/ research/papers/2015/new-estimates-value-land-united-states

Here's How America Uses Its Land. (2018b, July 31). Bloomberg.com. https://www.bloomberg.com/graphics/2018-us-land-use/

Girardin, M. (2023). Top 10 Investment Banking Companies. *Forage*. https://www.theforage.com/blog/companies/investment-banking-companies

Fillion, S. (2022, August 10). Meet The World's Best Management Consulting Firms 2022. *Forbes*. https://www.forbes.com/sites/ stephaniefillion/2022/08/10/meet-the-worlds-best-management-consulting-firms-2022/?sh=62056f842888

Index of Economic Freedom: Promoting Economic Opportunity and Prosperity by Country. (n.d.). Index of Ecnomic Freedom. https://www.heri-tage.org/index/

World Bank Open Data. (n.d.). World Bank Open Data. https://data. worldbank.org/indicator/NY.GDP.MKTP.CD?locations=ZJ

Introduction - The World of 1898: The Spanish-American War (Hispanic Division, Library of Congress). (n.d.). https://loc.gov/rr/hispanic/1898/ intro.html#:~:text=Representatives%20of%20Spain%20and%20 the,from%20Spain%20for%20%2420%20million.

Migration data in Central America. (2021, October 7). Migration Data Portal. https://www.migrationdataportal.org/regional-data-overview/migration-data-central-america

Remittances: Funds for the Folks Back Home. (2019, February 5). IMF. https://www.imf.org/en/Publications/fandd/issues/Series/Back-to-Basics/Remittances

15. Climate Solutions

Orcibal, J., & Jerphagnon, L. (2000, January 12). *Blaise Pascal | Biography, Facts, & Inventions.* Encyclopedia Britannica. https://www.britannica.com/biography/Blaise-Pascal

Pascal's Wager (Stanford Encyclopedia of Philosophy). (2022, September 11). https://plato.stanford.edu/entries/pascal-wager/

Kiefer, P. (2021). See 24,000 years of climate history at a glance. *Popular Science.* https://www.popsci.com/science/24000-years-of-climate-history-gif/#:~:text=The%20planetary%20change%20that%20accompanied,of%20the%20retreating%20ice%20sheets.

Sea Level in the Past 20,000 Years | Coastal Processes, Hazards, and Society. (n.d.). https://www.e-education.psu.edu/earth107/node/1506

Stips, A., Macías, D., Coughlan, C., Garcia-Gorriz, E., & Liang, X. S. (2016). On the causal structure between CO2 and global temperature. *Scientific Reports, 6*(1). https://doi.org/10.1038/srep21691

Editorial team. (2020, July 16). *5. Why does CO2 lag temperature? – Climate Change Action Team.* http://climatecat.eu/ufaqs/5-why-does-co2-lag-temperature/

Progress Cleaning the Air and Improving People's Health | US EPA. (2023, May 1). US EPA. https://www.epa.gov/clean-air-act-overview/progress-cleaning-air-and-improving-peoples-health#:~:text=Between%201970%20and%202020%2C%20the,the%20air%20that%20we%20breathe.

Imperial War Museums. (n.d.). *How Britain Hoped To Avoid War With Germany In The 1930s.* https://www.iwm.org.uk/history/how-britain-hoped-to-avoid-war-with-germany-in-the-1930s#:~:text=NEVILLE%20CHAMBERLAIN&text=Instituted%20in%20the%20hope%20of,as%20a%20policy%20of%20weakness.

BBC News. (2023, March 20). Why did the US and allies invade Iraq, 20 years ago? *BBC News.* https://www.bbc.com/news/world-64980565

Metcalfe, T. (2022). What is mutual assured destruction? *livescience. com.* https://www.livescience.com/mutual-assured-destruction

Tesla. (2023, March 2). *2023 Investor Day* [Video]. YouTube. https://www.youtube.com/watch?v=Hl1zEzVUV7w

https://www.jpl.nasa.gov/. (n.d.). *Emission Reductions From Pandemic Had Unexpected Effects on Atmosphere.* NASA Jet Propulsion Laboratory (JPL). https://www.jpl.nasa.gov/news/emission-re-ductions-from-pandemic-had-unexpected-effects-on-atmo-sphere

Frazin, R. (2022, November 6). The Hill. *The Hill.* https://thehill.com/policy/energy-environment/3719265-four-ways-a-gop-led-congress-will-take-on-energy-environment/

Tongia, R. (2023, March 22). It is unfair to push poor countries to reach zero carbon emissions too early. *Brookings.* https://www.brookings.edu/blog/planetpolicy/2022/10/26/it-is-unfair-to-push-poor-countries-to-reach-zero-carbon-emissions-too-early/

Reall, J. (2023, May 16). Seaweed-based straw maker Loliware scaling up with new financing. *Plastics News.* https://www.plastics-news.com/news/seaweed-based-loliware-scaling-new-financing

Chinapower. (2022, March 17). *How Is China's Energy Footprint Changing? | ChinaPower Project.* ChinaPower Project. https://chinapower.csis.org/energy-footprint/

Deaths from natural disasters by type. (n.d.). Our World in Data. https://ourworldindata.org/grapher/number-of-deaths-from-natural-disasters

Southwest Land Border Encounters. (n.d.). U.S. Customs And Border Protection. https://www.cbp.gov/newsroom/stats/southwest-land-border-encounters

16. Competition for Global Talent

Constitutional Rights Foundation. (n.d.). https://www.crf-usa.org/bill-of-rights-in-action/bria-26-2-the-debate-over-world-population-was-malthus- right.html#:~:text=Malthus%20applied%20this%20doubling%20rule,would%20redouble%20to%2028%20million.

Everett I.L. Baker Library: Border Studies: Cultural Assimilation. (n.d.). https://norwalkcc.libguides.com/c.php?g=572609&p=3998124#:~:text=Assimilation%20is%20a%20much%20contested,benefit%20from%20full%20citizenship%20status.

What History Tells Us about Assimilation of Immigrants. (n.d.). Stanford Institute for Economic Policy Research (SIEPR). https://siepr.stanford.edu/publications/policy-brief/what-history-tells-us-about-assimilation-immigrants#:~:text=The%20gradual%20adoption%20of%20American,came%20to%20identify%20as%20Americans.

Gelatt, J. (n.d.). *Do Employer-Sponsored Immigrants Fare Better in Labor Markets Than Family-Sponsored Immigrants?* https://muse.jhu.edu/article/777520

Employment policy | Fact Sheets on the European Union | European Parliament. (n.d.). https://www.europarl.europa.eu/factsheets/en/sheet/54/employment-policy

EconPort - Comparing Unemployment Among Countries. (n.d.). https://www.econport.org/content/handbook/Unemployment/Comparing.html

Immigrants to the U.S. Create More Jobs than They Take. (2020). *Kellogg Insight.* https://insight.kellogg.northwestern.edu/article/immigrants-to-the-u-s-create-more-jobs-than-they-take

Job Openings and Labor Turnover Summary - 2023 M03 Results. (n.d.). https://www.bls.gov/news.release/jolts.nr0.htm

Innovation in the United States and Europe – Report on the Digital Economy. (2020, August 25). https://gaidigitalreport.com/2020/08/25/innovation-in-the-united-states-and-europe/#:~:text=The%20United%20States%20is%20the,outpaced%20its%20counterparts%20in%20Europe.

Facilitation of Illegal Immigration | Europol. (n.d.). Europol. https://www.europol.europa.eu/crime-areas-and-statistics/crime-areas/facilitation-of-illegal-immigration

IIE Open Doors. (2022, November 14). *International Students - IIE Open Doors.* IIE Open Doors / International Students. https://opendoorsdata.org/annual-release/international-students/#:~:text=China%20and%20India%20remain%20the,year%2Dover%2Dyear).

Tin, A. (2023, April 27). U.S. reports no new mpox cases for first time since outbreak began. *CBS News*. https://www.cbsnews.com/sacramento/news/no-new-mpox-cases-in-us/

Naturalization Statistics | USCIS. (2022, September 21). USCIS. https://www.uscis.gov/citizenship-resource-center/naturalization-statistics

Statista. (2023, January 17). *Number of persons naturalized U.S. FY 1990-2021*. https://www.statista.com/statistics/247069/number-of-persons-naturalized-in-us/#:~:text=In%20the%20fiscal%20year%20of,citizens%20in%20the%20United%20States.

Non-immigrant and tourist visas | USAGov. (n.d.). https://www.usa.gov/non-immigrant-visas

Gelatt, J. (2019, July 2). *Explainer: How the U.S. Legal Immigration System Works*. migrationpolicy.org. https://www.migrationpolicy.org/content/explainer-how-us-legal-immigration-system-works

One-child policy | Definition, Start Date, Effects, & Facts. (2023, March 28). Encyclopedia Britannica. https://www.britannica.com/topic/one-child-policy/Consequences-of-Chinas-one-child-policy

Smil, V. (1999). China's great famine: 40 years later. *BMJ, 319*(7225), 1619–1621. https://doi.org/10.1136/bmj.319.7225.1619

Iacurci, G. (2023, February 1). 2022 was the 'real year of the Great Resignation,' says economist. *CNBC*. https://www.cnbc.com/2023/02/01/why-2022-was-the-real-year-of-the-great-resignation.html

International Entrepreneur Rule | USCIS. (2023, March 17). USCIS. https://www.uscis.gov/working-in-the-united-states/international-entrepreneur-rule

Conclusion: Achieving Unity

Rothman, L. (2018, December 1). The Story Behind George H.W. Bush's Famous "Read My Lips, No New Taxes" Promise. *Time.* https://time.com/3649511/george-hw-bush-quote-read-my-lips/